SECURITY IN DISARMAMENT

SECURITY IN
DISARMAMENT

EDITED BY RICHARD J. BARNET
AND RICHARD A. FALK

PRINCETON UNIVERSITY PRESS
PRINCETON, NEW JERSEY
1965

PREFACE

MANY of the chapters in this volume grew out of working papers prepared for the Woods Hole Summer Study of 1962, in which the editors were participants. The Summer Study was commissioned by the United States Arms Control and Disarmament Agency and administered by the Institute for Defense Analyses. Because of the importance of some of the analyses and findings that emerged from the study (published in a limited edition under the title *Verification and Response in Disarmament Agreements*), we have asked several of the participants to revise and bring up to date a number of contributions to that effort. In addition, we have included revised versions of three papers prepared for another contract study commissioned by the Arms Control and Disarmament Agency and conducted by the Peace Research Institute, titled *Quis Custodiet? Controlling the Police in a Disarmed World*. We have also added several papers not connected with either study but which bear on important facets of the problem of maintaining security in disarmament.

Earlier versions of Chapters VI and IX appeared in the journal *Disarmament and Arms Control*, of Chapters XII, XIII, and XIV in a report of the Peace Research Institute, of Chapter VIII in the *Proceedings of the American Society of International Law*, and of Chapter X and of the second part of Chapter VI in the *Journal of Arms Control*. Permission to use this material in altered form here is gratefully acknowledged.

We wish to acknowledge the support of the Center of International Studies of Princeton University and, particularly, the advice and encouragement of its Director, Klaus Knorr. Richard J. Barnet, who was appointed as a Research Associate of the Center especially to work on this book, also wishes to acknowledge the support of the Institute for Policy Studies, Washington, D.C.

CONTENTS

CONTENTS

SECURITY IN DISARMAMENT

INTRODUCTION

THESE essays have to do with the technical and political feasibility of choosing arms control and disarmament as a national security strategy. During the past four years several events have occurred which have increased general interest in arms control and disarmament and have thrown new light on the problems and possibilities of controlling the arms race.

First and most important, the leaders of the great nuclear powers have publicly recognized that the nuclear arms race is a dead end. President Kennedy told the American people that 300,000,000 people would die in the first exchange of a nuclear war and Chairman Khrushchev put the figure in his public warning to the Chinese at 700 to 800 million. After years in which both the US and the Soviet Union have proclaimed decisive leadership in the arms race, both now agree on the proposition (and defend it against powerful factions in their own countries or among their allies) that victory in a nuclear war is impossible.

Second, the strategy of brinkmanship—threatening nuclear war for specific political purposes but stopping short of the actual use of nuclear weapons—has come to look like an increasingly unsatisfactory way of conducting international relations. The Kennedy administration's handling of the Cuban missile crisis of October 1962 was a brilliant success, but the incident made apparent the fragility of an international system based on the manipulation of the nuclear threat.

Third, several significant steps toward disarmament have actually been taken in these four years. These measures, including the establishment of the "hot line," direct communications link between Washington and Moscow, a pledge by the US and the USSR not to station nuclear weapons in outer space, and the partial ban on nuclear testing, raised hopes that further measures to control the dangers of the arms race might be possible. Both the US and the USSR in early 1964 unilaterally cut their defense budgets by about 4 per cent and made quite substantial cuts in the rate of production of fissionable materials.

Finally, the arms race appears to be entering a new phase. The forward momentum of the military competition between the US and the USSR has slowed considerably. The US has not put a major new weapons system into operation for four years (although it is increasing the number of existing systems like Polaris and Minuteman). While the Soviets are also apparently adding to their force, they do not appear to be attempting to match the commanding lead of the US in nuclear weapons. The Soviets have important domestic priorities for the resources which an all-out military effort would take. And the United States, too, has urgent needs in its own society, which constitute natural limitations on its investment in the arms race.

But just as the principal arms race appears to be abating somewhat (and this hazardous prediction would be quite wrong if either side were to embark upon a major crash program to develop anti-ballistic-missile devices) new arms races involving other powers are now visible on the horizon. In the absence of nuclear controls, the end of the sixties will witness widespread proliferation of weapons. Such nightmares as the arms races between India and China and between Israel and Egypt, and nuclear rivalries among some of the nations of West Europe have stimulated a genuine interest in arms control among the great powers.

All of these developments have raised a number of issues that will be increasingly discussed in the next few years if, as we believe, the search for disarmament continues with increased seriousness. Public understanding of these issues is essential since, as the Senate hearings on the nuclear test ban in 1963 and the statements on disarmament made during the 1964 Presidential campaign make clear, these questions are more and more entering the area of political debate.

We have selected three areas in which we believe the issues are particularly important and in which some significant progress in analysis has been made during the past four years. The first group of issues deals with getting started toward disarmament. These questions have a great deal to do with inspection, which, as will be seen, is far more a political than a technical problem. The second group of issues revolves around the fear of national governments that they will be "locked in" to a disarmament agreement that will jeopardize their interests. These questions involve a discussion of sanctions, other means of enforcing, and other options available to nation-states under a security system based on disarmament. The third group of problems has to do with the special problems of drastic disarmament (the substantial elimination of national military capabilities). A look at this possibility can tell us a great deal about the role of inspection and enforcement in the disarming process.

PROBLEMS OF GETTING STARTED

To initiate disarmament it is necessary to find ways to be sure that the other side complies. A solemn pledge is not enough. In the negotiations with the Russians and in the political debate in the US great emphasis has been given to inspection. An inspection system is supposed to give parties confidence in the reliability of disarmament promises and to provide continuing sources of reassurance and warning throughout the life of disarmament agreements. Inspection makes trust less essential, perhaps even unnecessary.

As a series of abstract propositions the logic of this analysis has been persuasive. But it may now be worth asking whether this view of the role of inspection in disarmament makes political sense. For it may turn out that inspection is neither the only way nor the best way to provide a deterrent to would-be violators of disarmament obligations or to offer reassurance to those who have come to rely on disarmament for their national security. We have heard a good deal about Soviet resistance to inspection, but as President Eisenhower asked ten years ago, "Are we ready to open up every one of our factories, every place where something might be going on that could be inimical to the interests of somebody else?" The closer we get to implementing real measures of disarmament, the greater will be the incentive to find a variety of techniques to verify compliance other than the systematic, intrusive surveillance which we have come to think of as a sine qua non of disarmament. Where inspection is thought of as a principle rather than a technique, opportunities to conclude disarmament agreements that can enhance national security may be lost.

The Fear of Getting Locked In

There is a considerable fear within the government and particularly among the public that the cleverness of our adversaries or the near-sightedness of our own leaders would cause us to make highly disadvantageous disarmament agreements. One of the principal questions raised is the continued ability of the United States to pursue its foreign policy goals or to meet specific challenges, such as guerrilla warfare. In the present world, of course, no nation has complete confidence that it can defeat challenges to its interests. Indeed it is the recognition of their powerlessness to impose their will by force that has made the great nations consider disarmament as a possible strategy. Yet when a disarmament measure is under consideration, both the policy-maker and the citizen tend to demand a near-perfect confidence in the ability to control the future.

How can confidence be created that a nation can pursue its reasonable interests without being unduly hampered by the unforeseen strictures of disarmament agreements? One means is to permit easy withdrawal. Article IV of the Test Ban Treaty provides that where "extraordinary events, related to the subject matter of this treaty, have jeopardized the supreme interests of its country" a party can decide to withdraw by giving three months' notice. This provision offers an answer to possible concerns about being locked in to a seriously disadvantageous agreement, but it does not give any guide as to how to respond in the event of withdrawal by the other side or how to repair the damage that such a withdrawal might inflict on international society. The search is for a flexibility of response that can at the same time keep alive the disarmament system and protect the security of all the parties.

The essays in Part Two discuss a range of possible techniques to protect national security under a disarmament agreement. Such questions would usually arise in the event of a violation of the disarmament agreement by another power. There is clearly no single response in such situations. Indeed, what is needed is a series of possible responses appropriate to widely differing situations. The authors in this part are attempting to offer some general rules for thinking about responding to international crises under disarmament.

SPECULATION ABOUT DRASTIC DISARMAMENT

In this part the authors examine some of the special problems facing international society in the event the nations of the world were to undertake a disarmament program so drastic as to remove all national military capabilities. While disarmament on such a scale does not appear conceivable in the near future, there are several important reasons for focusing on such a contingency. In the first place, such analysis can tell us a great deal about the possibilities and limitations of the institutions we have come to think of as essential features of a world that has outgrown the war system, as, for example, inspection systems and police forces. Secondly, thinking about such a future can help us to prepare for the major changes in international life that would accompany drastic disarmament. And finally, while progress toward disarmament is most likely to be made by a series of steps rather than a single comprehensive treaty, it is most important to have a context within which to evaluate such steps. Without a theory of how international society might function in a warless world, it is difficult to determine whether particular measures of arms control or disarmament are leading in a desired direction.

The Editors

PART ONE

THE FUNCTION OF INSPECTION

INTRODUCTION TO PART ONE

THE essays in Part One focus on a question that until recently has rarely been asked in discussions of disarmament: what is the function of inspection? True, even the first postwar disarmament negotiations assumed that inspection would help to maintain security during the disarmament process, and all of the authors represented here would agree with this proposition when stated in such general terms. But what has been missing from official debates and from scholarly commentary is an analysis of the specific ways in which inspection might support the disarmament process in a variety of concrete situations. Abstract evaluations of the role of inspection, unrelated either to the political environment of a disarming world or to the changing nature of military technology, have produced singularly sterile debate on this subject both at the negotiations in Geneva and in discussions within our own country. One of the primary reasons for this is that inspection has generally been viewed not as part of a process leading to a particular set of desired ends, but rather as an end in itself. Only now are attempts being made to relate inspection to other means of assuring security such as international police forces and non-military sanctions and, most important, to a vision of the world we would like to see at the end of the disarmament process.

Part One is a contribution to the effort to understand how inspection might actually work. The authors attempt to define the role of inspection in the disarmament process—both its possibilities and its limitations. On the basis of various assumptions about the nature of a disarmed world, the first two chapters analyze the range of tasks an inspection arrangement might be expected to perform. Chapter I argues that the functions of inspection will vary according to the basic conception of the disarmament process. Chapter II takes a critical look at the proposition that inspection can serve as a "substitute for trust."

Chapters III and IV attempt to apply some of the general principles concerning the functions of inspection to two concrete arms control situations. The first situation is a limitation on strategic delivery vehicles, a measure in which both the US and the Soviet Union have shown interest. Since the Soviets have proposed a disarmament arrangement under which "agreed and limited numbers" of missiles would be retained by the US and the USSR until the end of the disarmament process and since the US has proposed a "freeze" on the future production of such weapons systems, the prospects for an agreement of some kind in this general area appear more encouraging now than in the past. Thus it is especially important to begin thinking about the peculiar inspection requirements associated with such an agreement.

Similarly, Chapter IV deals with one of the other more promising measures of arms control: a production cutoff of fissionable materials for weapons use. In April 1964, President Johnson and Chairman Khrushchev announced that the two nuclear powers would make substantial cuts in projected fissionable materials production without inspection. It is quite possible, therefore, that a complete cutoff might be negotiated in the coming period. Chapter IV analyzes the need for inspection in such a measure and the kind of inspection that might be appropriate. It examines some of the special problems involved in working out inspection arrangements for agreements that do not materially affect the military security position of either side.

Chapter V takes up the problems of organizing and administering inspection arrangements. As a result of the protracted test ban negotiations, the organization of the disarmament inspectorate has received serious consideration. The major question in this area is whether the inspectorate should be international in allegiance and in composition or whether it should be based on the principle that one country inspects another.

Chapters VI and VII discuss the relationship between the kind of inspection needed and the range of actions a nation might wish to be able to take in the event that a violation of a disarmament measure is discovered—what we call in this volume "the response."

Finally, Chapter VIII examines some of the principal concepts about inspection in relation to a major historical event—the Cuban missile crisis of October 1962—that offers lessons for the development of practical disarmament arrangements.

CHAPTER I

INSPECTION: SHADOW AND SUBSTANCE

BY RICHARD J. BARNET

O F all the issues surrounding disarmament that have divided the US and the USSR, none has seemed more critical than inspection. From the days of the early discussions of the Baruch Plan in 1946, the words "inspection and control" have evoked the picture of dreary sessions at Geneva at which little has been exchanged but recriminations.

The United States has insisted that reliance on inspection and control serve as a substitute for reliance on arms. Thus, as a nation progressively abandons its dependence on armaments, it turns increasingly to inspection as a source of confidence that the disarmament arrangement is protecting its security. Inspection is designed to provide assurance that the other parties to the disarmament agreement are fulfilling their obligations, under the proposition that a powerful nation should not weaken itself militarily unless it has confidence that other states are actually carrying out corresponding obligations.

The Soviet Union has never taken issue with this proposition as long as it has been stated in general terms. The whole debate has centered on two questions: what is the degree of confidence that one nation can reasonably expect to have, under a disarmament agreement, about the military establishment of a rival nation? and what are the appropriate means for establishing this confidence?

The United States came to the postwar disarmament discussions demanding high confidence, although it had only vague notions as to the means that would provide it.

RICHARD J. BARNET

The quest for foolproof solutions, although self-deluding, was a product of the times. The United States emerged from the war with the fearful memory of Pearl Harbor inflamed anew by the vision of Hiroshima. The single bomb that could destroy a city—and soon perhaps an entire country—offered an unprecedented incentive to treachery. In the past, the surprise blow could be absorbed. The Japanese violations of the Washington Treaty on Naval Limitations, if they had any effect at all on the United States, merely delayed the Pacific victory. Even the attack on Pearl Harbor was far from decisive. But now it seemed that an aggressor could retain a secret stock of a few atomic bombs to blackmail or fight its way to world supremacy.

Fears that such an aggressor actually existed were becoming increasingly concrete. While the Soviet Union did not possess nuclear weapons, it was recognized that in a matter of years it would. As the US-Soviet conflict deepened, the spectre of a hidden Soviet stockpile that would remain after the United States had eliminated its own began to dominate American thinking.

However, the planners of early postwar disarmament policy were skeptical that inspection alone could go very far toward preventing or detecting clandestine activities under a nuclear disarmament arrangement. In developing the Acheson-Lilienthal plan, which became the basis for the Baruch proposals, Acheson pointed out that inspection would not be adequate if the production of fissionable materials were allowed to continue in national hands. "The cops and robbers theory of control," as he called it, would break down "because the people charged with policing the agreement . . . couldn't possibly know as much as those they were trying to police."[1] The alternative solution, in which inspection was to play only a subordinate role, was international ownership of all nuclear materials including weapons and production facilities. And Robert Oppenheimer, testifying in response to Congressional concerns that nuclear weapons might soon be secretly introduced into the United States in ordinary packing crates, replied that the only scientific instrument he knew of for detecting such weapons at the port of entry was the screwdriver.

Thus, while American thinking on disarmament immediately centered on the problem of deterring violations and responding to them, it did not at first lay heavy emphasis on inspection. This emphasis grew, however, as the disarmament debates wore on. The United States program increased its reliance on inspection as the prospects for its more radical solutions faded. When discussions on the Baruch proposals ended, it was clear that neither international ownership of nuclear materials nor a veto-free right of the majority of signatory states to punish a violator (as Baruch also proposed) would gain acceptance. Compared to these, inspection appeared a more promising avenue.

Essentially, the American position on inspection included a demand for free access throughout the Soviet Union. Great stress was placed on the right to conduct pre-emptory inspections on the ground that an element of uncertainty in the locus and time of surveillance strengthened the deterrent. Thus, inspectors should conduct inspections at times of their own choosing and should not be obliged to follow a prearranged schedule.

[1] *International Control of Atomic Energy: Growth of a Policy* (United States Government Printing Office, 1946), p. 37.

The Soviet Union found this concept of virtually un-limited rights of inspection completely unacceptable.

The Soviet Union also took issue with another US idea about inspection: that the inspection arrangements go into effect in advance of those disarmament measures that they were to verify. The US explained that unless the inspection apparatus was in place and working before disarmament occurred, there would be no way to verify compliance with the disarmament steps that had been agreed upon. The USSR retorted that inspection without disarmament was espionage. The numerous Western proposals that the disarmament process begin with declarations of existing arms inventories and with a census of military personnel provided some substance to Soviet charges that the West was more interested in probing Soviet secrecy, a highly prized military asset, than in disarmament. Later proposals for aerial inspection unaccompanied by any disarmament (the Eisenhower Open Skies proposal) increased their suspicion.

The Russian view of the proper connection between inspection and disarmament was vague. While agreeing "in principle" that there should be some proportionality between inspection and disarmament, they opposed inspection within the territory of the Soviet Union until the end of the third stage of their own program for general and complete disarmament. The USSR said that at the end of the program, when all national military forces beyond limited internal security contingents would have been eliminated, it would be willing to submit to any system of control the West desired. Proportionality would thus be achieved when disarmament and inspection reached the 100 per cent level, but the Soviet Union was never willing to discuss the relationship between arms reduction and surveillance prior to the completion of the disarmament process. A US effort to find a formula for progressive implementation of inspection—a scheme for inspection in a gradually increasing number of zones—was rejected with the curious charge that it did not offer enough inspection!

*

The deadlock on inspection goes far deeper than the dispute on phasing. Indeed, most of the official discussions on inspection have dealt with differences of technique and detail that are merely symptomatic of basic differences in approach. It is not, however, that the two sides have sharply clashing ideologies of inspection but rather that they do not have a sufficiently clear picture of what they hope to achieve by it.

Curiously enough, in forty years both the United States and the USSR have completely reversed themselves, and each has adopted the position of the other. During the disarmament conferences of the 1920's, the Soviets favored an inspection system that involved territorial surveillance. The US in the same period opposed inspection on the now familiar grounds that inspection is an affront to national sovereignty and that parties to an agreement should trust one another without it. The US view of the twenties coincided with the traditional approach to disarmament. With a single exception, the few disarmament or arms control agreements that had been reached did not include provisions for inspection.

Most agreements were declaratory in nature. The Hague Conventions, which established certain rules of warfare and prohibitions on the use of weapons, included no inspection provisions; violations were self-evident. The

Treaty of Kuchuk-Kainarji between Russia and Turkey, which restricted fortification of the Black Sea, and the Rush-Bagot Agreement between the United States and Britain, calling for the demilitarization of the US-Canadian frontier, are examples of arms agreements for which no inspection was sought.

The only arms limitation agreement with elaborate inspection provisions that dates from the pre-World War II period was the Versailles Treaty. The Allies demanded extensive rights of inspection and control with respect to production, training, and deployment of German military forces.

It is most unlikely that any nation would have voluntarily agreed to such provisions. The Versailles Treaty was, of course, scarcely a negotiated instrument.

The experience under the Versailles Treaty suggests several conclusions. First, inspectors did not, both because of political obstacles and lack of personal initiative, exercise most of the inspection rights accorded under the treaty. Second, the inspection process did not deter widespread evasion. Third, within a short time after the systematic evasion of the arms restrictions commenced, inspection was not needed for detection; independent of inspection, governments obtained sufficient information about the violations to enable responses and countermeasures. Failure to act was unrelated to the failure of the inspection system to uncover the violations.

The record of Japanese and German violations of the Washington Naval Arms Limitation Treaty of 1922 also suggests that, although violations of a disarmament agreement can occur, *secret* violations are not particularly likely. While the Germans and the Japanese made some attempt to conceal their naval building programs, most of their efforts were devoted to devising ingenious variations of those vessels prohibited under the treaty—variations that would fall outside the letter of the prohibition.

The hypothesis is supported by the limited experience of the postwar period. The Korean Armistice contained a prohibition against the introduction of weapons of improved type into either North or South Korea. The Communists, who had only reluctantly agreed to the provision, soon began to violate it openly. No effort was made to conceal the introduction of new weapons in North Korea, and the United States promptly became aware of the violation and responded in kind. The case of the Soviet "violation" of the nuclear test moratorium is also suggestive. The Soviet action was not, of course, a technical violation since there existed no legal obligation to maintain the moratorium; this interpretation seems particularly compelling since the United States had also declared itself free to resume testing. The precipitous Soviet action did, however, violate the reasonable expectations of those with whom the Soviets were at the time negotiating. The USSR made no attempt to conceal its sudden resumption of atmospheric testing. The act was overt, and the Soviet Union attempted to defend it openly.

I am not suggesting that clandestine violations are not a danger. Under general and complete disarmament, the potential gains from such violations would increase markedly beyond what they have been in the past or what they would be under any disarmament arrangement short of the total elimination of nuclear weapons from national arsenals. Rather, I am suggesting that in the postwar period the United States has been obsessed with a special case in the disarmament problem—the clandestine violation—which the admittedly meager history on the subject indicates is an improbable one. Thus, the inspection problem has come to dominate the entire disarmament issue, creating obstacles where none need exist and diverting attention from more serious problems that also demand solution.

*

The lack of clarity in thinking about inspection, which has contributed so much on both sides to the impasse, is the result of two basic conceptual problems. The first is the difficulty that each has in understanding the position of the other. Thus, the popular view in the United States is that the Soviet reluctance to accept inspection indicates a basic intent to cheat. "If their intentions were honest, they'd accept inspection." I expect that the counterpart of this view in the Soviet Union would be something like this: "If they were serious about disarmament, they wouldn't ask for unreasonable inspection." It is unfortunately true of the disarmament negotiations that the demands for and the refusals of inspection have themselves intensified suspicion. There has been no real dialogue despite the interminable debates. Each side has read more into the position of the other than was warranted, since surely each has had substantive reasons for its position on inspection beyond a desire to outwit the other or to block disarmament. Because these objections have not often been articulated little effort has been made to explore them.

The Russians have been particularly evasive in discussing their objections to extensive or intrusive inspection. They base their case largely on the familiar charge of espionage. Although they are seldom specific, their concern embraces a number of separate points. First, they fear the disclosure of military targets. Such disclosure has been a particularly dangerous problem for them since the United States has enjoyed a significant numerical superiority in strategic delivery vehicles. Presumably, this will decrease as the Soviet Union develops increased numbers of hardened or concealed missiles.

Espionage also includes political intelligence. The Soviets feel that they have an advantage in maintaining the secrecy that surrounds the formation and the development of their policy. Shielded from the Russian public and from the prying eyes of foreigners, the Soviet government can exercise greater control than it could if it had to take such opinion continually into account. Secrecy has been regarded historically as a diplomatic asset in Russia's dealings with other nations.

The Soviets have other reasons for seeking to avoid territorial inspection that may be even more significant for them. The early inspection proposals of the West were greeted with charges that they violated national sovereignty rather than that they opened up the Soviet Union to spies. In the strong internationalist climate of the immediate postwar period, resistance to foreign inspection by an appeal to the principle of sovereignty had an archaic ring. It was bad propaganda, and it put Russia in a reactionary light. The propaganda emphasis shifted to the espionage charge. Nonetheless, it appears that the USSR has viewed inspection as a serious affront to national sovereignty chiefly because it would reduce the extent of political control that the Communist leadership could exercise on its own territory. An international inspection authority, even if its powers were limited, would have some of the attributes of a government. It could conduct searches, question individuals, and demand production

23

of documents. Its principal mission would be adverse to that of the territorial government since its primary target would be the discovery of violations undertaken by or attributable to that government.

Toleration of a foreign government operating on its own soil with rights over its own citizens requires a remarkable degree of self-confidence for any government. As President Eisenhower pointed out in 1955, it is by no means clear that we would favor such a thoroughgoing inspection here. Our ambivalent attitude toward the International Court of Justice is disclosed by the retention of the Connally Reservation; this suggests not only that we do not welcome the operation of supranational authorities on the territory of the United States but also that we are reluctant to give up sovereign control over what we regard as our own business.

The Soviet Union evidently regards the establishment on its soil of a legitimate authority with attributes of a rival sovereign as having profound symbolic significance for their system. The exclusiveness of party control is a fundamental and an explicit tenet of Soviet theory and practice. The right of an international inspectorate to challenge this exclusive claim to power poses a problem in itself, quite apart from the consequences that might flow from the exercise of the right. For the first time a sector of Soviet life would be beyond the exclusive control of the party. And the party itself would have acquiesced in this change.

In the Soviet view the symbolic problem posed by territorial inspection is compounded by current facts of international life. For the foreseeable future the Soviet Union is likely to remain a minority in any international organization. Refusing to believe that individuals can be insulated from the prejudices of their own countries, the Soviets deny that an international authority will be impartial, and they fear that the inspection system will be used against them. This could happen in many ways. Ambiguous events—of which there will be many in any disarmament agreement if only because even a reckless charge is sure to receive a hearing—could be interpreted so as to resolve doubts consistently against the USSR. Inspection could also reveal a good deal of information about the operation of the Soviet system. Some of this information would belie official propaganda and could therefore be used for counterpropaganda once it became international property.

Because of the amount of information about the West that is available without any inspection at all, the Soviets would probably rely very little on inspection to verify the compliance of others. Therefore, from their viewpoint there are few advantages to balance the disadvantages.

That the Soviets have little to gain from inspection and good reasons to oppose it does not, of course, mean that they will necessarily reject it. The postwar negotiations record a gradual softening of their opposition, culminating in the recent offer to accept three on-site inspections on Soviet territory in association with the test ban, an arms control measure of marginal importance. Their consistently grudging position does suggest, however, that they regard inspection as a unilateral advantage for the West that should be accepted only in association with disarmament measures of considerable value to the Soviet Union. For this reason, the acceptability of a particular inspection proposal cannot be judged except in conjunction with a concrete disarmament proposal in its political context. Thus, a test ban with on-site inspection can be wholly unacceptable one year and acceptable the next —probably for reasons having more to do with the general political environment than with the merits of the test ban.

While the United States policy has not given sufficient attention to the factors that shape Soviet attitudes on inspection, the Soviets, for their part, have attributed our insistence on inspection wholly to sinister motives and have adamantly refused to admit the existence of our own legitimate concerns. They have underrated the extent to which the "lesson of Pearl Harbor" has been learned. Fear of surprise attack, the sudden act of treachery that alone can make a great power vulnerable, is exceedingly strong in this country. Preoccupation with the surprise attack problem has resulted in the magnification of the role of inspection.

The United States has also strongly favored inspection because of the fear that it will be trapped by a disarmament treaty precipitously abandoned by the other side. Inspection is needed to provide "turn-around time," i.e., sufficient advance warning so that appropriate countersteps such as rearmament or redeployment may be prepared. The United States feels at a distinct disadvantage in entering a disarmament arrangement with the Soviets, because the political requirements of our system make it essential to base a major step such as abrogation upon evidence that will be credible to our own population and to many other nations whose favorable opinions we solicit.

The principal reason for our insistence on inspection is, however, our profound distrust of the Soviet Union. A basic premise of our policy has been that, but for the risks of detection provided by an inspection system, the

Soviets, more probably than not, would cheat. Below the threshold at which the inspection system becomes effective, therefore, the conservative planner assumes that the Soviets will cheat.

The absence of moral inhibitions against cheating and the presence of a positive incentive to violate are, however, two different things. US thinking on inspection has generally looked at Soviet capabilities to cheat without adequately examining the incentives. On the analogy of military planning, which assumes the worst and prepares for it, this would appear to be sound and conservative. In the search for disarmament, it is self-defeating. If the assumption that the Soviet Union will enter a disarmament agreement for the purpose of violating it and thereby of achieving a military advantage is valid, it should be sufficient to preclude all disarmament agreements with the Soviet Union, since no inspection system is capable of deterring a nation with a high incentive to cheat. The simple assumption that any capability for evasion will be automatically translated into violations strikes me as highly dubious, but it lies at the heart of US thinking on inspection. Since the Russians surely do not view themselves as acting in this way, the assumption confounds and annoys them.

*

The failure of governments to determine for themselves what they hope to achieve from disarmament makes it difficult for them to agree on any disarmament measures at all. Since the advantages are only dimly perceived, the risks stand out like shadows at twilight, breeding a host of fears that paralyze initiative. Confusion as to the purposes of disarmament greatly complicates the inspection problem. Since inspection is not an end in itself but a technique for disarmament that is itself a means of establishing new relationships among states, the degree of inspection that is appropriate depends upon what the new relationship is conceived to be.

It has been customary in the past few years to characterize those who look to substantial changes in armaments levels as "disarmers" and those who look only to modest changes in the present military behavior of states as "arms controllers." Another difference in viewpoint on disarmament that is even more crucial to the inspection issue can be described in terms of this dichotomy: those who see disarmament serving modest goals and those who believe that disarmament will contribute to a radical transformation in international relations. The first group shares objectives for disarmament that, if completely achieved, would not in themselves change existing political relationships. One such modest objective is the creation of a more stable military balance. Under this view, disarmament may be used to eliminate peculiarly dangerous weapons. Thus, those airplanes and missiles that are vulnerable to surprise attack should be replaced with weapons that are less vulnerable on the theory that their existence would reduce the temptation to launch a surprise attack.

What kind of inspection is appropriate for accomplishing this objective? The only information that would appear necessary would be a general idea of the military building programs and the deployments of the other side. All that either side could expect would be some degree of assurance that the other was adhering to the rules of the game—that both, in effect, have the same general understanding of the agreement. If one side or the other should fail to make the changes in its military posture required by the agreement, the result would be insignificant, since the other side would be placing virtually no reliance on the fulfillment of the pledge. Moreover, unilateral intelligence can by itself make reasonably accurate determinations of the general trend of military programs, even in a country that makes a fetish of military secrecy.

Nor is inspection needed, as is sometimes asserted, to establish a precedent for further disarmament agreements, since such agreements as we have described do not constitute a "first step" to significant arms reduction. They proceed on quite different assumptions: the arms race is to continue indefinitely; the quest for military superiority is not to be abandoned; there is no effort to build trust in a political sense. Indeed, both sides assume that it is the military balance and the technical characteristics of weapons that alone keep the peace and that, without these, each side would have a strong incentive to strike. If this is the basic nature of the relationship, inspection cannot increase confidence nor provide a basis for further measures of disarmament. In fact, inspection is likely to have the opposite effect, since it will disclose some general military information that nations traditionally keep secret, such as targeting data.

A second modest objective is the reduction of damage in a war. If this purpose is to be achieved, inspection must play a somewhat increased role. The reason is that very substantial disarmament will be required to accomplish this objective. Nuclear stockpiles (including delivery systems) are presently so high that without reductions that are substantially in excess of 75 per cent, no appreciable difference in damage levels can be expected. Some inspection is needed to detect gross violations of such mag-

29

nitude that they change the anticipated level of damage.

But a building program of such magnitude as to be significant here is likely to come to light through normal intelligence operations. Presumably, such a disarmament agreement would also include a production cutoff, since it would be absurd to cut stocks by over 75 per cent and still continue production. Inspection would thus be needed to monitor the production cutoff and to ascertain that the reductions promised had actually occurred. The degree of inspection necessary would depend upon the confidence that each side had in its own estimates of the stockpile of the other at the start of the agreement.

Turning to the more ambitious objectives for disarmament, we first encounter the traditional view that the goal of disarmament is to render nations incapable of making war. Thus, under total disarmament great powers will be restrained from initiating armed conflict by the simple fact that they have deliberately divested themselves of the instruments of warfare. Stated in this simple form, this objective appears unattainable. If nations have the incentive to make war because of outstanding disputes, conflicts of political goals, or other reasons that they themselves may not understand, they will not disarm. Unless they are prepared to accept the political preconditions of a warless world, they will not willingly put themselves in a position in which they will lack the favored means of transacting international business: the manipulation of military power. Even if by some chance they should try disarmament without any other changes in existing relationships, the capability for war would not be abolished. Inspected disarmament alone cannot do away with weapons any more than Prohibition, even if perfectly enforced, could rid society of alcohol. The counterpart of bathtub gin would be suitcase bombs, garage-built rockets, and botulinus toxins cultured in home kitchens.

The inspection necessary to enforce total disarmament and even to approach the problem of crude weapons production is staggering if we assume a high incentive to cheat. A relationship of intense hostility and rivalry in which each side contemplates the use of force to bring about the elimination of the other cannot be effectively enforced—by inspection or any other technique. This is a popular model of a disarmed world, but it is a wholly unreal one. Nations will not divest themselves of armaments unless they have concluded that new relationships, not dependent upon arms, serve their interests. The very act of arms elimination would indicate a high incentive to make the disarmament system work. This does not mean that a power that embraced disarmament might not change its mind, particularly if it found that the arrangement was working to its disadvantage. It does mean, however, that no power is likely to enter a disarmament arrangement with a fixed intention of using disarmament to win a military victory, if only because of the uncertainties involved. For this reason, therefore, the inspection system accompanying comprehensive disarmament should concentrate not on providing absolute assurance that no war-making capabilities exist, but rather on encouraging existing incentives to make the new relationship work and on discouraging changes of heart. Inspection requirements should be judged on the premise that disarmament has come about as a result of a decision to create a new relationship based on a recognition that major armaments are impractical instruments for carrying on national rivalries. It should not be assumed that disarmament has been grudgingly accepted merely as a mechanical device to put weapons beyond reach.

The principal function of inspection in total disarmament is *reassurance*. An auxiliary function is deterrence, but this role is quite secondary. If the relationship depends to any significant degree on the "cops and robbers" approach, it will not survive, since the necessary incentive will be lacking. Moreover, if compliance depends to any significant extent upon deterrence through exposure, compliance is unlikely, since exposure of significant violations cannot be assured at low armaments levels.

What sort of reassurance should an inspection system communicate? It cannot provide reassurance that no clandestine weapons are being produced or that another country is incapable of inflicting substantial harm if it chooses. It has been frequently pointed out that even total elimination of all weapons merely postpones the capability to make war. It does not remove it for all time. The knowledge of nuclear technology and the potential of any industrial nation for rearmament cannot be eradicated. If radical disarmament builds new relationships among nations, it will not be because these nations have passed a point of no return. Rather, it will be because their values and perceptions have been profoundly changed by the experience so that there is little interest in returning to the jungle world they have left. For this reason, inspection should be more concerned with providing reassurance as to intentions than with providing reassurance as to capabilities.

It is essential that an inspection system communicate intentions as accurately as possible. Difficult as this is, it is less difficult than verifying the absence of weapons. It is far more important for a government to know whether its partner in the agreement is interested in blackmail as a national policy than whether it has destroyed every missile it said it would. To be sure, failure to destroy a missile is powerful evidence that something is wrong. But this evidence may not be as significant as many other indicators that are easier to observe, such as diplomatic activity, internal propaganda, and changes in the organization of society. Detection of clandestine weapons would not itself provide conclusive proof that the violator intended to attack or blackmail other countries. If we imagine one situation in which we were to discover clandestine weapons in Britain and another in which we were to discover them in the Soviet Union, it becomes clear that the existence of the weapons is not the primary factor affecting our judgment, since our evaluation of the two situations would be quite different.

A somewhat different theory of disarmament starts with the assumption that it is impossible to render nations incapable of making war and then treats arms reduction as an enforced cooling-off period so that nations will have to take time to rearm if they wish to launch any more war. Under the cooling-off theory, the primary function of inspection would be to provide reassurance as to intentions, as in the case just discussed, and also to develop confidence among the parties that they were all operating under roughly equal handicaps. Thus, the rearmament capabilities of the parties and the role such capabilities might play in their political and economic life would be as important an area for surveillance as existing military capabilities.

There is a third theory of disarmament that makes major claims for arms reduction but that falls short of asserting the elimination of war-making capability as the goal. Its objective is the reduction or elimination of the importance of weapons in the political relations of states. Under this view, the level of armaments is not so important as the fact that the arms race has come to a halt and that weapons of mass destruction, including armies, no longer dominate political competition. Some weapons would remain, but nations would become increasingly indifferent to them as threats declined and energies were diverted to other causes. In discussing disarmament in 1926, Salvador de Madariaga pointed out that the great dangers of the modest arms race then being carried on were not only the waste of economic and human resources but particularly the great commitment of intellect and energy to war.

Preoccupation with military approaches to political problems frustrates political solutions and increases the risk of war. A disarmament arrangement that could not only end the forward momentum of the arms race but also provide the basis for untangling international politics from the restraints of military power would bring about a major change in relations among states. Proponents of this theory assert that when it becomes a matter of indifference how many missiles remain—and only then—will it become possible to eliminate missiles.

The function of inspection in such an arrangement would be to provide reassurance that all states had, in fact, entered into a new relationship under which some means of coercion might remain, but in which their importance would be downgraded and the use of threats would cease. True, no inspection is needed to determine whether one nation attempts to use threats or blackmail against another, whether its diplomats contemplate the use of force, whether it seeks to derive prestige from the possession of weapons, or whether it uses military power as the basic criterion for according respect to other nations. However, inspectors might be able to supply additional data that would confirm or deny the impressions derived from general observation.

If all parties are seriously interested in creating a relationship in which military power will play an increasingly subordinate role, they should share an incentive to communicate as much reassuring information about their intentions as possible. The extent to which they have complied with disarmament obligations would be an important index of intentions. An inspection system for such an arrangement should provide maximum opportunity for self-disclosure, since relevant information freely communicated would probably do more to create a satisfactory climate for the arrangement than the right to conduct free-wheeling inspections. In the event of compliance with a ban on missile production, for example, inspection could turn up only negative findings that would be, of course, ambiguous. They could mean either that no missiles were being produced or that the inspection was inadequate to find them. Self-disclosure is a useful complement to adversary inspection, not a substitute for it. Inspection is inadequate to verify compliance. There will always be a considerable area of uncertainty. It may turn out that a better function for inspection is the verification of disclosure rather than the verification of compliance. The administration of the income tax offers a possible analogy. In some countries, the tax administrator attempts to verify compliance by checking the taxpayer's income and deductions and by computing the tax for him. The results are often unsatisfactory. The government lacks the personnel required to do the job effectively. The taxpayer feels no responsibility to cooperate. Evasion is a perfectly respectable as well as a profitable pursuit. In the United States the emphasis is on self-disclosure. The primary task of the tax administration is to police the system of self-disclosure.

There may be other analogies and other approaches to inspection. But they will not be acceptable until we and the Soviets talk a common language on the objectives of disarmament.

CHAPTER II

INSPECTION, TRUST, AND SECURITY
DURING DISARMAMENT

BY RICHARD A. FALK

THIS essay considers several related issues. First, it considers the proper way to correlate the amount of inspection with the amount of disarmament. Second, it questions whether adequate inspection, however specified, will provide reasonable security to disarming states that distrust one another. And third, it suggests that important changes in the character of international relations may be the only way to provide for the security of states during the final stages of disarmament, thereby implying that no inspection system, however extensive, can by itself give reasonable assurance of compliance with a commitment to engage in drastic disarmament.

One inspection issue—how much inspection?—has been at the center of our efforts to understand what kinds of special machinery are needed to make disarmament agreements compatible with both the objective requirements of national security (actual security) and the subjective requirements of domestic political acceptability (perceived security).

An important attempt to correlate inspection and disarmament has been made by Jerome Wiesner. "The level or intensity of inspection required to monitor a disarmament agreement is in some way proportional to the degree of disarmament."[1] This is a verbal statement of

[1] Jerome B. Wiesner, "Inspection for Disarmament," in Louis B. Henkin (ed.), *Arms Control* (1961), pp. 112-140, at 113.

what has come to be known as the Wiesner Curve.[2] The basis for Wiesner's correlation is the reasonable assumption that a complying nation grows progressively more vulnerable as the disarmament process proceeds. However, the reliance upon inspection as *the way* to offset this vulnerability seems far less reasonable. This emphasis upon inspection follows from another assumption made by Wiesner, namely, that "the hope for disarmament in a context of acute distrust lies in solutions to the problems of inspection."[3] Wiesner's statement is rather similar to the maxim of conventional wisdom that inspection is a substitute for trust.

There are several explanations of the popularity of the Wiesner Curve: (1) it is simple; (2) it confirms common sense; (3) it is very comprehensive, applying to every stage of the disarmament process; and (4) it is responsive to Soviet contentions about inspection and yet appears to uphold the Western position. Perhaps this fourth explanation needs some comment. The Soviet Union has been contending that the West demands a great deal of inspection in exchange for very little disarmament. The Wiesner Curve seems to formulate the West's demands in their most reasonable form. For only as security risks increase does the inspection capability grow. Thus, at the outset of disarmament, only a relatively "little" inspection is sought. At the same time, the inspection allowed, however "little," is presumably enough to eliminate the security risks that are attributable to the reduction of forces and the destruction of weapons at the particular stage.

[2] *Idem,* at 137.
[3] *Idem,* at 140.

These considerations favoring the adoption of the Wiesner Curve as an approach to the relevance of inspection to the disarmament process do not strike me as convincing. An initial objection involves the excessive generality of the Wiesner Curve. It might be plausible to argue that, to monitor agreed reductions and retained levels of stockpiles and production facilities for nuclear weapons and fissionable materials, there should be maintained a directly proportional relationship between the amount of inspection and the amount of disarmament. But even in this rather simplified case, the argument is not especially persuasive. There is no evidence to support the assumption that a functional relationship subsists between inspection needs and disarmament deeds. In fact, it seems more plausible to assume that at the early stages of disarmament there is no significant impairment of security at the strategic level, even in the event of substantial non-compliance. What can an enemy do with the extra weapons it has retained or produced during Stage I in violation of the agreement to disarm? The complying state will retain both the ability to rearm and a sizable minimum deterrent. It is hard to imagine a state willing to risk the instabilities of a disrupted disarmament process in order to gain some slight advantage in the arms race; this is especially the case since research and development activities, the most vital sector of competition for military superiority, are left undisturbed, at least in the current proposals, until late in the disarmament process.

Clandestine intelligence sources would almost certainly detect gross violations, whereas minor violations would have no more than slight strategic relevance. It should be emphasized that the augmented military capability achieved by cheating cannot normally form part of that state's deterrent capability as long as disarmament continues. Since it is the threat to use nuclear weapons, not their actual use, that creates a political role for nuclear weapons, the secretness of a violation in Stage I would eliminate much of the incentive to violate. Only later in disarmament, when a genuine counterforce possibility exists, would it make much sense to violate disarmament provisions dealing with the stockpiling and production of nuclear weapons. Early, the incentive is small, the risk of discovery is large, and the dangers of serious instability in the event of discovery are great. The Wiesner Curve makes an assumption that security requires an upward inspection slope without specifying why in military-strategic terms.

The Curve also lumps together all kinds of disarmament measures. Thus, it presumably applies equally to a test or missile ban, military uses of outer space, controls over the use, development, and possession of biological and chemical weapons (BWCW), removal of foreign military bases, and budget reductions, as well as to a comprehensive disarmament process. In each of these disarmament situations, the extent, if at all, that inspection is *necessary* or *feasible* is not readily apparent. For example, as the agreement on the limited nuclear test ban presupposes, information about violations can be acquired by a combination of unilateral monitoring and clandestine intelligence. In contrast, no inspection system, however well designed, promises to detect and verify with any reliability the presence of violations in the BWCW area, even though this category of violation may be quite disturbing to the military balance, especially if committed by unstable states of secondary power such as China, India, Indonesia, Pakistan, or the United Arab

Republic. The non-inspectability of certain kinds of violations may turn out to be an insurmountable obstacle to disarmament progress; but it is certainly unresponsive to propose reliance upon an expanding inspection capability to meet this danger of the uninspectable violation. For if something is virtually uninspectable, an increase in the quantum of inspection makes only a negligible contribution to the security of the disarming states. Perhaps it is less than negligible, since an operating inspection system takes one off guard without warrant.[4] We need a series of specific studies about the relevance of inspection to security during disarmament, studies that are clustered about such topics as the following: delivery vehicles, conventional weapons and forces, fissionable materials, production facilities, research and development, and chemical and biological weapons. The relevance of inspection must be ascertained for each arms category with regard to whether the agreement calls for declaration, destruction, surveillance, freeze, or transfers of military weapons to non-military uses. The objective would be to produce a series of specific correlations between the need for inspection and the type of disarmament measure.

But even if one overlooks the need for functional specificity in the design of an inspection system, another, perhaps more significant, criticism can be made of the Wiesner Curve. The main postulation of the Wiesner Curve is that as the level of inspection gets higher so does the quality of security. The reason that we want more inspection later in disarmament is because we need more protection against violations—that is, the security requirements have increased because vulnerabilities are greater. But is there any basis for supposing that an in-

[4] See Chapter XII for further discussion.

crease in the level of inspection necessarily increases the probability of detecting violations in all disarmament environments? Can an inspection system, however augmented, hope to cover the globe's surface in search of weapons caches and illegal facilities for the production and delivery of biological and chemical weapons? If one regards the potential violator to be any state, not just the rival superpower, then the security task is considerably complicated—complicated above all by the almost necessary condition of obtaining and sustaining universal participation, an achievement not nearly attained for even so modest a venture as the limited nuclear test ban.

The Wiesner Curve also assumes that the request for inspection is completely a function of the need for security. Thus, when the security requirements are low, at the outset of disarmament, then the inspection capability can be small, whereas when the security requirements rise, so must the inspection capability increase. We have already criticized the Wiesner Curve for suggesting that an increase in inspection would produce a proportionate increase in security during the final stage of disarmament. But we have not mentioned the opposite difficulty, namely, that inspection requirements might be relatively high during the initial stages of disarmament because *perceived* security needs are great at the start of the disarmament process. The Wiesner Curve does not distinguish between actual and perceived security during disarmament. If the demands for inspection were to be based on perceived security, then the general trend would probably be almost the opposite of that envisaged by Wiesner. For, at the start, maximum distrust exists and any kind of cheating, however implausible, would be viewed by the West as a threat to its security. There need not be a high incentive to cheat nor an understanding of how the violator proposes to gain military advantages in a disarming world. There is, instead, a more naïve perception. The Russians cannot be trusted to keep international agreements. Therefore, it is wrong to rely upon their pledge in the critical context of disarmament. A foolproof inspection system, or at least its approximation, is desirable and essential because it makes it unnecessary for the West to trust the Russians.

This correlation of distrust and insecurity is no more grounded in fact than is Wiesner's inverse correlation of inspection and security. The fact of distrust does not suggest a danger of violation unless a high military payoff exists for a violator. At the outset of disarmament, the incentives to violate do not seem nearly as great as do the risks of instability that might be expected to result from a discovered or verified violation of any magnitude. Part of the reason why the incentives are low is that vulnerabilities are not much greater than before disarmament commenced; there is not much to be gained by a violation.

Nevertheless, the perceived security needs are likely to influence greatly, if not actually determine, the amount of inspection that a disarming state regards as necessary. And, as we have suggested, perceived security is a product of the entire political environment and is not merely a reflection of an analysis of what it is necessary to be assured about so that the military balance will not be overthrown to our disadvantage during disarmament. Therefore, initial distrust and hostility require that we have reasonable confidence that our inspection system is good enough at the outset to detect a violation by a diligent violator. Such an approach, then, sets initial inspection requirements high and includes a demand that declara-

43

tions about retained levels of weapons and forces be verified, that is, that the whole of the participating society be subject to close surveillance. To be confident about compliance with a disarmament process is as difficult at the outset as later on, even if confidence is less important to actual security. Thus, when there is relatively little disarmament, there must be comparatively great inspection.

The acceptance of this need for reassurance makes somewhat plausible the Soviet exaggeration of the Western approach as inspection without disarmament, as well as the Western exaggeration of the Soviet approach as disarmament without control. Neither is accurate; each has some plausibility, depending upon how one feels about being assured that the other side is complying early in disarmament. The Soviets claim that, late in disarmament when, presumably, vulnerabilities would be high and control necessary, they would be willing, in principle, to accept any control arrangement. This difference in viewpoints reflects differences in the character of perceived security, unless one is prepared to make a Machiavellian interpretation of one or the other or both sides. The Soviet Union apparently associates its sense of security with the impenetrability of its territory, whereas the West associates its sense of security with knowledge about what "the other" is doing. Both positions are irrational if measured by the military dangers that are likely to arise as a consequence of disarmament, but both positions are realistic projections of national character.

Knowledge about these two negotiating positions also allows us to make predictions about the basis for *acceptable* disarmament. It is necessary either to satisfy the mutual needs established by perceived security requirements or to change the perceptions of the actors. Since the perceived requirements of the superstates are presently incompatible, we have tried to change both sets of perceptions by education and persuasion, hoping to reach an eventual and reasonable compromise, rather than to demand a complete conversion. Part of the psychological environment of the negotiations is a widespread public awareness that a failure to disarm is also inconsistent with the middle- and long-term security of the big states. This gives an incentive for states to seek perceptions of the character of security during disarmament that are more compatible with one another.

The relevance of perceived security needs to the acceptability of disarmament can also be appreciated from the perspective of American politics. An agreement requires a ratifying consensus of two-thirds in the United States Senate; a prudent President would probably want an even higher level of support, at least by the time of treaty signature. A President would want, above all, to avoid having the United States reject a disarmament treaty that was acceptable to other states and to its own governmental representative. If political acceptability depends upon perceived security and if perceived security depends upon being reasonably sure about compliance from the outset, then the United States demand for inspection is likely to remain high in proportion to disarmament.

One could contend that Wiesner is trying to educate us so that our conception of perceived security is more closely in line with the requirements of actual security. In this sense, his approach is a contribution, if confined to the first half of disarmament. (As has been said, the Wiesner assumption that actual security would benefit from multiplied inspection in the second half of disarmament seems dubious; at least it is unsupported by evidence.) It might be more rational for the American public to accept the idea that one does not have to be assured that a state we distrust is complying, so long as there is no reason for apprehension that potential non-compliance is likely to do us great damage. An armed world includes the risks that one's rivals may be gaining the military upper hand by producing more weapons than we know about. How is the character or relevance of this risk changed when the shift is made from arming to disarming? It seems proper to disjoin security from the presence of trust, as well as from the adequacy of inspection. If one contends, as Wiesner does, that inspection is a substitute for trust, then one needs, contrary to his proposal, an elaborate kind of inspection at the outset to give information about non-compliance. Our position is that actual security early in disarmament depends neither upon trust nor upon inspection.

Perceived security needs, however, continue to require the West to ask for enough inspection to identify non-compliance reliably from the beginning. If this perception is maintained, then it is likely to produce a special attitude toward inspection late in disarmament. Instead of asking gradually for more inspection, it is likely, if early disarmament goes well, that the original suspicions will gradually disappear. Inspection is central only so long as distrust prevails; but should trust emerge, then there may well be less and less political insistence upon reliable inspection despite the increased vulnerability of disarming states to violations. That is, perceived security is correlated with active distrust rather than with threats to actual security, so that the removal of distrust should tend to satisfy the sense of security of disarming states. Where active trust is present, it has never occurred to states that disarmament should be accompanied by inspection; the agreement between Canada and the United States on the demilitarization of the Great Lakes is a case in point. In one respect, this way of thinking about security during disarmament may be the only way to achieve a sense of security and yet to entertain seriously the prospect of general and complete disarmament. For, as we show elsewhere,[5] no amount of inspection would seem to give states protection against violations in Stage III. Therefore, only if protection were regarded as unnecessary, would its impossibility not constitute a permanent barrier to drastic disarmament.

This leads to one final thought. If the process of disarmament, once commenced, were to continue, it would almost necessarily transform both the attitudes of states toward one another and the general character of international society. It seems most implausible to postulate as constant the political atmosphere that exists today during the course of disarmament from beginning to end. Either trust and harmony would emerge to a much greater extent than they exist today or the disarmament process would not proceed very far. That is, we must accompany the idea of disarmament with an expectation of political transformation, the nature of which cannot be anticipated with any precision. But there is one consequence of this assumption that is particularly relevant to our discussion, namely, that security requirements and their perception would be changed by the political transformations accompanying a successful disarmament process. Therefore, a theory of inspection that projects into the last stage of disarmament the security needs that are calculated in light

[5] See Chapter XII.

of the conflicts in the contemporary world is almost certain to be misleading. One can say, to emphasize this aspect of our disagreement with Wiesner, that, if we ever should reach Stage III, we would probably no longer correlate security with the adequacy of our inspection system.

In conclusion, there are several ways to improve upon our manner of thinking about inspection. First, if we are concerned with actual security, then we should conduct specific studies of the relationship between different kinds of violations and the maintenance of military stability. Second, if we are concerned about perceived security, then we should recognize that the inspection system is expected to deter and detect cheating at all stages, not just when the complying side grows vulnerable. Third, if active distrust persists, no inspection system can protect actual security needs in Stage III. Fourth, if active distrust disappears, perceived security is not likely to depend upon inspection nearly as much as it now does. Fifth, if active distrust does not disappear during the early stages of disarmament, then, regardless of how much inspection is agreed upon, drastic disarmament is unlikely to take place. Sixth, it is difficult to imagine the success of early disarmament without the resultant transformation of international society. Seventh, although the character of this transformation cannot be anticipated in detail, it will influence the conception of security in subsequent stages of disarmament.

The tenor of these conclusions suggests that it is unrealistic to think about drastic disarmament as something separable from the overall condition of international politics. It seems reasonably plain that the design of an adequate security system during disarmament depends upon the success of our efforts to transform international society into a more harmonious and stable political system. These efforts are needed prior to disarmament and throughout its process; and, as they succeed, the character of perceived security correspondingly changes.

CHAPTER III

VERIFICATION OF REDUCTIONS IN
THE NUMBER OF STRATEGIC
DELIVERY VEHICLES

BY THE COMMITTEE ON STRATEGIC
DELIVERY VEHICLES, WOODS HOLE
SUMMER STUDY, 1962*

THIS chapter appraises a disarmament agreement between the United States and the Soviet Union that commits each side to make major reductions in strategic delivery vehicles. For purposes of illustration and analysis, it is assumed that the agreement calls upon each side to retain no more than two hundred delivery vehicles. The analysis will treat the method of reduction, the type of substantive violations that could occur, the stability of the resulting military environment, and the kind of inspection that might appropriately form part of the agreement. This analysis discloses that such an agreement would require a significant but not unlimited amount of inspection and access.

The strategic inventories of the US and the USSR as of January 1, 1963, were estimated by the Institute for Strategic Studies as follows:

	US	USSR
Heavy bombers, ICBM's, Polaris-type missiles	1068	265
Medium bombers	840	1000

* The members of the committee were Richard J. Barnet, Lincoln P. Bloomfield, James Fletcher, David Frisch, Leonard S. Rodberg, and Louis B. Sohn. This chapter, however, does not necessarily reflect the views of all committee members.

The relative strengths of the two sides are far from equal. The United States has many more long-range vehicles, and its medium bombers are far more effective due partly to the world-wide network of SAC bases.

There are a number of strong incentives for reaching an agreement to reduce these inventories. Either force is capable of destroying a large fraction of the other's population on a first strike. The asymmetry between the forces could provoke intemperate moves on either side, while the likelihood of accidents would be reduced by decreasing the size of the force. Continued reliance by the superpowers on unrestricted forces will increase the incentives of other countries to develop nuclear delivery capabilities. For these reasons, as well as others, it appears to be in the national interest of the United States to work toward an agreement with the Soviet Union to reduce significantly the level of strategic armaments.

It is probable that such an agreement, which would necessarily involve a significant amount of inspection, cannot be achieved without a move toward strategic equality between the US and the USSR. If such a move is to be made, then the conventional and tactical nuclear forces of the United States and its allies must be capable of meeting any reasonable threat without resort to the use of strategic nuclear weapons. This may require a reduction of defense requirements by insisting upon a prior settlement of the Berlin problem or even upon a wider European settlement. This settlement might include some strengthening of NATO's conventional forces or involve an agreement obliging the Soviet Union to reduce its conventional strength. Whatever the change may be, it must permit the United States to adopt a pure deterrent strategy in which it will not use its strategic nuclear weapons except in retaliation against an attack with nuclear weapons (a "no-first-strike" policy). This emphasizes that an agreement such as that examined here involves not simply a reduction in arms but also a major change in United States strategy, which now depends significantly on creating a credible threat of a nuclear strike as a response to a range of non-nuclear provocations.

In order for an agreement such as we are considering to be acceptable to the Soviet Union, it must also neutralize the tactical delivery vehicles that both sides maintain in Europe. These include the tactical aircraft and IRBM's maintained by NATO and the Soviet Union, as well as the carrier attack forces of the United States Sixth Fleet, now stationed in the Mediterranean. Both the United States and the Soviet Union recognize that NATO "tactical" aircraft can strike the Soviet heartland and that these aircraft are, therefore, equivalent to other "strategic" forces of the West. At the same time, Soviet intermediate-range missiles effectively hold Western Europe hostage. An agreement such as that envisioned here, involving the maintenance of limited forces of bombers and long-range missiles, will probably be acceptable to both sides only if these other nuclear delivery vehicles are also included in the terms of reduction.

In analyzing such an agreement, one can sensibly consider only the immediate future, since, in the absence of a production cutoff, changes in weapons and defense systems or in the military and political environment cannot be anticipated with confidence. Therefore, the following three assumptions are made: (1) The use of strategic nuclear forces for anything except retaliation against strategic nuclear attack has been renounced; (2) Nuclear delivery vehicles that threaten long-range attack in Europe have been limited; (3) The agreement takes place during the next five years, that is, before major changes in the nature of strategic forces are likely to take place.

THE AGREEMENT

The disarmament agreement to be discussed is primarily between the United States and the Soviet Union; however, restrictions imposed on Great Britain, France, and Germany would be included in the assumed agreement on tactical vehicles. The relevant parts of the agreement are as follows:

1. The strategic armaments of the United States and the Soviet Union will be progressively reduced to two hundred strategic delivery vehicles each. The following will be considered as strategic delivery vehicles: (a) armed combat aircraft having an empty weight of 25,000 kilograms or greater; (b) missiles having a range of 5,000 kilometers or greater; (c) submarine-launched missiles having a range of 300 kilometers or greater. Within the quota of two hundred there will be no restriction on the number of any particular type of vehicle remaining at the end of the reduction. The reduction will take place over a period of three years. During each six-month period, a number of delivery vehicles equal to one-sixth of the difference between the initially declared number and two hundred will be destroyed.

2. The production of strategic delivery vehicles will be halted except for production, within agreed limits, of replacement parts required for maintenance of the retained vehicles.

3. The development and testing of new types of delivery vehicles will be halted. The flight testing of existing types of vehicles will be limited to agreed quotas.

4. The production of other specified types of armaments, including tactical delivery vehicles and defensive systems, will be halted except for production, within agreed limits, of parts required for maintenance of the retained armaments.

5. The production, stockpiling, and testing of civilian aircraft having an empty weight of 25,000 kilograms or greater and boosters for space vehicles will be subject to agreed limitations.

6. Procedures for modifying the agreement in the light of changed technological circumstances will be established.

The United States treaty outline of April 18, 1962, includes air-to-surface missiles in the category of long-range delivery vehicles and requires reductions in these as well as in other types of vehicles. Since the agreement described here fixes the level of strategic forces, the inclusion of missiles that are launched from long-range bombers implies a double-counting of these bombers. To avoid difficulties arising from this circumstance, the agreement may provide that each nation can maintain only a limited inventory of air-to-surface missiles.

Production will be limited to what is necessary to produce spare parts. Besides inhibiting a qualitative arms race, this provision will prevent a transition to high-yield or high-accuracy missiles. However, if the agreement should provide that any parts produced must be exactly identical with the parts they are to replace, it would probably impose requirements that no feasible inspection system could satisfy. The agreement should be based on a sufficiently broad definition of "replacement" so that verification of this restriction will not produce endless argument and dissension. At the same time the conception of replacement should be framed to prevent significant changes in the vehicles.

An important part of the agreement will consist of a restriction on the flight testing of strategic delivery vehicles. Major changes in components that could give either side an improved capability will, in most cases, require flight testing before they can be used with assurance. A ban on flight testing of new types of vehicles should inhibit most potentially destabilizing changes.

If the strategic forces are to be maintained at a fixed level, then neither side can be permitted unilaterally to build extensive defense systems against them. While, for political reasons, reductions in defensive systems probably cannot be included in the agreement, the agreement can impose production restrictions on defensive systems similar to those imposed on delivery systems. This will permit each side to maintain those defenses existing at the time the agreement becomes effective but will not permit it to expand these defenses thereafter.

It is necessary to limit the production of vehicles for peaceful purposes, since a nation might produce a vast number of "space boosters," which could be used as military missiles. Limits might be agreed upon each year, so that a country could place a yearly quota on its production of these items.

Force Structure

If the United States were constrained to hold its strategic forces to a level of two hundred delivery vehicles, it would probably select a mix of different systems, each possessing both a high degree of survivability if subject to direct attack and a considerable ability to penetrate existing defenses. A mix ensures that no single technical innovation or violation by the other side could significantly degrade the retaliatory capability of the other side's force.

A sample mix is the following:

B-52	60	(20 maintained on airborne alert)
Polaris	60	(30 submarines, each carrying 2 missiles)
Titan II	40	
Minuteman	40	

Some of the factors behind this choice of a force structure are the following: (a) the large delivery capability of the B-52 and its invulnerability to long-range attack while airborne; (b) the invulnerability of Polaris to direct attack but its vulnerability to some types of anti-missile defense; (c) the hardening of the storable-fueled Titan II and its ability to carry decoys, making it less vulnerable to anti-missile defenses; (d) the hardening of the solid-fueled Minuteman and its relatively small delivery capability, permitting greater flexibility in the use of the force.

If only two missiles were carried on each Polaris submarine (which can ordinarily carry sixteen missiles), some means would be required to give assurance that a clandestine cache of missiles, ready for instant emplacement, was not being maintained. One obvious precaution would be to render the submarines incapable of carrying more than two missiles without major overhaul and repair.

Some Types of Violations

One can conceive of a number of different violations of this agreement, including outright abrogation, clandestine construction of large forces, minor deviations from allowed production levels, and inadvertent delays in the destruction or replacement of vehicles. In order to gain some appreciation of the verification requirements associated with this agreement, only intentional clandestine violations will be considered. The possibility of other types of violations would have some effect upon the design of the inspection system and the way it gathers and reports data, but this will be considered only tangentially.

Four major types of violations will be discussed here: (1) clandestine production of missiles; (2) clandestine production of aircraft; (3) conversion of civil aircraft; (4) deployment of an anti-missile system. Any one of these violations might indicate a danger that a counterforce capability was being secretly developed. Each type of violation could reduce the size and effectiveness of the force that would survive an attack by the evader.

The possible development of such a capability represents the primary source of instability under an agreement to reduce delivery forces to low levels. If major nuclear powers entered such an agreement, they would need assurance not only that such a capability could be detected but that its development could be detected soon enough to permit appropriate countermeasures short of nuclear attack. The verification required to provide reasonable assurance against each of the four types of violations must now be examined.

CLANDESTINE PRODUCTION OF MISSILES

The production and deployment of missiles is the most direct way of developing a counterforce capability against hardened missiles. In deciding to develop a clandestine missile force, a nation could choose to produce missiles identical with those it had built prior to the agreement, or it might decide to build a new missile that would be easier to produce under the added constraints of the agreement. For instance, it might use simpler materials or fewer low-tolerance parts. In the first case, about eighteen months might be required to prepare new production facilities to produce an old-model missile, assuming that the former production facilities were not available— that is, assuming that the former production sites had been fully declared and were being kept under effective surveillance. In the second case, a minimum of thirty to forty-eight months might be needed to develop and begin producing a new missile. Additional time, say, twelve to eighteen months, would be required to produce and deploy the missiles.

The ban on missile testing is important in simplifying the problem of detecting clandestine production. A new missile will require extensive flight testing before it is either a usable weapon system or a credible threat. Such testing must occur about a year before final production is begun; hence the detection of these tests would give more than a one-year warning before a significant force could be deployed. The potential violator, therefore, must expect that its violation will be revealed long before it is operational. Several choices are open: it can secretly develop the missile and make preparations for production; it can openly abrogate the agreement, giving an additional one- or two-year warning; or it can produce an old tested model.

The third choice is likely to give much less warning to the other side, since it requires less flight testing. If the violator wants to produce missiles and to use or threaten to use them without flight testing, then it will certainly wish to make use of the same techniques and, if possible, the same facilities and personnel that have been involved in previous production. In the design and production of any complex system such as a missile, there are a large number of unforeseen problems that only experienced personnel could handle well. Without flight testing, it would be essential to rely on such personnel.

For these reasons, it is important that an inspection system should be able to verify that facilities previously producing major subsystems and components are engaged only in allowed production or peaceful activities and that the personnel previously working on them can be accounted for. Major production facilities that appear to be undergoing significant changeover in equipment or personnel should be subjected to close scrutiny.

CLANDESTINE PRODUCTION OF AIRCRAFT

The facilities in which long-range aircraft are produced are unique and sufficiently easy to detect so that it is unlikely that a violator would attempt to carry on clandestine production of aircraft. The facilities must have extensive floor space and high bay areas to accommodate the aircraft, and they must be located near an airfield that permits the aircraft to fly away. A violation involving aircraft production could be detected so readily that a potential violator would most probably not choose to go to the trouble and expense of attempting clandestine aircraft production, but either would not attempt to conceal its violation or would develop some other system.

In the missile age, moreover, there is little motivation for such clandestine production. Aircraft are no longer effective in performing a counterforce mission. The long warning times in the event of a bomber attack would permit the launching of retaliatory missiles and bombers before a significant part of this force could be destroyed.

CONVERSION OF CIVIL AIRCRAFT

The Soviet Union maintains a large civilian fleet of jet and turboprop aircraft. Many of these could be converted to bombers in a relatively short time.

However, the availability of the aircraft does not mean that a usable military force exists. For such a force to be employed, especially in a surprise attack situation, it has to be trained and tested in order to create a high degree of confidence that it will perform effectively. A converted civil fleet is not a military instrument until pilots have been trained in the use of the aircraft and have flown practice missions against simulated targets with a reasonable degree of success. This means that a verification system, whether using unilateral means or an agreed inspection system, should be alert to any changes in the use patterns of civil aircraft and to evidence of special training or special personnel being employed on these aircraft. (The pilots to be used in an attack mission would probably have to be specially selected, if only to assure that the nature of the activity was not divulged.)

DEPLOYMENT OF AN ANTI-MISSILE SYSTEM

One way to nullify a strategic retaliatory force is to construct an effective AICBM and air defense system. If such a defense were possible, a country might decide to deploy it, either in violation of a restriction or by some device that could evade the language of the agreement. In any case, the deployment of such systems is a long, expensive, and easily observable process involving the construction of extensive radar facilities and launching sites in the vicinity of principal targets. It has been estimated that five years would be required for the United States to deploy a satisfactory AICBM system, and one may expect that the Soviet Union would require a similar period for such deployment.

Vulnerability of Force to Violations

A two-hundred-vehicle force of the mix suggested above is highly survivable against all but very large and varied counterforce attacks. As will be seen, the violator's force must include both offensive and defensive systems in order to have any hope of a successful counterforce strike.

First, suppose that the violator constructs a clandestine force composed of missiles, each carrying a twenty-megaton warhead and having a circular probable error (cep) of one nautical mile. A missile hardened to withstand a pressure of 300 psi has a 50 per cent probability of surviving an attack by such a weapon. In order to provide 90 per cent confidence that no more than five of the original 80 missiles will survive, the attacker must be able to deliver 390 missiles. Since these missiles will not be perfectly reliable, the ability to launch such a force requires a somewhat larger initial force. For instance, if they are 80 per cent reliable (an optimistic figure in view of present performance records) and if the attacker is able to retarget some of its missiles to take account of the 20 per cent that will probably misfire, it will require a force of 490 missiles. (If it cannot retarget, but must use redundant or multiple targeting, it will require 530 missiles.) A nation beginning with a force of 200 missiles having the above characteristics would have to construct and deploy 290 additional vehicles effectively to destroy the hardened missiles of the other side.

Second, aircraft that are maintained on the ground are subject to destruction by missile attack, provided no warning of the attack is received. The bomber force might be dispersed among some ten or twenty bases, even though this is inefficient from the point of view of maintenance and personnel. Such dispersion would require the attacker to expend about twenty missiles on these bases.

The only way at present to prevent retaliation by the bombers on air alert is by normal air defense, that is, by ground-to-air missiles and fighter-interceptors. The attacker would probably not expand its air defense system, since such efforts would be an easily observable violation of the agreement. It would most probably place its air defense crew on alert status, increase their training and readiness, and otherwise show increased concern over an attack. Nevertheless, most estimates are that, with normal penetration aids and countermeasures against defensive radar, a significant fraction of the retaliatory force could survive. Since aircraft carry large yields and can attack several targets, even a reduced form of retaliation has significant deterrent value.

Finally, the Polaris component of the force is invulnerable to all presently available forms of attack and defense. It is doubtful whether there is an anti-submarine system in existence that can, with a high degree of confidence, find and destroy a submarine force such as that pictured here; and the use of longer-range missiles for nuclear submarines makes it unlikely that such a system can be developed in the near future.

A number of technological advances are possible during the 1965-1970 period that could require major alterations in the agreement or the force structure discussed here. Among them are the following:

1. It may be possible to achieve very much smaller cep's than are presently attainable. There are some who believe that a cep of a few tenths of a mile will be possible within the next ten years. If improved accuracy were attained, missiles at known locations would become highly vulnerable, and it might not be desirable to include fixed land-based missiles in the force.

2. A reliable technique for detecting and locating submarines might be developed. Although it would still be enormously difficult to find and destroy submarines carrying long-range missiles, this does represent an area in which technological development might alter present calculations.

3. An effective AICBM system might be developed. While advances in decoys and penetration aids would be proceeding concurrently, the presence of large numbers of AICBM systems might produce enough uncertainty in the penetrability of the retaliatory missiles to make an agreement such as the one under consideration untenable.

In the absence of such developments, the force that would survive a surprise attack would represent a potent deterrent, even if one assumed substantial clandestine violations. Thus, suppose that a country did succeed in developing the kind of clandestine force described earlier in this section. Then one might expect that the surviving vehicles would include 5 Titan II or Minuteman ICBM's, 60 Polaris missiles, and at least 20 B-52 airplanes (those maintained on air alert). Assuming reasonable reliability factors and air defense capabilities, the force that reached its target might include 3 ICBM's, 10 B-52's, and 30 Polaris missiles. Since each aircraft can carry several bombs, about 50 separate targets could be attacked. Since each weapon has a yield in the megaton range, one can estimate the casualties that would be suffered by counting the total population subjected to attack in the event that each target was a city. In both the United States and the Soviet Union, the 50 largest cities have a total population of about 35,000,000 people. Thus, even in the presence of a gross undetected violation, the force that would survive a surprise attack could still inflict massive damage upon the aggressor. The danger of such violations would not be that the violator could not be punished, or even that he would not reasonably anticipate effective retaliation, but that the populations of the other parties to the agreement might panic. But this likelihood would depend not upon the degree of inspection, but rather on the general political climate and, in particular, the rapport between the "victim" governments and their populations.

Verification of the Agreement

As was suggested earlier, the reduction to the final level of two hundred vehicles would be carried out in proportionate steps of six months duration each over a three-year period. During each six-month step, the United States and the Soviet Union would effect one-sixth of the reduction necessary to bring it to the agreed final level. The reduction would probably be accompanied by an initial declaration of the total inventory. The declaration would be necessary solely to determine the number of vehicles to be destroyed during each step. Therefore, it might be made implicitly by delivering the vehicles to be destroyed rather than through the explicit deposit of a written document.

As we have suggested, military considerations alone require no inspection other than verification of destruction and of declared production facilities. Even unilateral intelligence capabilities could probably discover violations serious enough to affect the deterrent capability of the other side. Nevertheless, there are a number of reasons (aside from domestic political ones) why formal inspection is desirable. It would provide continuous reassurance to each party that it could continue to abide by the agreement and it would give sufficient warning to permit a number of limited responses (including the initiation of more thorough investigations) should suspicion of noncompliance develop. It seems clear that for long-term stability of the agreement some agreed forms of access and information transfer are essential.

Great concern has been expressed by many people that the Soviet Union would not declare all of its vehicles. In making a declaration of initial arms levels, the Soviet Union would be constrained within rather narrow limits to make an accurate declaration. The declared strength could not be too high since this would require the destruction of added numbers of vehicles. At the same time, it could not be too low since it would have to be compatible with information from intelligence sources presently available to the United States. Furthermore, a major production facility could not be left undeclared, both because the USSR could not then account for the production of the vehicles in its inventory and because any plant left out of the declaration might be known in advance by United States intelligence.

During the first three years of agreement, the inspectors would observe the destruction of delivery vehicles and would inspect all declared production facilities. Even this amount of inspection would require a large increase in access within the Soviet Union compared to what is available today. The inspectors would also establish procedures for verifying the absence of clandestine production and stockpiles. Although the discussion in the previous section suggests that there would be no military necessity for conducting such inspections during this initial three-year period, it might still be desirable early in the process to establish the precedent of gradually increasing the freedom with which inspections were conducted. This might be done by permitting a limited number of inspection teams to carry out inspections within some of the larger cities or industrial centers. The number of such teams and the territory covered might be slowly increased during the period of the reduction.

At the end of this period, inspection procedures should be established that could provide reasonable assurance that the number of delivery vehicles was being held within the agreed limits. One factor affecting the magnitude of the inspection effort required is the type and extent of the industrial capacity currently devoted to producing delivery vehicles by the US and the USSR. The United States has about twenty plants producing engines and final assemblies, with about one hundred more producing major components and auxiliary equipment. The United States missile industry employs about 200,000 people, of whom about 10,000 are engineers.

The Soviet missile industry is likely to be of comparable size. This suggests that the industrial complex involved in the delivery vehicle industry is not so large as to require great numbers of inspectors to monitor its activities. At the same time, the industrial complex required to support a major effort to produce delivery vehicles (on a scale necessary to have a significant effect) would be quite

difficult to hide from a trained inspectorate or from unilateral detection techniques.

The inspectorate might be given the right to conduct a
total of perhaps one hundred inspections per year at selected industrial facilities, in addition to a continuous
monitoring of declared production facilities and of test
activities associated with related peaceful programs. An
important purpose of the inspection system should be to
check on information acquired by other means, such as
unilateral intelligence. This would serve the interests of
both sides if such an inspection tended to allay suspicions.
The inspectors should thus be able to conduct a number
of pre-emptory inspections without being required to
present supporting evidence.

Since there already exists a large body of information on
existing forces and production facilities, major clandestine production programs would be the primary targets
of the inspection system. The inspectors thus would need
only limited access privileges. For instance, their inspection visits might consist simply of tours through selected
factories and interviews with plant personnel, with no
monitoring of records, blueprint examination, or hardware testing. Assuming three-man inspection teams stationed at declared facilities, travelling between several
facilities, or inspecting for clandestine production, a total
of between 150 and 300 inspectors (50 to 100 teams)
would be sufficient.

These inspectors would fulfill a number of functions
besides verifying the type and amount of production.
These would include: (a) a selective monitoring of the
activities of professional personnel, especially those presently associated with aircraft and missile programs; (b)
the occasional inspection of sites suspected to contain

67

hidden stockpiles; (c) the verification of the scope and extent of defensive measures, including air defense, anti-missile defense, and anti-submarine systems.

As discussed earlier, a missile test ban is an important part of the agreement. It might be monitored by pre-launch inspections designed to reveal the purpose of each booster test and by the employment of a radar net capable of detecting launchings that have not been reported.

CHAPTER IV

VERIFICATION REQUIREMENTS FOR A PRODUCTION CUTOFF OF WEAPONS-GRADE FISSIONABLE MATERIAL

BY HANS A. LINDE

CONTEXT

THIS paper illustrates the study of hypothetical disarmament or arms control measures. The measure under consideration is an agreement between the US, the USSR, and perhaps other nations to end production of weapons-grade fissionable material.

THE HYPOTHETICAL RULE

The rule assumed to be agreed upon is a prohibition against the production of weapons-grade fissionable material. Stated more precisely, it is a cutback of uranium enrichment to levels adequate for peaceful uses but substantially below weapons grade and a prohibition on the military use of plutonium produced in operating reactors.

PURPOSE AND SCOPE OF THE RULE

The evaluation of the rule and the requirements for verifying compliance with it may depend on whether an international or merely a bilateral US-Soviet agreement is involved. For the bilateral agreement on a production cutoff, it may be generally true that as the two adversaries' stockpiles of weapons-grade fissionable material are perceived to approach the limits of military usefulness ("infinity"), the military interest in verifying compliance with the cutoff (in fact, along with the military interest in the agreement itself) approaches zero. At this point, the analysis of political objectives and of political verification requirements becomes one that is common to all similar hypothetical conditions: under what conditions, if ever, is an agreement on a militarily non-significant disarmament measure, with or without verification, worthwhile?

The more interesting version is a multilateral agreement not to produce weapons-grade fissionable material, i.e., one that is relevant to the "nth country" problem. An international production ban accepted by the US and the USSR would probably be signed by many other nations. There is the question whether, or under what conditions, it would be signed by two classes of significant nations: (1) those significant to the East-West strategic confrontation, i.e., China, France, Germany (or Western Europe generally), and (2) those that may pursue local military-political objectives that could seriously involve the US, the USSR, or both, e.g., Egypt-Israel, India-Pakistan, South Africa, and Latin American nations. Another question is whether or not such an agreement should be accompanied by a ban on transfers of weapons and weapons-grade material to nations that do not have them. We may assume that there would be a very substantial military interest in verification of such a ban, i.e., in knowing whether or not the various nth countries did or did not have nuclear weapons. Verification provisions of the agreement itself would then be calculated from the familiar factors of the importance of knowing the acceptable degree of uncertainty, the adequacy of other sources of information, the feasibility of adding agreed verification procedures to those other sources, the political estimate of the intentions of the potential transferors and of the nth

70

countries involved, and the nature of the price the US was paying for the agreement.

VERIFICATION TECHNIQUES

With respect to the hypothetical production cutoff, considered apart from questions of a ban on transfers, it appears that verification does not present insuperable technical difficulties. This results, for weapons-grade uranium enrichment, from the magnitude of the facilities involved and the relatively simple and non-intrusive techniques for checking sufficiently on the degree of enrichment—enough to make "cheating" too expensive relative to the insignificant amounts to be gained. In the case of plutonium, its production is a function of the power of the reactor, and its separation requires a complex technology, both of which are such that nth country "illegal" plutonium production may not be a militarily significant problem in the near future.

A military interest in verification of a production cutoff arises when an nth country acquires a large-scale, complex reactor technology while at the same time not having a national nuclear weapons material stockpile. Whether this interest rises to the level of a verification "requirement" depends on the calculation stated before. Similarly, an increased interest in verification of compliance, gradually approaching a verification "requirement," develops when a production cutoff is coupled with a significant reduction of existing stockpiles by the US and USSR. Again, this will be recognized as merely another application of the truism that you care about verifying those military conditions that matter and not those that do not matter militarily.

Nevertheless, perhaps one meaningful relation exists

among the different measures: it may be recognized that, where a number of measures are tied together, acceptance of the militarily most significant measure probably controls the others. It is more difficult to verify a ban on transfer or a reduction to an agreed stockpile than a production cutoff. A stockpile reduction by specified amounts may not be harder to verify but will be perceived as substantively more significant than a production cutoff. Accordingly, if either of these measures is successfully negotiated, the question of coupling a production cutoff agreement with it will not hinge on difficulties over verification—either because a more significant degree of verification has been accepted for the more critical measure or because the more critical measure has proved acceptable without much verification, so why not the less critical one.

Political-Psychological Verification Requirements

Apart from actual requirements of military security, what reasons, if any, give rise to a requirement that compliance with an arms control arrangement be verifiable?

A related question is: why conclude militarily trivial agreements in the armament field at all (such as, by hypothesis, a production cutoff not coupled to a stockpile reduction, at a time when the adversaries' stockpiles are perceived to approach practical "infinity")?

One political interest in verification is to determine whether or not the other side is keeping the agreement, i.e., compliance as a test of political intentions rather than of military capability. Likewise, the agreement itself, if not militarily important, may have been sought and accepted only for political reasons, e.g., as a symbol of willingness to undertake and carry out *some* agreement in the arms field. Again, in the case of a weapons-material cutoff, a point may be reached, now or in the future, where an end to further production may be unilaterally advantageous, if only to free resources for useful purposes. Nevertheless, the US government may perceive it to be politically impossible to stop production of even redundant materials that represent a theoretical threat to its adversaries without obtaining some "quid pro quo," even one that (by the hypothesis of near-infinite stockpiles) is equally valueless to the USSR. This concept of an elaborately negotiated agreement with one's adversary to permit oneself to take steps of even unilateral self-interest, while an engaging notion, does not commend itself as a major premise of rational policy. (An international agreement that is designed to meet the nth country problem, perhaps including rules on transfer, has real military as well as political significance.)

What, then, is the utility of an agreement that is seen essentially as a militarily non-significant "experiment" or "first step"? The political gains claimed by "optimists" for such an agreement might include: (1) reduction in tension from the mere fact of agreement with the USSR; (2) reduction in tension from an apparent "first step backward in the arms race"; (3) reduction of suspicion (development of mutual confidence) from an acceptance of the principle of verification; (4) experience with verification processes, particularly with administering an international system if one is used; (5) reduction of suspicion (development of confidence) from the fact of compliance with the agreement, i.e., from apparently successful verification; and (6) implications for other strategic and political confrontations between the US and USSR, e.g., recognition that some community of interest may

73

exist, such as possible tacit consensus on status quo in areas of vital concern. "Pessimists" have, in turn, seen these same results as involving the assumption of dangerous political risks: (1) false sense of accomplishment attaching to the mere fact of agreement with the USSR over an insignificant matter; (2) false sense of relaxation arising from an apparent breakthrough in reversing the arms race; (3) devaluation of the principle of verification by the precedent of accepting minimal procedures where we do not care much; (4) danger of a bad precedent in the design of an international inspectorate when we do not care much, which would be inadequate for critical measures, and danger of unnecessary friction and disputes over the operation of verification machinery; (5) false sense of confidence in Soviet intentions and in the capabilities of a verification system, resulting from Soviet compliance with a measure imposing no real restraint; and (6) detrimental effect on allies and others relying on US support to resist Soviet pressure as a consequence of the apparent political implications of the agreement. These arguments for and against negotiating a militarily nonsignificant arms limitation indicate the nature and importance of political requirements for verification of compliance with the formally agreed limitation even if verification is militarily insignificant.

ACCEPTABILITY

It is characteristic of the disarmament discussion, at least the discussion of "first measures," that it presupposes a continuation of antagonism and hostility between the disarming parties. For this reason, it is necessary to meet the psychological need for assurance that the agreement is being complied with, thus to retain a posture of distrust vis-à-vis the adversary in connection with any "first step." But this need can be met by any method of verification pronounced to be adequate by national leaders and experts. However, some special verification requirements may emerge as essential.

Such requirements might be particularly evident with respect to the actual or potential participation of Communist China, assuming Chinese adherence to be an important interest in the negotiation and in its acceptance of a production cutoff treaty.

At present, it may be more likely that China (and other nations planning to produce weapons-grade material) will refuse to sign the treaty than that they would sign and then cheat. Nevertheless, the minimum verification procedures accompanying a production cutoff agreement to be offered to all nations for accession will be those considered appropriate for an agreement with that nation for whose compliance one wants the most verification. For the US, that would be China, and if a multilateral production cutoff agreement is to be offered for Chinese accession, this will presumably determine the minimum political verification requirements for the draft convention whether or not China actually adheres to it.

PRECEDENT AND "PRINCIPLE"

The elevation of inspection to the status of a "principle" has, no doubt, been exaggerated to the point where it rigidifies and hampers rather than helps US disarmament policy. The extent of our national policy commitment to this principle adds to the political verification requirements of a US position, both domestically and internationally. Nevertheless, in rejecting the self-imposed constraints of a no-disarmament-without-inspection principle, it would be a mistake to conclude at the other extreme, that there is no serious precedent-creating effect in the design and operation of a disarmament measure.

Different degrees, methods, and systems of verification can unquestionably be designed to provide the requisite assurance needed for different disarmament measures. But politically, no matter what efforts may be made to state clearly that each measure and its verification stand on their own feet, the "precedent" of one measure will be cited by the party to whom it would be advantageous in the design of another measure—and not only in the disarmament context. Thus, it was reasonable for the US to be concerned about the effect that serious consideration of the USSR's "troika" approach to the nuclear test ban organization would have upon the simultaneous fight taking place over the USSR's troika proposal for the UN Secretariat. The US position should be flexible on the design of different verification provisions appropriate to the actual needs of specific disarmament measures. But it is not unreasonable to recognize a political requirement that these different verification provisions be explainable as variations on a single, consistent policy.

BASIS FOR RESPONSE

Another political verification requirement is to establish some identifiable occasion that raises the question whether or not a response to non-compliance is called for. The proposition is stated in this awkward way because of the narrow connotations that references to "responses" generally seem to bring to mind. What is meant here is not a matter of "sanctions," of UN or other international verdicts, of US abrogation in case of "cheating," or of any other specific response. In the case of the hypothetical production cutoff, the actual need for the US to do something about suspected or known non-compliance is probably minimal. By the same token, there is maximum US freedom to choose what to do, including doing nothing. Nevertheless, it is important for the US to be in a position to consider and choose a policy if an agreement, such as the production cutoff, is not being kept. To that extent, there is an apparent political requirement that compliance be verifiable by some process that will trigger a signal for US consideration in case of doubt.

RISKS IN VERIFICATION PROVISIONS

The costs and risks of these verification procedures should always be weighed against the gains of satisfying verification requirements. Among the costs may be substantial financial ones. The risks include the substantial danger that there will be frequent, difficult, and bitter controversies over the operation of verification procedures unrelated to any real issues of substantive compliance with the agreement. There is reason to believe that intrusive verification procedures could become a great source of friction and international tension that would eliminate any possible gain resulting from an agreement on a relatively innocuous disarmament measure. The US may be confronted repeatedly with the need to decide how to respond to "violations" of the verification provisions rather than, as is usually imagined, to violations of the substantive provisions of the agreement. It is not necessary to spell out in detail the way in which such situations influence domestic and international politics, perhaps forcing US policy into undesirable steps not required by any national interest in the substantive disarmament measures as such.

SOME CONCLUSIONS

Certain conclusions suggested by the foregoing may be summarized here for further discussion.

Political verification requirements increase with the formality of the agreement. If one starts with our assumption that a weapons-grade material cutoff is not of great military importance to either the US or the USSR, it may be a mutually desirable step to take if this cost for a formal commitment upon a secondary matter is not too great. Accordingly, an agreement may be desirable at a political level not requiring much militarily unnecessary verification.

Both the formality of the cutoff agreement and verification requirements are likely to increase with the number of parties involved; political verification requirements may increase sharply if the agreement is designed for the contemplated adherence of strategically less important nations, particularly China and Germany. But the strictly military verification requirement is not changed by this (since we have at least the same information about nth countries with, as without, an agreement and since the US is giving up nothing militarily in agreeing to stop weapons-grade production). Accordingly, if an international cutoff agreement can be drafted for signature by the US and the USSR and other willing nations *without* increasing verification provisions beyond the minimal techniques that are mutually acceptable and more than adequate in the context of the US and USSR stockpiles, an international agreement may be a desirable form of bilateral cutoff that will simultaneously exercise substantial pressure against proliferation of weapons-grade production capabilities.

On the other hand, if minimal verification techniques are politically non-acceptable in a draft treaty open to the adherence of China (or other major nations), then it may be preferable to end weapons-grade production in the US and the USSR under a bilateral agreement that involves a lower level of formality and to rely on the political fact of this cutoff rather than on the existence of a formal draft convention to exert political pressure upon nth countries to discourage them from seeking weapons-grade production capability.

Pragmatic, ad hoc verification procedures tailored to the needs of the specific substantive measure are easier to design and accept on a case-by-case basis. When measures are combined and offered as part of a "plan," questions of "principle" and the drive to achieve consistency in policy tend to increase political verification requirements and to rigidify positions around some single model of an acceptable verification procedure. By the same token, the precedent value and significance of any particular verification procedure is minimized, facilitating the outlook of pragmatic flexibility, if a measure can be separated and dealt with on a level less formal than the "Geneva" meetings and as something independent of other disarmament measures. This treatment might be possible for a production cutoff—with or without related measures to inhibit the spread of nuclear-weapons capabilities—particularly if there is present no idea of establishing the notion of an International Disarmament Administration. To create an administering agency would make formal negotiations and treaties inevitable and, to that extent, would maximize the political standards that must be attained by the verification provisions.

CHAPTER V

ORGANIZATION OF A "MIXED" NATIONAL AND INTERNATIONAL INSPECTORATE

BY HANS A. LINDE

BACKGROUND

Most discussions of verification of compliance with disarmament agreements by inspection have assumed the necessity for an international disarmament organization. IDO has become almost a synonym for inspectorate. However, the characteristics of the IDO itself have not often been subjected to analysis. When discussion of inspection has been more technical—for example, on detection techniques and capabilities, on personnel and equipment requirements, and on degrees of access—the organization of the inspectorate has been tacitly assumed to resemble the Secretariat of the United Nations or one of its specialized agencies and to be somehow related to the United Nations.

It is possible, however, to envisage an inspection system operating on an *adversary* rather than an *impartial* basis. The adversary inspector represents a government that has undertaken reciprocal disarmament obligations with the inspected nation and that has a direct interest in the latter's compliance with the agreed measure. The impartial inspector, on the other hand, is selected because he has no prior commitment to any party to the agreement but only to the proper functioning of the arrangement. Neutral governments (Sweden, Switzerland, and India) *or* neutral individuals (the head of the International Red Cross or ad hoc arbitrators), as well as formal international organizations, may serve as impartial inspectors, but the concept usually brings to mind the international civil servant working for an international organization.

The advantages of the two alternative principles of organization should be evaluated in terms of specific disarmament agreements. If the United States assumes militarily important disarmament commitments in reliance on disarmament commitments by the Soviet Union, China, or another state, the crucial requirement of verification is that it support a high level of confidence that the potential adversary is continuing compliance with the agreement and that the United States will receive reliable and timely signals of present or impending violations. If a verification arrangement meets this requirement, other potential gains might include the encouragement of an international response to violations and the development of worthwhile international institutions or projects. Such secondary objectives may even outweigh reliability of verification for a limited disarmament measure not substantially affecting national security. The balance of advantages may not be the same for the Soviet Union, which has more "open" information about the United States and needs less verification of US compliance, nor for smaller nations, which rely on third-party support more than on their own unilateral capacity to protect their national security.

An adversary inspection system may permit a higher degree of confidence in the reliability of its operation. The inspecting nation has greater control over the internal functioning of the system: it may choose and replace personnel, furnish them with reliable and technologically up-to-date equipment, and place great reliance on their reports. There is no risk of internal obstruction of the system through falsifications, cover-ups, slowdowns, vetoes, or refusals to vote adequate budgets or to pay the funds voted. The precise capabilities of the system, within the limits set by the terms of the agreement and by technology, are within the knowledge and control of the inspecting nation but not necessarily known to the inspected nation. This may mean a reduced vulnerability to countermeasures and a gain in inducement to compliance.

Impartial (international) inspection, on the other hand, may have advantages in acceptability, and this must be weighed against the lesser confidence in its reliability. An international system may be more negotiable, particularly in connection with multilateral agreements among nations that do not fall clearly into adversary groups. International inspectors may be granted wider access and greater freedom of movement than inspectors identified ab initio as adversaries. The presence of international personnel may be more acceptable to the host country than inspectors from a nation considered hostile, for example, Soviet inspectors in the United States. The reports of impartial inspectors will carry greater persuasiveness for a third-party and international opinion than complaints and allegations emanating from an adversary-type inspection system operated by the complaining nation. Obstruction by the host nation of impartial inspection operations may be restrained by a potentially greater political penalty than obstruction of adversary inspection. (Compare, for example, North Korean attitudes toward the Swedes and Swiss, on the one hand, and toward the United States representatives, on the other.) But this constraint should not be exaggerated. (The Soviets have refused to admit a UN mission to Hungary, and there are other examples of Communist obstruction of neutral observers.)

The potential design of *mixed systems* that will combine characteristics of both the adversary and the impartial principles of organization seems to be the most promising approach. Which components should (from the US standpoint) be adversary and which impartial can, in the first instance, be determined from the priorities assigned to the two types in relation to the particular object of verification. This initial "optimum" mixed design would, in turn, be subject to qualification by all the contingencies of political acceptability, such as negotiability, favorable or adverse precedent effect for other measures, and cost.

The outstanding detailed design of an inspection system that has been subjected to the tests of actual policy decisions and of negotiation has been the international verification system proposed by the US for the nuclear test ban treaty in 1961. The history of the test ban negotiations shows that neither the Soviet nor the Western positions had any clear or consistent theory of the operations of the international organization to be set up to monitor compliance with the test ban. In the Western treaty draft for the international inspection system for a nuclear test ban in all environments, the United States was driven by Soviet insistence on political representation within the administration structure to compromise the international principle for the adversary one in ways that impaired the former without gaining for the United States the important advantages of the latter.

The Functional Levels of Verification and Response

A variety of concepts has been used to describe those disarmament operations whose functions are to provide assurance and safeguards to the disarming nations, such as disarmament "controls," "inspection," "verification," "inducements to compliance," "response," and "sanctions." But the functions and the operations are not always clearly distinguished. In an adversary system, this is not critical, since the single crucial operation is to get the required raw data into the information channels of the inspecting side whether by voluntary disclosure, by external verification, or by permitted inspection. In an international or a mixed system, clarity about the functions of the various components is important.

For a complex system, the simple notion of "detecting a violation" and "responding" may mean several distinct functions, such as (1) collecting the relevant raw data, (2) collating diverse sets of data, (3) factual interpreting of the data, (4) evaluating the interpreted facts, that is, whether they constitute a discrepancy, (5) evaluating the discrepancy, that is, whether it constitutes a "violation," (6) deciding on a response (or no response) to the violation, and (7) executing the response. In deciding what operations are to be performed by international, adversary, host-national or third-party personnel, it is essential to consider what function the operation serves and how it is related to other functions. There is a natural inclination to consider this in chronological order, from data input to the ultimate response. But the design and the negotiation of a disarmament control system must recognize that the logical order of functions is the reverse. The decision on a response is logically a function of the available responses. The judgment of "violation" is related to a potential decision on response. The evaluation of discrepancies will consider the consequences that may follow. The specifications for the fact-finding process depend upon the requirements for evaluation and judgment, not vice versa. And data collection and transmittal procedures should provide for fact-finding within the prescribed limits of confidence.

This appears self-evident, but no such recognition of the functional hierarchy was apparent in the organization of the nuclear test ban verification provisions proposed by the Western side. The IDO provisions perfectly illustrated a design based on painstaking and conservative attention to the technical capabilities of detection hardware, while the organization of the functions above the level of data collection appeared to have received no analytical attention by either side, reflecting only routine concepts and political arguments about secretariats, voting strengths, lists of decisions subject to veto, and so forth.

THE ROLE OF RESPONSES

An understanding of the foregoing hierarchy of functions from response to data collection—makes clear the importance of having explicit and realistic assumptions about the role of response in any given disarmament plan. There has been a good deal of "conventional wisdom" about the "enforcement" of disarmament through inspection and response to violations, both with respect to initial measures in the present world and even more in a substantially disarmed world. The following propositions are meant to suggest that some common assumptions, though perhaps true for some situations, are not *necessarily* true—that the conventional premises need examination in each case.

1. *International disarmament agreements need not necessarily be guaranteed by international responses to violations.* If the US is confronted by Soviet (or other) non-compliance with an arms control agreement, inter-

national support for its position and collective action in response, if attainable, are certainly desirable. But the safety to the United States of a militarily significant arms control measure depends on the availability of a secure US response to non-compliance, not on an international response. (Less powerful nations threatened by another's violation may, of course, be dependent on US or other third-party, i.e., a collective or international, response.)

Parties to an agreement that has been violated may join in response to a violation, if willing to do so, without express procedures for such joint action being provided in the agreement. In the case of arms control agreements, institutional channels for such an international response could also be found under the United Nations Charter. But a decision in advance to institutionalize responses to apparent disarmament violations is not necessarily fruitful. Many governments may be glad to accept and abide by an agreement imposing certain limits on armaments, and they may also be willing to join in an international organization for that purpose. But any subsequent occasion for taking action in response to apparent violations of the agreement will pose quite different decisions of foreign policy for these governments. If provisions for an international determination of and response to violations are written into a treaty, this may give a nation charging another with non-compliance a claim to receive international support. But at the same time, it may inhibit an independent response in the absence of such support and thus place the United States (for instance) in the position of needing the votes or other support of third parties to whom the claimed violation is far less important than other demands they have against the US, its allies, or the Soviet Union. These political dynamics of international organization are a familiar part of the experience of the United Nations.

2. *International responses do not necessarily become more essential in long-range projections of substantial disarmament.* A stable international order at substantially lower arms levels does not necessarily depend on substitution of an international force for national forces in order to maintain the agreed state of disarmament. The contrary assumption rests on the questionable notion that an advanced state of disarmament can be reached by an agreement among hostile adversaries to shift the control of predominant military force from themselves to some administrative and voting mechanism *while persisting in their mutual hostility and distrust.*

The large powers that are able to rely on national armed strength for their security will not substantially reduce their national armaments unless they are convinced that they can pursue their national interests with at least equal security at lower levels of armament. The capacity to respond to rearmament steps by potential must be a national one. But national capacity to respond is itself only one element in the confidence necessary to reach and maintain arms control or arms reduction. Such confidence requires a political judgment of the intentions of the other major governments, their policies toward existing or predictable areas of dispute, the likelihood that these disputes may flare into violence, and other factors—but, ultimately, a judgment as to whether the potential adversary will continue to perceive the arrangement to be in *its* own interest. (In the light of its neighbors' traditional fears, German rearmament in the 1950's was made subject to control by the WEU—but French, Belgian, Dutch, etc. acceptance of German rearmament, in fact, rests on sources of confidence other than the WEU controls.) If the environment appears politically stable for a considerable period into the future, substantial arms reductions may be feasible and consistent with mutual security at a lower level of military stability. The imposition of external enforcement machinery to coerce compliance will not only seem unnecessary; it will introduce unknown risks to the existing political stability. If, on the other hand, the preconditions of fairly long-range political stability are lacking, the alternative of an international force to coerce compliance with disarmament will be neither negotiable nor acceptable.

Creation of an international force more powerful than those of any nation or alliance is not a logically deducible "stage" in a linear development of a disarming world but only one of several theoretical conceptions for a far-reaching transformation of international society. It is not a sine qua non of substantial disarmament. Thus, it is not a necessary characteristic of initial, partial disarmament measures that they be organized in a manner facilitating later international enforcement of subsequent, more radical measures, and this criterion need not affect the acceptability of otherwise desirable steps toward disarmament. Rather, the responses deemed necessary for any stage of disarmament must reflect realistic assumptions about the political, and not only about the military, environment that take into account the conditions necessary for those stages to be reached, as well as the anticipated political effects of the disarmament process itself. Both of these—preconditions as well as consequences—will include a substantial re-evaluation of the assumptions of mutual hostility and distrust. And new steps toward mutual arms reductions will be taken only if these are found to be reduced—i.e., in reliance on a political basis for confidence rather than on increasingly effective detection-response mechanisms in case of non-compliance.

In short, the detection-response capability is most significant when mutual hostility and distrust are at their highest—at the beginning of the disarmament process—since reliance then is primarily on national response. Substantially lower arms levels are possible only in an environment of considerable political stability, when confidence in the security of the arrangement is based much less on the detection-response capacity; thus, no increased need for international enforcement machinery can necessarily be postulated.

3. *International responses may be valuable for maintaining operation of an arms agreement rather than for "punishing violations."* It is important to recognize the distinction between responses to suspicious events, obstructions, propaganda charges, etc., that arise in the course of an arrangement that retains a reasonable life expectancy, and responses to overt abandonment or covert evasions that signal the substantive end of the arms control arrangement and that threaten international security. It is the latter case ("cheating") that has received the attention in the analysis of responses. For that case, the United States must rely on its capacity to make a timely national response. But the former case—controversies in day-to-day life under the agreement that do not necessarily involve non-compliance with its substantive arms limitations—may realistically be much more common and quite troublesome. For such controversies, an added international response may be valuable.

In the present world, it may be assumed that nations outside the Soviet bloc and the Western alliances will act on a policy of doing everything to keep an arms control agreement among the large powers in existence and nothing to support one large power in any action to "enforce" the substantive agreement or to end the agreement and penalize the "violator" for its non-compliance. This assumption has significance for the design of arms control organizations: the proper role of "neutrals," for example, might be based on a recognized bias against finding substantive violations, but in favor of facilitating verification and otherwise inducing compliance by the parties with agreed procedures, at least up to the point where further insistence would threaten the agreement. A "mixed" design could reflect this objective of furnishing bases for an international response to "procedural" non-compliance, while assuring parties of the opportunity to decide on a national response if another party should end its substantive compliance.

Such a mixed design should therefore select national or international elements on the basis of clear and rigorous assumptions about whether the operation of each element would be essential to a national response to substantive non-compliance or to maintaining international pressure for compliance with a verification procedure. There may be cases in which it will be desirable to facilitate an international response even at some cost of inhibiting national capabilities for unilateral response.

DESIGN OF MIXED ORGANIZATIONS FOR DISARMAMENT VERIFICATION

The wide range of possible arms control measures naturally involves many wholly different techniques of obtaining the information necessary for verification of compliance at acceptable confidence levels. Depending on the nature of the arms control measure, these techniques may rely more or less on sensors and other instruments, depend on few or many individuals, and require more or less access to the territory of (or other cooperation by) the inspected nation. Irrespective of the technical means employed, however, the human element in the verification system is essential to an evaluation of its chances of performing its functions. People have to design, order, install, adjust, operate, service, and pay for machines, and people have to read, transmit, interpret, evaluate, and report the information obtained from them and decide what to do about disputes over the operation of the verification system. Thus, the confidence that may be placed in a system of verification operations depends at least as much on its organization as on its technical capabilities.

The major functions of verification, as stated before, are to contribute to the confidence in compliance that is needed to sustain an arms control agreement among adversaries and to assure timely opportunity for response in case of non-compliance. For both purposes, the product of verification processes—the information confirming compliance or signaling non-compliance—is of primary interest to national governments, as long as nations make the basic choices of foreign and military policy. From the standpoint of the United States, the information obtained by verification techniques must reach the US government in a manner that will best assure the US of Soviet compliance or give timely warning of non compliance with a substantive arms control measure. In addition to this essential requirement, it is desirable that the information be politically usable as a basis both for national action and for claiming international support.

Thus, the functions of verification, like the functions of the arms to be restricted by the control measure and like the responses to possible non-compliance with it, are essentially adversary in principle. It is possible to organize mutual surveillance of compliance with arms control, as with any other agreement, on this principle. But another principle is deeply ingrained in Western thinking: that of the objective ascertainment of fact by impartial agencies whose commitment is to the truth and to a larger community encompassing all adversaries. This is the theoretical foundation of Western law enforcement, which is so readily assumed as the appropriate analogy in Western plans for disarmament and other international peace-keeping organizations. Neither the analogy nor its philosophical premises is shared, however, by the Communist world and not even by all other non-Western nations. Thus, the international organization of verification —e.g., inspection by the impartial personnel of an international disarmament organization—cannot be taken for granted as a self-evident principle. It may offer very important and attainable advantages toward making a verification system effective and toward enhancing its life expectancy. But its advantages and limitations must be identified and measured along with those of adversary verification arrangements. And the advantages of the two principles of organization can be combined if the objectives for which each is best suited are clearly identified and used in making the allocation of functions within the mixed system.

The premise of any mixed design is that there are some functions of the total system that should be organized internationally and others for which national (adversary or host-national) operations are appropriate. These allocations will vary for different measures and for different nations. The United States, relying on its own military capability for its national security, will not delegate the functions of decision and execution of response with respect to any measure that has material significance for US national security. For such measures, the United States must be able to form a judgment about "violations," that is, to assess its own confidence in the continued compliance of others with their disarmament commitment. It would be desirable to have third-party (allied, neutral, or international) judgments and responses. But if the United States has critically based its security on a disarmament commitment by another nation, any verification procedure must be organized to facilitate a US judgment concerning compliance. Organization of the fact-finding functions below that of judgment must be designed so as to protect this essentially adversary function, whatever other desiderata and constraints may bear upon the possible design.

References to "adversary" and "international" components in a mixed organization denote the operations of the components, not the nomenclature of appearance of the organization. It is possible to have adversary components within an international organization. In fact, it is necessary and customary to have their participation at the level at which the political nature of decisions is clearly recognized, such as, for example, the "Commission" and the "Conference" in the proposed nuclear test-ban organization; this is perceived to be characteristic of, rather than inconsistent with, the principle of international organization. There is no intrinsic reason why an organization that performs the operations of verification on an adversary principle cannot possess some of the important characteristics of an international system. The theoretical criterion for such a "mixed system," subject, of course, to the compromises of negotiability, is to use adversary elements of organization to perform adversary functions and impartial elements to perform impartial functions and to give the system international status and acceptability.

How can a mixed system be organized to perform its fact-finding operations most reliably from the standpoint of the adversary parties while making maximum use of the additional advantages of international systems? For the purposes of this discussion, it is assumed that a substantive disarmament measure is accepted by the United States and the Soviet Union and perhaps by other nations and that verification of compliance with the agreement is to include an inspectorate conducting various operations within the inspected countries. How might the components and operations of such an inspectorate be organized?

PERSONNEL

The confidence that the inspecting nation can place in the reliability of a system becomes greater as its own personnel come closer to the basic level of data collection. An optimum design for the United States would use adversary (American, possibly allied NATO) inspection teams in the Soviet Union. Soviet or other Communist teams would operate in the Western nations.

These adversary inspectors would not need to operate alone. They could be accompanied by host-nation and, if desired, by third-nation or by international personnel.[1]

[1] Throughout this discussion, "international personnel" means an international civil service whose personnel are obligated to maintain independence from national influence including their own

94

The adversary inspection personnel might best have international status; for example, they might be US nationals assigned or on loan to the IDO, wear blue IDO uniforms, and travel on IDO identification papers and passes. It would be important that they be clearly entitled to report to, receive instructions from, and be replaceable by their national government (perhaps through its representatives in the IDO).

International inspectors might usefully be added to mixed inspection teams whenever the signatories to the agreement do not fall into two adversary "sides"—to represent the "neutral" signatories of an agreement, that is, more than Western and Soviet-allied nations. International personnel might comprise the administrative staff of the IDO under an international secretary-general to act as the secretariat for conferences, to keep records, to publish reports, to handle support operations such as buildings, travel, personnel health and welfare, to conduct open research and testing, and to participate directly in inspection functions if requested to do so by the parties to the agreement.

Equipment

A separation of adversary and international (or host-nation) components should reflect the importance ascribed to assuring that the equipment is accurate, technically up to date, always available, correctly calibrated, and foolproof—factors that obviously depend on the nature of the specific equipment and inspection processes involved. Another factor could be the advantage to the inspecting nation if the inspected nation did not know

---

governments; third-nation personnel represents an agreed upon, presumably "neutral," government.

the full capability and results of the equipment, as against the inspected nation's objections to espionage capabilities.

To illustrate, one possible "mix" could use small, portable equipment furnished by the inspectors themselves (that is, on the adversary principle), while heavy equipment and service facilities (airplanes, darkrooms, laboratory equipment) were international. Again, variations are possible. Fixed stations, particularly buildings, within inspected territories could be owned by the host nation—possibly under lease to the IDO. Examples of essential components that would, under normal conditions, be furnished by the host nation are transportation and communications, though the right to use planes and radio frequencies when needed might be provided to the IDO.

International equipment might be made subject to periodic checks by adversary personnel. Adversary equipment might be made subject to checks by international personnel. Where inspection by mixed teams and equipment is important, controversy over equipment might be headed off by allowing the use of duplicate equipment by the disagreeing inspectors. Two conditions are important for the adversary part of the "mix": that adversary use of necessary equipment not be subject to obstruction either in input or in output and that the adversary inspectors be able to report on the reliability of the equipment they are using.

BUDGET

The risk of degrading the originally assumed quality of the inspection system by financial starvation, either for reasons of economy or as a means of obstruction, is often overlooked. When the need for verification is asymmetrical, interest in economy and obstruction in the process of agreeing on a budget can work against the nation most desiring high-system performance. Yet if the Soviet Union constantly opposed a large budget for the IDO (note the significance of the veto issue here) or refused to pay its share of a budget it considered excessive, the United States could not reasonably conclude that the reason was a desire to violate the substantive disarmament agreement in an undetected manner.

In a pure adversary system, this problem is solved by letting each party pay the costs of the amount of inspection it conducts. In a mixed system, the same principle should be recognized by charging to the account of the inspecting nation the costs of its adversary operations— for example, inspectors' salaries, equipment costs, and use of transportation and communication facilities. If the mixed system operates as an IDO inspectorate, these accounts might be handled through the international secretariat rather than by the inspecting nation through direct payments; this would also be the easier way to determine fair charges made for host-nation services. The adversary components must be able to continue to operate when underwritten by national shares of the budget. The international budget requiring agreement would be reduced to a fraction of the total cost of the inspection system by the allocation of adversary and international components and operations suggested in the present mixed system.

Operations

Assuming the above mixed inspectorate of adequately equipped and financed personnel, adversary and impartial principles can also be integrated into the conduct of inspection operations.

HANS A. LINDE

ACCESS RIGHTS

In the adversary system, the access rights defined in the agreement belong to the inspecting nation. In the mixed system, these rights will probably be granted to the IDO. Nevertheless, the access provisions should be designed to guarantee at least the required access for the adversary personnel of the inspectorate and to flag obstruction if access is denied. For instance, an inspection team may consist of an adversary national accompanied by a host national. The agreement may specify that the agreed access rights be exercised by either member of the team alone; if the other member disagrees with the demand, he may record his protest and transmit it to a higher administrative or political organ. If this is unacceptable, the agreement might provide that the adversary inspector may demand that a third inspector (neutral or international) be dispatched to demand access or to accept the reasons against it—with the losing side having the right of protest, and so forth. Three-man inspection teams would fulfill the same function.

The use of international arbitrators is preferred, however, only in cases of disagreement. Their absence places greater pressure on the adversary team members to agree between themselves rather than routinely to carry each individual decision to the impartial member; it permits keeping international inspection personnel less numerous and less expensive, but more expert and important when needed.

REPORTS

It is essential that each individual inspector—adversary, host-nation, or impartial—be free to make his own report and that the national governments have direct access to the data reported by their nationals within the system. This is the chief purpose of the adversary components of a mixed inspection system. In a purely adversary system, the inspecting personnel would simply make their reports through the most direct or most secure communication channel available, for example, by reports to embassy attachés or by whatever happened to be the "read-out" of the particular method of adversary data collection. Such adversary reports might have to be shared with the other party (that is, copies of inspectors' reports might have to be given to the inspected nation). While such a requirement could not be enforced to the extent of preventing additional "debriefing" of adversary inspectors by their own governments, it might nevertheless be useful in fixing the overt record on which any charges of obstruction, discrepancies, and so forth would be based.

When impartial components are added to the adversary system, similar questions arise that may be solved by various arrangements. Adversary inspectors' reports and data may go in duplicate channels with copies to the national governments and to the international secretariat. Alternatively, they may be transmitted to the governments *through* IDO channels, where these channels meet the characteristics of reliability and efficiency associated with adversary operations. A significant question in considering the mixed system is to what extent, and under what conditions, adversary reports gain some kind of unearned authenticity, politically though not legally, by having been made to, or transmitted by, an IDO. Inspectors' reports *not* made to the IDO will not be useful as a basis for making complaints of obstruction, asking for further verification of discrepancies, and so forth.

ADMINISTRATIVE DIRECTION

A mixed organization may present problems of "command and control" that should be anticipated and given careful attention in planning the inspection system. In the pure adversary model, inspectors are employees of the inspecting government and responsible solely to it. In the international model, all personnel below the governing body of political representatives are international civil servants responsible solely to the secretary-general and independent, theoretically, from any national influence. If a mixed system is designed to place national personnel performing adversary inspection functions within an IDO containing international components under an international administrator, the responsibilities of the national personnel toward higher national and international levels must be carefully specified to reduce the inevitable problems of dual control. Here, as elsewhere, the problems vary with the size and complexity of the mixed organization.

A very simple model of a mixed system might consist of two or more sets of national inspection personnel acting as adversary inspectors abroad and as host-nation "controllers" at home. The "mixture" might consist only of additional sets of inspectors designated by nth country "neutrals" to be available to act as impartial inspectors when called upon to do so under specified conditions (the Korean armistice system). This does not involve any international administrator. International administrators can be added to the above model without serious problems of command and control as long as they perform limited service functions clearly separable from the inspection functions of the adversary teams acting under direction of their respective governments. The problems become more complicated when the adversary personnel are to be given international status as members of an IDO and when their operations are more closely integrated with those of the international personnel (for example, on three-man inspection teams, within data-processing or in equipment-maintenance facilities). It may be better to design the national channel of adversary operations to flow into the IDO rather than to have governmental directives come to their own nationals in the IDO from the outside. The proposal of the Soviet Union in their suggested comprehensive test ban organization to have "political" deputy administrators might have been exploited for this function had the US been willing to compromise the principle of a pure international system.

To protect the international secretary-general in cases of conflict, all IDO personnel must in the first instance abide by his orders, but personnel performing adversary functions would report to their national representative, who could take up the issue with his opposite numbers and with the secretary-general at the political level. Again, the adversary principle does not demand that national inspectors do everything they judge themselves entitled to do. They must be both able and free to report to their government on whatever obstructions or shortcomings they meet in their inspection operations and thus permit the government to assess the reliability of the inspection system and to deal with its problems at the political level.

POLITICAL CONTROL AND RESPONSIVENESS

The foregoing paragraphs are not exhaustive, but they illustrate how the data-collecting operations of inspection might be organized to satisfy the needs of the adversaries for reliable data and, at the same time, to gain many of the advantages of an international organization. Beyond the design of data-collection machinery itself, there remains the problem of political control of the inspection system and of procedures for dealing with discrepancies and with other issues arising from the inspection operations. For these purposes, national and international modes of organization can be mixed on the same basic principle: that the minimum essential freedom of adversary choice of response not be impaired and that desirable international components and procedures be added to achieve advantages while protecting the essential adversary principle.

THE POLITICAL LEVEL

In a small, relatively simple inspection system that produces usable reports without extensive detection machinery and data processing, the political level can be very close to the basic operations. In the simplest adversary form of organization, that is, mutual inspection through the "attaché system," they are, in effect, the same: any issue arising in the course of routine inspection operations can be taken up between the embassy and the foreign ministry. No pure adversary model needs more elaborateness than this. If inspection is performed by more numerous adversary personnel accompanied by host-nation inspectors, the first-stage political level of dealing with inspection procedures, of receiving mutual reports or complaints, and of planning for the continued effective operation of the system might be built into the system itself. At this stage, adversary representatives, meeting on call or on schedule, might be assigned the task of deciding whether newly built factories should or should not be placed on the list of inspectable facilities. At the level of political control, the adversary system relies on the continued desire of the adversaries to make the disarmament agreement and its operations, including verification, work.

If a disagreement occurs that cannot be settled by the political representatives and is not settled by built-in voting procedures, the respective governments will decide or act accordingly. This is, in fact, the most common arrangement for facilitating the operation of on-going international agreements that may raise routine issues. An analogy can be found in the grievance procedures of collective bargaining contracts in which third-party judgment—arbitration—is invoked only after the exhaustion of lower-level, bilateral settlement procedures. Even though this arrangement is easier to visualize in a bilateral confrontation, it need not be different in principle in a multilateral treaty that does not rely on international inspectors.

Political control becomes difficult as soon as the political direction of an international organization is at stake. At this advanced level, the familiar and existing problems of the veto, troikas, voting formulas, and the selection of administrators and third-party members of the political organs become important. In the context of disarmament inspection, a mixed system lessens their influence on the disarmament process by establishing clear authority and modes of operation for the adversary components of the system and by assigning to international personnel those functions that are less essential to the day-to-day inspection operations.

There is a crucial distinction between the concept of a troika and the use of mixed inspection teams consisting of a host-national, an adversary, and (either regularly or when needed) an impartial member. There should be no objection to teams composed of two, three, or even more members at every data-collecting and data-processing stage of inspection, as long as each is free to transmit individual reports to his national or international principal. It is when an administrative decision, a judgment, or a joint conclusion is a required prerequisite for further operations that the troika has a capacity to block or delay. Thus, while a troika is unacceptable within an international administration, three-man teams, organized on the adversary principle, are not objectionable in inspection operations.

FUNCTIONS ABOVE DATA COLLECTION AND REPORTING

In the simple adversary system, data are reported to the national governments, who interpret and evaluate the reports, form judgments about obstructions, discrepancies, and possible "violations," and decide what, if anything, is to be done on the basis of the reports. Such an adversary system can be "mixed" with international components at various levels. Some functions are fairly conventional, including annual or more frequent conferences of the signatories of the agreement to discuss reports on the operation of the agreement. Resolutions at such conferences can exert political pressure toward cooperation with the inspection procedures. There may be an adjudication clause, compulsory or optional, for settling legal disputes about the interpretation of the agreement. The agreement may provide that reports of compliance and complaints about obstruction or violation of the agreement shall be made to the United Nations.

Less routine procedures may be designed. Impartial personnel (third-party or international) may be drawn upon for second-level inspection; that is, the agreement may provide that if unexplained suspicious data are discovered, the adversary inspector, or the host national, or perhaps both, may call for a further *and* an impartial inspection. International personnel can be called on to verify the calibration and the accurate use of equipment by adversary inspectors. International record centers can serve as depositories for copies of all data reported by adversary inspectors so as to serve as a check on the evidence that may later be offered in support of allegations of non-compliance. The important thing to recognize is that the main purpose of all such international procedures (beyond gaining improved acceptability) is to give the inspection process authenticity and persuasiveness with third parties, i.e., "world opinion." However, they carry a corresponding cost. They constrain the freedom of action of the adversaries. The choice in each case is whether the gains outweigh the costs.

The analysis and evaluation of gaining international status for the results of inspection fall within the area of responses rather than the operation of inspection systems. But the recognition (again aside from acceptability) that international components are important as bases for third-party responses—not to facilitate national responses —is important for the planning of inspection systems. In the prototype of the international system (the IDO) or the test ban organization, the hierarchy of functions was reversed: data collection and evaluation were painstakingly organized on an international basis, but no clear position on international judgment or response was worked out. Actually, reliance was placed only on an adversary response (primarily, the right of withdrawal). For an adversary response, international performance of all fact-finding and evaluating functions furnishes less reliability for and more obstacles to action. This would be especially true in the absence of an international judgment that was itself extremely vulnerable to obstruction, delay, falsification, and political short circuits. In the planning of mixed systems, international components should be added for lower functions only if they serve as a base for clearly understood higher-level international functions, unless the political requirements of negotiability cannot be satisfied in this manner.

CHAPTER VI

INSPECTION AND THE PROBLEM

OF ACCESS

BY LINCOLN P. BLOOMFIELD
AND LOUIS HENKIN*

I T is in the interest of the United States to terminate or temper the arms race by some form of disarmament or arms control. This is also in the interest of the Soviet Union. However, the Soviet Union will apparently not accept any arms control arrangement that requires either deep penetration into its territory or drastic alterations in its social organization. (The United States, too, may in the end find objectionable some inspections in the United States.) It appears, however, that many arms control measures in the common interests of both powers can be monitored without significant access to the territory or interference in the affairs of participating nations. With present and immediately foreseeable technology, and by combining several services and techniques of intelligence, it is even possible to verify compliance with many measures of arms control to a relatively high level of confidence by unilateral, external means.

Some of these measures might serve strong substantive interests of the United States. Even an arrangement that furthered only minor interests might be desirable both because of the political significance that would attach to

* The authors wish to acknowledge that Section II of this chapter was written and published in a slightly different form by Leonard S. Rodberg under the title "Graduated Access Inspection" in the *Journal of Arms Control*, 1 (1963), 139-144. Mr. Rodberg has kindly consented to its inclusion in this chapter.

any genuine agreement today and because it could serve as a first step toward more important arrangements. The United States might best achieve progress in disarmament and arms control by proposing measures that could be monitored with minimum internal access in the Soviet Union. It is important also to take into full account that it now appears that far-reaching disarmament measures might be adequately verified with less internal access than has been previously supposed necessary; this means that successful negotiation of more ambitious measures may also now be more feasible.

Of course, the obstacles to the achievement of arms control and disarmament agreements transcend American-Soviet disagreements about inspection. Resolution of the inspection problem would not automatically assure meaningful agreements, since there are other important disarmament issues upon which the two sides are divided. Nonetheless, the disagreements on verification and inspection have been so fundamental that they have been sufficient by themselves to frustrate progress toward disarmament. Elimination of the inspection obstacle would make it possible to consider proposals strictly on the merits of their relevance to national security and international peace. It would also clarify whether the inspection question was a bona fide obstacle or only pretext, and facilitate the development of arms and arms-control policy.

DIFFICULTIES OF HIGH-ACCESS INSPECTION

Soviet resistance to territorial inspection in the Soviet Union rests on several considerations. Military security is a primary one. Territorial access might yield additional target information for the United States and presumably improve the United States capability for a counterforce strike against the Soviet Union. The development of hardened, mobile, and sea-based missile systems, however, should reduce this particular concern. The Soviet Union has recently indicated that it would be willing to permit inspection of the missiles that were retained during the first stage of a disarmament agreement. However, certain types of inspection would still pose a military security problem for the Soviet Union because they would probably reveal its overall military position.

Inspection involving deep penetration into Soviet society also appears to present serious political problems for Soviet leadership. The Soviet Union fears that contact with foreign inspectors might intensify disaffection among the Soviet population, reveal deficiencies in the Communist system, and generally contradict the picture of Soviet society that it wishes to convey to the outside world.

A doctrinal but fundamental objection to internal penetration is the reluctance of Soviet leadership to admit a source of legitimate authority on Soviet territory that would not only be free of its control but would actually have a primary competence that was superior and might be adverse to the interests of Soviet rulers, namely, the detection of government-sponsored violations.

It may be assumed that an arms control measure affecting the Soviet Union that could be monitored, say, in the United States, over the high seas, or in outer space would be more acceptable than one requiring penetration of Soviet society. It is probably also true that, in regard to verification of American compliance, arrangements that did not require the presence of foreign inspectors inside American laboratories, arsenals, or plants would be more acceptable to the United States.

Conversely, verification requiring unlimited access by foreign inspectors throughout both countries, with rights of access to the most sensitive installations and with wide-ranging rights of interrogation and search affecting both plant records and personnel, would represent maximum penetration and would seem to entail the greatest disruption and change in the internal arrangements of a society. Due to Soviet concerns with secrecy, particularly regarding matters of military security, these types of inspection must be assumed to be least acceptable and, therefore, least negotiable.

Clearly, not every verification technique that avoids extensive territorial access can be made the basis of formal negotiations with the Russians. For example, the use of reconnaissance satellites may not involve internal penetration but may, nevertheless, be regarded by the Russians as a non-negotiable verification technique in view of the strong position they have already taken against the use of space for intelligence activities. But, as in the present test ban treaty, inspection methods which do not require the agreement of the other side need not be a subject of negotiation at all. Some methods may require some co-operation or acquiescence (at least, a policy not to frustrate inspection, say by "jamming"), but these need not necessarily be negotiated either. The Soviet Union may refuse to authorize the use of reconnaissance satellites in a formal treaty, but it may tacitly accept their use, particularly if the United States is thereby led to accept disarmament measures desired by the Soviet Union without requiring territorial inspection. Later attempts to frustrate such inspection might be treated as some evidence of a purpose to violate.

It must be recognized that reliance on unilateral capabilities for verification rather than on inspection systems established by treaty may inhibit responses to some violations since information obtained from such sources often cannot be publicly revealed. The recent Cuban missile crisis revealed how necessary it may be to present publicly evidence of the violation. Even if this information is usable in influencing world opinion, it might be a less persuasive justification for action than would information obtained by an international inspectorate. However, the information on the Soviet missiles in Cuba and the accuracy of US announcements about Soviet nuclear weapons tests, made on the basis of unilateral sources, have not been challenged. Information obtained from unilateral sources might be highly persuasive both to the American public and to American allies; their attitudes more than the attitudes of Communist or non-aligned countries are likely to be important for decisions based on such information.

A SCALE OF THE DEGREE OF INTERNAL ACCESS

In order to arrive at mutually acceptable verification procedures, it may be desirable to grade types of inspection according to the degree of access to the internal life of a nation that each entails and thus to prepare a scale of "intrusiveness." The following is one such scale:

External Verification—Unilateral. This category refers to verification that could be accomplished by personnel or instrumentation located outside the territorial limits of a country, also outside its territorial waters and air space. Included are techniques of verification that could be operated unilaterally and, if necessary, covertly, although explicit agreements to verify by extra-territorial techniques are not excluded. Such techniques would involve the use of sensors sufficiently sensitive to record events inside the boundaries of the target country. The equipment might, for example, be mounted in orbiting satellites or in aircraft such as those that collect atmospheric debris. This level of inspection is considered to be the least unacceptable to the Soviet Union because it would not require the presence of foreigners on Soviet territory. Since the machinery of verification would be located outside the sovereign area of a country, such inspection would not necessarily require cooperation or even acquiescence by the country being inspected. This form of verification could monitor a nuclear weapons test ban, a missile test ban, and limitations on the transfer of weapons or military personnel to foreign countries.

External Verification—Cooperative. Inspection in this category would also be conducted outside the territory of a nation, but to be effective it would require a certain degree of cooperation or acquiescence from that nation. It would include mechanical or electrical "monitoring" from the outside, which could be frustrated by "jamming" and related devices; it would be necessary, then, that the government inspected agree not to "jam." A different example is the transmission of adequate budgetary data to an international organization for analysis in order to determine the gross trends with respect to military budgeting. The verification of agreed destruction or divestment of some declared military items by means of "bonfires" outside of national territory is a simple and promising possibility. Demilitarized or denuclearized zones outside the US and USSR also would not entail access to those countries but might, of course, involve considerable penetration of other countries.

Existing Internal Verification. This category refers

to territorial inspection, under existing restrictions, by presently acceptable personnel including military, naval, and air attachés attached to existing embassies and legations, journalists, and other travellers. These individuals, operating under present conditions, would have the opportunity to observe various activities and to obtain gross impressions that would be correlated by technically qualified people to produce significant indices. This is the first instance on the scale that contemplates verification activities on the soil of the inspected country. But the degree of access called for would be no greater than is now accepted and, therefore, would not represent any *additional* penetration into the internal life of a country. The limiting factor is that its continuation would be in the exclusive control of the host nation, as indeed would be all inspection techniques involving higher levels of access.

Invitation to Witness Destruction or Divestment of Declared Items. This category includes observation of the destruction of armaments at specified depots or stockpile areas within a nation's territory. Even though these observations might take place deep inside national territory, this level of inspection would not involve penetration into the fabric of society, since the inspectors would have strictly limited functions and could not conduct searches outside the sites where the destruction was taking place.

Significantly Increased Internal Verification. The next category includes more intense levels of inspection which, even though they involve significantly increased access into the internal life of a nation, would not require a large-scale transformation of the Soviet system. The access would still be limited since the activities of the observers and the sites they could visit would remain largely within the control of the host country. Such types of inspection would require a change of policy by the Soviet Union. Each represents a degree of access that the Soviet Union has not yet been willing to grant foreigners.

This level of verification would involve an agreement to open certain areas now prohibited to foreign travel and to permit regularly-accredited attachés as well as journalists and tourists to visit significantly greater portions of the Soviet Union. Over the years, the degree of freedom of travel allowed within the boundaries of the Soviet Union has varied appreciably. A significant relaxation of travel restrictions would not require major changes in Soviet society or even the existence of an explicit agreement. However, since it would reflect significantly greater self-confidence on the part of the Soviet Union, a relaxation of restrictions would probably depend upon some degree of détente between East and West. With significantly increased access for presently accepted types of personnel, gross indicators of compliance with or violation of an arms control agreement could be evaluated with considerably greater confidence than would be possible under present restrictions.

A different and highly significant variation would be freedom of overflight within the national sovereign airspace by agreement similar to that envisioned by the "Open Skies" proposal offered by President Eisenhower in 1955. While such penetration would involve less political intrusion since there would be no contact on the ground with political dissidents and no revelation of social, economic, or other internal difficulties, military secrecy would be impaired. It is possible, however, that the advent of high resolution observation satellites might make overflights by aircraft unnecessary.

Access to Declared Facilities. This level represents minimum but significant access resembling techniques included in several Soviet arms control and disarmament proposals since the Second World War. The country being inspected would declare its facilities, including, for example, factories, launching sites, and military installations. The inspectors might also have the right to interrogate personnel or to examine records at declared locations. This represents a fairly high level of penetration since it implies the identification of sensitive installations as well as the right to observe activities and equipment within them. However, the choice of the sites to be inspected would remain within the control of the host country, and, perhaps for this reason, the Soviet Union has accepted inspection of specific types of declared facilities as part of its disarmament plan.

INSPECTION OF UNDECLARED SITES

The remaining level on the access scale consists of the main area of present disagreement between the United States and the Soviet Union. These involve inspection at sites to be selected by the inspectorate, but it is at just such undeclared sites that one might expect to find clandestine production or armaments caches. One would need a form of inspection that would deter violations of this kind and would provide assurance to all parties that significant quantities of armaments were not being produced or stored at undeclared sites. But these inspections entail a degree of access that has hitherto been unacceptable.

Here, too, focus on the problem of access may increase the likelihood of agreement. Perhaps a solution might lie in a program of inspection that would represent a gradual increase in the degree of access as disarmament proceeded. Such inspection would be designed to detect militarily significant violations throughout all stages of disarmament, recognizing that the types of violations that are militarily significant change as disarmament progresses. During the early stages of disarmament, violations are militarily significant if they provide a violator with a sizable additional military capability; after disarmament has progressed to later stages a lesser capability obtained by violation might also be significant. A militarily significant violation early in the disarmament process might depend upon a clandestine evasion that would be a cumbersome undertaking involving extensive resources, personnel, facilities and transportation, and requiring an extended period of time during which the evasion would have to remain concealed. As disarmament progressed, however, significant military advantages might be obtained by small-scale evasions with reduced logistics requirements.

INSPECTION VARIABLES

It is easiest to describe the higher levels of access in terms of the general ways in which access could be graduated. Specific plans can then be formulated, using different levels of access for each characteristic of high access.

Perhaps the most obvious characteristic is the number of inspectors involved. A large number of inspectors would increase the intensity of the inspection that could be conducted, permit a finer search for prohibited activities, and achieve a progressively increasing penetration into the inspected country. Among other ways in which access could be graduated are:

Size of the Area Subject to Inspection. Inspection could be conducted initially in a limited area, the inspected area being gradually expanded throughout the disarmament process. This is the concept underlying the method of progressive zonal inspection that has been suggested by the United States government.

Sensitivity of the Area Subject to Inspection. While a large part of the inspected country could reasonably be opened to inspection, there are likely to be installations and facilities that each country would wish to close to inspection during the early stages of disarmament. These might include weapons laboratories, missile sites, communication centers, and military and governmental command centers. The progressive increase in access to areas and facilities could begin with areas presently open to foreigners and proceed to areas open to citizens of the host country, specified types of industrial production facilities, research laboratories, military bases and launch pads, military communication centers, and, finally, military and governmental command centers.

The agreement might specify the facilities to which access was allowed or those where it was forbidden. Alternatively, each party to the treaty might designate restricted areas containing the facilities that would be opened progressively to inspection. Access to the remainder of the country and perimeter inspection of the restricted areas could be maintained to provide a reasonable degree of confidence that significant violations were not taking place during the early stages.

Inspection Techniques. Different inspection techniques would require different degrees of access and penetration into the inspected country. Mobile ground inspection represents the most direct means of detecting violations; it would allow varying degrees of access and search. Records-monitoring and personnel interrogation could assist ground teams in finding clandestine production facilities and undeclared armaments but might require increased contact with the economic and social life of the inspected country. Aerial inspection might be of use in order to direct ground inspectors to the most likely sites of either production or deployment violations. In some instances, aerial inspection might itself detect specific types of violations. These forms of inspection are very different; they might be introduced gradually as each was recognized to be a legitimate and appropriate method of inspection.

Access Rights of the Inspectors. The access rights of the inspectors might be progressively expanded to provide an opportunity to detect significant violations with no more penetration than was required at each stage. Throughout the disarmament process, the inspectors could travel on thoroughfares to observe major military shipments, convoys, and the perimeters of restricted areas and facilities. Such observation could concentrate upon specific sites at which prohibited activities would be most likely to occur. These access rights could begin with perimeter observation of areas and facilities and arranged tours of specified facilities; they could progress to unannounced tours of facilities, inspections of transportation centers and the contents of transportation carriers, and, finally, to detailed searches of facilities (to implement agreements including those for dismantling of equipment and facilities). This progression would permit the detection of significant production activities and armaments stockpiles without unnecessary disclosure of technical intelligence information. At the same time, increasing access would provide an increasing ability to detect small-scale production and undeclared armaments caches in violation of the treaty.

In order to verify agreed levels of armaments, the inspection system could use a procedure in which identification indices were assigned to each declared armament and military unit. These might be normal serial numbers attached to all such items. Each inspection team would have a master list of all armament numbers; and the possession either of an item that did not bear a number on the master list or of two armaments bearing the same number would constitute a violation. The object of the inspection would be to discover undeclared armaments rather than to count the declared ones. This would permit the use of sampling techniques, thereby reducing both the required number of inspectors and the unnecessary disclosure of military intelligence information.

Scope of Obligatory Inspection. In its nuclear test ban proposals, the United States has insisted that each side should be able to conduct on-site inspections at specific sites on the territory of the other when certain criteria indicating suspicious events were satisfied. These criteria involve characteristic readings on a seismograph. In the more general case of inspection for clandestine production and hidden armaments in a comprehensive disarmament agreement, it is unlikely that such data would be available. A country might wish to conduct an inspection because suspicion had been aroused by an informer's report, by information obtained through the open literature, or by information obtained through unilateral intelligence techniques that the country would not wish to reveal. Thus, nations might wish to initiate inspections without the presentation of supporting evidence. This procedure was followed in Korea, where, in theory, each side was able to direct the neutral nations inspection teams to locations where it thought violations were occurring, without the prior need to present evidence.

Even if a country should be permitted to initiate such inspections as a matter of right, it does not seem realistic to expect the host country to permit inspections within any facility that the other side should choose. On the other hand, the side conducting the inspection would not wish to be bound by the necessity of submitting evidence before conducting an inspection. It thus seems that a trade-off would be necessary: the nation initiating the inspection would not be required to produce evidence, and the nation being inspected should be entitled to deny access to certain facilities. Alternatively, one could compensate for the absence of initiating evidence by creating a class of inspections that would be conducted on the basis of a request to the host country. Each side might be able to request inspection of certain facilities or areas, and a denial of this request would not constitute a violation of the agreement. In this way, the class of facilities to which the inspectors could potentially have access might be broader than if obligatory rights had to be spelled out. At the same time, however, the security of the host country would be protected.

One can then envision three types of access that might be provided under the agreement: (1) access by right, including travel on major thoroughfares, inspections within certain facilities, and perhaps aerial inspection; (2) access by request, including inspection of other facilities and military installations; and (3) no access to certain very sensitive facilities, at least during the early stages of disarmament. In a disarmament process, the areas to which the inspectors would have access by right would be gradually increased with the progress of disarmament.

ADVANTAGES OF THE GRADUATED ACCESS PRINCIPLE

Inspection using graduated levels of access has a number of advantages that make it appear desirable from the point of view of the United States and potentially acceptable to the Soviet Union. The inspection process can be closely related to the risk resulting from possible violations at each step in the disarmament process. Thus, inspection can be instituted to provide at each step whatever information is needed to provide assurance of compliance at the level of arms reduction that is reached. In this way, the inspection procedures permit the parties to maintain the agreement even if progress in disarmament is interrupted.

A nationwide inspection system using teams with agreed access rights can investigate suspicious facilities or equipment identified by other sources of information. By permitting each party to request inspections of particular areas, the system can rapidly check on suspected violations and provide information to facilitate an appropriate response if violations are found.

The approach minimizes the complexity of the inspection system and requires a minimum number of trained personnel during the early stages of a disarmament agreement. Any disarmament agreement will have a major impact on the relations between the parties. Thus, in the interests of making the transition to that new situation as free from trouble as possible, it is desirable to strive for simplicity in the verification arrangements

The system involves minimum interference with the military, economic, and social structure of the host country during the early stages and requires little change in the manner in which it conducts its internal affairs. A minimum release of intelligence information, especially of a technical nature, is required. Furthermore, the activities of the inspectors could initially be analogous to accepted forms of mutual surveillance such as liaison missions and military attachés.

This approach can easily be adapted to a variety of different arms control and disarmament agreements. It can be used on partial measures, or comprehensive but limited disarmament agreements, or in connection with a treaty for general and complete disarmament. It can be used to implement either an international inspection system or one set up on an "adversary" or reciprocal basis between the parties.

CHAPTER VII

THE POLITICS OF ADMINISTERING DISARMAMENT*

BY LINCOLN P. BLOOMFIELD

IF our aim is enlightenment rather than polemics or propaganda, the issue of disarmament controls makes sense only against the background of the contrasting Western and Soviet approaches to international organization. Behind these contrasting attitudes toward institutions lie more fundamental views on the arrangement of political power in the world. For this reason the two sides are, perhaps, in greater disagreement on the institutional implementation of disarmament schemes than on any other aspects of this subject.

Present Western disarmament policy is guided by the fundamental assumption that significant disarmament or other agreed regulation and limitation of armaments cannot be safely undertaken unless supranational machinery comes into existence to oversee, monitor, supervise, and otherwise manage the program. This assumption has two roots. First, it grows out of the view particularly characteristic of American thinking that international relations and arms control primarily involve problems of organization, i.e., matters to be regulated and, ideally, controlled by appropriate organizational structures. Second, pervasive historic suspicion of Soviet motives has focused Western arms control proposals on organizational frameworks that would minimize the possibility that the Communists

---

* The initial research for portions of this article was done under the auspices of the Institute for Defense Analyses.

could cheat. The Western powers have consequently emphasized both the need for structured international controls over disarmament and for international forces and international peace-keeping institutions as corollaries to comprehensive disarmament—in a word, world government without the name.[1]

The Soviet view of international institutions differs from ours in significant ways. By any authentic interpretation of Communist doctrine, a powerful non-Communist supranational organization at this stage of history can only mean a plot by the capitalist powers to check Communism's forward momentum and to destroy its hard-won gains. This interpretation suggests that existing international organizations such as the United Nations must be checked when they go beyond a purely servicing function. If they cannot be checked, the Communists generally prefer that they be eliminated. Moreover, unlike the West, the Soviets do not accept a necessary relationship between disarmament and world government.

Thus, whether or not the Soviets really want some significant disarmament, they tend to view with profound suspicion any attempt to impose a new and, by definition, anti-Communist international order that, under the guise of disarmament controls, would frustrate their revolutionary movement. It is not even a question of degree. At the level of minimum arms control the issue is still that of penetration into Soviet society by a necessarily hostile power. And when one goes up the scale of disarmament measures toward truly comprehensive programs, the conflict sharpens acutely between the Western assertion that supranational institutions are required and

[1] See the author's article, "Arms Control and World Government," *World Politics* (July 1962).

the Soviet determination to oppose them, as well as between the equally conventional Western thesis—and its converse—that the amount of inspection needed goes up with the degree of disarmament.

Clearly, then, whatever the disagreements on anything else—and they are formidable—there is no real common meeting ground either on the matter of international political institutions or on the related matter of intensive inspection under an arms control agreement. As long as this is so, it is difficult to test whether a consensus exists on regulating the arms race. It is enough to complicate the matter for one side to set as a precondition for reciprocal arms reductions the radical rearrangement of power and authority in the political world. What is particularly troublesome is that the West may not really want this rearrangement once conditions actually favor arms reductions. We can attack the problem through three avenues, all intimately related: inspection; enforcement; and administration. Are there new ways of thinking about each that might be in the common interest?

The key to the control issue is inspection—that is to say, verifying to one's own satisfaction that agreed measures have, in fact, been carried out by the other side. All else flows from this need.

Inspection is now generally recognized to serve two principal purposes, and its dual nature has complicated our thinking about control institutions. The most commonly cited purpose of inspection is to discover and warn against violations. In this sense the system is a deterrent to crime. It is this meaning that has dominated Western thinking thus far.

The second purpose of inspection, particularly important where there is a high degree of suspicion, is to reassure others that a potential or actual violation will surely be detected. Under those conditions the *belief* that crimes will be detected is the important factor. A degree of penetration of the Soviet Union significantly greater than would be needed to detect a major preparation for war would not necessarily deter the Soviet Union any more than a lesser but adequate penetration, but it would have the political virtue of substantially greater reassurance for the West.

The high degree of mutual mistrust makes it uncommonly difficult to estimate the objective requirements for adequate detection. But until and unless that objective need can be separated from the psychological need for reassurance we cannot be certain of having developed a disarmament position which does justice to our own priority interest in reducing the level of armaments, the danger of accidental war, and the proliferation of nuclear weapons. Mistrust, the need for reassurance, penetration of national societies, and the question of sovereignty are all links in the chain of political logic here.

The Western position correctly asserts that if we cannot discover whether the other side is complying or not, it would be foolhardy and even dangerous to risk a reliance upon Soviet honesty. By this reasoning, someone other than a Soviet national—whether a UN inspector or a Western observer—must be permitted to verify Communist compliance, and vice versa. But because of the great suspicion between the two sides we have gone considerably beyond the essential minimum in our approach to inspection. Some Westerners believe that only through uninhibited access, that is, only by transforming the Soviet Union into an open society, can we have confidence sufficient to reverse substantially the arms race.

This was the real meaning of the American position taken after the Soviet resumption of testing in the fall of 1961 that any agreement on testing must contain inspection provisions ensuring that no nation could ever again secretly even prepare to test, an obviously unmanageable position that was subsequently dropped.

The central logic of the matter is essentially uncomplicated. The Soviet system will, we fervently hope, be altered by time and by such influences as we can bring to bear; but it is unlikely to be altered as part of an arms control agreement unless we are prepared to crush the USSR in battle, which we are not. At the same time there is general agreement that Western and Soviet security would, in fact, be improved by reasonably safeguarded controls on the arms race. We must conclude, however reluctantly, that such an improvement in our security cannot be achieved if our price is ideological and political surrender on the part of the Soviets.

If we are to find a sound position for achieving our objectives regarding arms control, we need to understand better the Soviet view of inspection. Doubtless military secrecy is a prime component. But Soviet resistance to intrusion by "foreigners" goes deeper. The very matrix of control by the present Soviet regime depends above all on the monopoly of authority it enjoys. The greatest danger to that monopoly could well lie in the sudden presence, under the mandate of a politically transcendent authority, of foreign inspectors with search and interrogation powers hitherto enjoyed only by the Soviet regime. This prospect, rather than pure considerations of military secrecy, may go far to explain the Soviets' violent resistance to inspection to the extent it intrudes and penetrates into the interior fabric of Soviet society.

It follows that, so long as Western demands for inspection appear to require maximum intrusion or disarmament is seen by either side as a device for politically defeating the other side, negotiations will be sterile. Western proposals should, then, consciously aim at as low a level as possible consonant with safety rather than at as high a level as possible out of idealistic, utopian, espionage, or excessively suspicious motivations. This is, of course, not a new insight. It seems, however, to require new understanding.

This understanding requires that we make a clear distinction between inspection that is essential to verify compliance and inspection that is proposed for other reasons. It is becoming possible to accomplish this on a basis that is technically persuasive.[2] Having done so, one can systematically re-examine disarmament and arms control measures to discern which of them can be verified with minimum access inside Soviet—and American—society, and which require a manifestly unacceptable degree of penetration.

One highly promising key to this "minimum-intrusion" approach lies in the unfolding technology of detection. The American observation satellite known as Samos could become the agent of a first stage disarmament agreement *most of which could be verified from orbiting satellites.* This revolution in information-gathering has limitations: present mechanisms are crude, objects can be hidden, and at best the ground resolution of prospective systems will not tell people everything they would wish in order to be wholly reassured.

[2] See report entitled *Verification and Response in Disarmament Agreements,* prepared by Institute for Defense Analyses for United States Arms Control and Disarmament Agency, based on Woods Hole Summer Study, Washington D.C., November 1962.

But within a relatively short time a significant degree of inspection by an observation satellite system may be technically possible with respect to such important objects as deployed ICBM's, anti-missile systems, the deployment of surface naval vessels and major military aircraft, and significant new construction on the ground. It is thus possible that these things could be verified with a reasonably high level of confidence by an agency *external to the sovereign territory, waters, and air space of a country,* or even over the objection of the country being inspected.

Other means of inspection exist that are equally non-intrusive compared with the proposed injection of alien inspectors into the interior fabric of a given society—for example, attachés, tourists, and other travellers. Soviet disarmament proposals have invariably included inspection of declared facilities, and this poses no real con-control problem, nor does the invitation to witness destruction of agreed amounts of military equipment. Obviously none of these is reliable or effective taken singly; but in combination with the fruits of the new technology, they might add up to a set of integrated means of verifying some, but by no means all, disarmament steps of importance. National intelligence systems, infrequently mentioned publicly in the disarmament context, are available to both sides to supplement information derived from agreed inspection arrangements.

The Western problem with inspection is usually stated this way: we may see them destroy stocks, and we may be posted at declared plants. But how do we know how much is left, and whether there is clandestine production and other unreported activities? How can we find out without having complete access? The answer, of course, is that it is never possible to have complete assurance. The only valid question is whether, risk for risk, contingency for contingency, we would be better off than we are today. A growing professional opinion says yes. In past and present disarmament plans each side has not very subtly arranged things to ensure that its presumed strategic advantage—whether in missiles, tanks, aircraft carriers, bases, or military manpower—was retained in the first stages. Clearly no such strategic advantage will ever be agreed to by the other side, and this fact has contributed mightily to the arms stalemate. More realistic proposals must rest on legitimate considerations of strategic balance; but with them ought to be the criterion of relative non-intrusiveness of inspection.

A new first stage would thus include as many measures as possible that can be verified with a satisfactory degree of confidence by external technical means, by inviting the sides to witness agreed destruction, and by the observation of attachés and tourists already permitted. All of this would be supplemented by continuing unilateral national intelligence. But such a first stage would not include measures that can be verified only with a high degree of penetration—as both US *and* Soviet current proposals do. Nor would it leave to an admittedly utopian third stage—as both sets of proposals now do—many measures that can readily be inspected with minimum intrusion. It would not include in the first stage *all* easily verified measures, but it would give far more weight to this criterion than in the past.

From such an approach it is possible to propose measures to modify and even to reverse the arms race—measures that have a chance of being negotiated through to agreement. They could comprise a single step or a new "Stage I" of Western proposals; their precise form is far less important than the general conclusion that significant disarmament might be achieved without conditions that make arms control a chimerical expectation.

Another fundamental stumbling block is often said to be *enforcement*, and the crux of enforcement is said to involve the question of the *veto*. Surely it is apparent that under present historical circumstances the most to be expected, even with substantial disarmament, is retention of the great-power veto—whether called that or not—whenever crucial political decisions, especially the coercion of sovereign states, are involved. Any other arrangement would surely be as unacceptable to the United States Senate and the people of France as to the Soviet Presidium and the ideologists of Peking.

The feasibility of enforcement invariably depends upon the relative power of the parties, the depth of feeling involved in the issues in dispute, and the strength of will of those who are committed to preserve the international system in the face of a challenge. This is true now; it would also be true if arms were substantially reduced or controlled. If these assumptions are valid, the question of a veto over enforcement turns out to be not particularly meaningful after all. If the Security Council is to be the final arbiter of violations, as most disarmament schemes seem to suggest, the built-in veto will remain; but the veto at the topmost political level does not hamper a disarmament scheme any more or less than it hampers international relations in a non-disarmament environment. The major powers in the postwar period adopted national, regional, and global collective security policies that discouraged military and expansionist adventures by the new imperialistic power they faced. Likewise, in a drastically disarmed world the purpose, resolution, and intelligence of the major governments would in the end surely determine the response of the community to violations.

Even today, under the present system, an effective majority of responsible powers has at its disposal instruments of coercion that could be fearfully effective if it chose to react against a clear violation of a disarmament agreement. The will to act is always more important than the modalities; this central lesson of politics is the one indispensable component in political analysis that no computer, no random theory of numbers, no matrix of game strategies can ever reproduce. Given that will, there exist even now embryonic international legislative and judicial organs, a somewhat better developed executive power, and a framework of moral persuasion and ad hoc political pressure which are, it is true, only partially effective, but which represent the outer limits of enforcement power presently acceptable to the principal nations.

One can then conceive of a comprehensive disarmament program based on obvious, minimal common interests, complete with an appropriate inspection and verification organization, even employing international civil servants in the territory of states—*but with no appreciable alteration in the present concept of national sovereignty and no real capability for enforcement in the sense of punishment on the part of the central authority.* If substantial disarmament can be envisaged *without* the necessity for world government—and that is my hypothesis—then it becomes possible to focus on the *other* political level, i.e., that level required for political control of the technical administration by the participating nations.

The place where the veto *is* inadmissible is in the collection and transmission of data on the basis of which the coercive political decisions we have discussed are to

132

be made. The veto can be exercised in the drafting of the agreement; it can be exercised in the appointment of administrative personnel to fill agreed top positions, as it is today in the UN; and it can and doubtless will be exercised in any collective political decisions about how to act on information. But it cannot exist at the level of securing and transmitting information. If the only way to verify compliance with a given measure is to witness it, it must be witnessed. If that witnessing is prohibited, frustrated, or "vetoed," tolerable procedures of verificacation are precluded.

But what about the intermediate level of international administration, between the point of direct observation and the interposition of the national veto? It is here that negotiations have periodically collapsed on the Soviet demand for a veto; it is here that Khrushchev has opposed the Western concept of a single neutral administrator and insisted upon a tripartite direction.

Unquestionably, an organization cannot function efficiently if it does not have a single, operationally responsible administrative head. The real question is whether the system can function in the terms of paramount substantive importance—*the accurate, reliable, and timely reporting and transmittal to the appropriate political authorities of the information gathered* with arrangements for administrative direction other than a single neutral administrator.

I happen personally to attach the highest value to the concept of the neutral man, specifically, the neutral international administrator.[3] But unless it is proved to be essential, we ought not to allow the urgent task of arms

[3] See the author's *The United Nations and U.S. Foreign Policy* (Boston: Little, Brown, 1960), pp. 149-156.

control to be dominated by the abstract concept of the neutral man, which on all the evidence is so remote from Communist ideology that no programs depending on its universal acceptance will bear fruit. The test for arms control organizations should not be, "Will the Soviets accept the concept of a neutral man?" but "Will the Soviets accept an administrative arrangement that will supply the essential information about compliance?"

The key to the problem may be found in conceiving of the flow of information from the field directly to the level of political judgment, where the information can and should be appraised, with minimum involvement of the senior technical level of administrative direction. It is precisely the function of appraising the technical information produced by the program that the administrative level could not perform and should not be asked to perform. If it can be demonstrated that such a flow of information and concept of organization is practicable, then the West will indeed have a new basis for negotiating with the Soviets.

It is not necessarily true that the information flow would be too complex for government representatives to handle. The political organ could be a working one, in permanent session. The complexity of the data itself will pose a problem, and the political organ will need the service of experts and the help of data-processing electronic equipment; but there would appear to be no intrinsic objection to a contributed joint staff, consisting of electronic engineers, programmers, economists, physicists, and mathematicians who could perform the service function of data-processing for the political organ.

I would not argue that such a system is perfect, or even desirable compared with a neutral secretariat. A joint staff or a secretariat under a committee or collegial type of direction would undoubtedly be less efficient, less orderly, and generally less satisfactory than the other way. Obviously, the advantages are balanced critically by the defects in such a scheme. The Soviets would not be subject to the whims of a single individual, and would presumably be disposed to accept such an arrangement. But the administration of the agency would be clumsy and could be crippled. The responsibility and the workload of the body corresponding to today's Security Council would be heavy. The delegates, representing governments, would have to make initial evaluations of data from the field themselves as a check on the evaluations of the same data by the secretary-general and his staffs.

But this independent parallel check might be desirable anyway since it would presumably save time. The government representatives might also have to resolve administrative questions normally left to the secretariat if one or several "secretaries-general" should be unable to resolve such questions. *But the only truly decisive value of a control scheme—timely and reliable warning of evasions—would under our stipulated conditions be satisfied.* If the essential condition of reliable and unhampered flow of necessary information is met, the question of whether the administrative manager of the organization can be trusted to be impartial, or should be single or collegial, becomes a secondary—though important—matter of administrative efficiency.

The information could of course take the form of a split or minority report from mixed field inspection teams. The essential point is that it come in. The system would be complemented by continued national intelligence operations, under foreseeable conditions the latter would supply reliable indications to us that the Soviet Union or any other party was generally complying with an agreement. Any potential violator would have to reckon not just with an international system but also with inevitable revelation of a significant violation to other powers that doubtless could still mount a damaging pre-emptive attack.

Another vital problem concerns the ability of the system to verify uncertain or troublesome information. Where it is absolutely essential to acquire indispensable information about compliance, the right of on-site inspection must, of course, be acquired. Failure to permit the on-site inspections when the agreement went into effect would simply signal that the agreement was not, in fact, being kept, and a rational party to the agreement would withdraw from it.

But if the procedures for verification are not left to the discretion of a neutral administrator, they must be spelled out with precision in advance. If the Soviet Union wants an agreement, it will make some concessions to permit verification, as it has done in the test ban negotiations (however inadequate those concessions were from our standpoint). To discover if the Soviets want an agreement, we must put the matter on this basis rather than on the basis of a powerful neutral administrator.

To sum up, we are clear that there can be no veto over the gathering of information agreed to be essential to verify compliance. But it is also clear that only a stalemate can result from confronting the Western concept of impartiality with the Soviet insistence that everyone is *parti pris*. There is an area of possible compromise with the Soviet notion of veto over administrative controls, *so long as the inspection system furnishes to the political authority that which is in our primary interest: unimpeded and reliable information.* It should be a matter of first priority to study this redefined technical requirement with a view to designing a scheme that ensures the latter without dependence on the day-to-day decisions of the administrative level.

Several avenues suggest themselves. One is that the agreement be as precise as possible, to minimize the need for the administration to improvise. Another is the concept of joint scientific and technical data-processing staffs. And the most fruitful will be the principle of "minimum intrusion," combined with maximum automation of the inspection process aided by the fantastic new technology of satellite observation.

No one can predict whether a new stand by the West on these matters would make an agreement more possible. If the Soviets wish an agreement, they will ultimately agree to a reasonable minimum of inspection, though undoubtedly not to an all-powerful directorate in the hands of some third party who by their definition is hostile. They will then support the concept of political judgment by the parties—not by a third-party administrator—of the information developed by inspection and verification. Above all, they will support the technical requirement for maximum specificity in the agreement, maximum automation of the information flow, and maximum capability of the representatives of government to make continuous assessments of the data. Similarly, if the United States genuinely wishes an agreement, it will focus on the essentials of the flow of adequate, reliable, and timely information to the nations concerned. It will not permit the negotiations to collapse on any issue which is not relevant to that central one.

It may be that the vital Western interest in defending

the office of the UN Secretary-General is overriding and that a precedent set in an arms control agreement would be too damaging and prejudicial to our position on the United Nations. This is an issue of national priority that can be decided only by Western political leadership. But that decision does not need to be complicated by the conviction we have hitherto entertained that there could be *no* arms control or disarmament agreement without Soviet capitulation on the question of a single neutral administrator or on what amounts to the surrender of the regime's total authority over its subjects. If this thesis is correct, the negotiating area can be defined with a good deal more precision than exists today.

CHAPTER VIII
THE CUBAN CRISIS AND DISARMAMENT: IMPLICATIONS FOR INSPECTION AND ENFORCEMENT

BY RICHARD J. BARNET

IMPLICATIONS FOR THE ARMS RACE

THE attempt of the Soviet Union to place strategic nuclear weapons in large numbers in Cuba provoked an extreme crisis because it shattered the expectations of the West. The abandonment of the familiar deployment patterns of the USSR, which hitherto had made it a practice to retain nuclear weapons only on its own soil, caused particularly serious concern, for in breaching one of their own self-imposed rules, the Soviet Union gave no indication of where they might stop. In his address to the American people in which he announced that the Soviet Union had placed IRBM's and long-range bombers in Cuba, President Kennedy compared the Soviet move to the Rhineland episode of 1936. He emphasized that the missiles were dangerous not only because they symbolized a willingness to take new risks. Such daring, if not effectively discouraged, could prompt further challenges to American power.

On several occasions before October 1962 some American politicians had suggested the possibility that the Soviets might place missiles in Cuba, but such a move had always been discounted precisely because it would involve a radical departure from familiar practice. One of the tacit rules of the cold war had always been that the

Soviets would not attempt to establish a military presence in the Western hemisphere, much less an offensive nuclear capability. The system to which the world had grown accustomed for fifteen years and in which, despite its obvious dangers, considerable trust was reposed, had broken down.

We shall undoubtedly have to wait many years before we can know what led Khrushchev to commit the Soviet Union to an act of adventurism on the other side of the world. The Soviet leader has stated that his purpose was to deter an invasion of Cuba, but the risks were so enormous in relation to Soviet interests there that one is tempted to speculate in other directions. The circumstances strongly suggest that one of Khrushchev's major aims was to symbolize his refusal to accept a position of permanent inferiority in the arms race. In the months before the Cuban crisis the United States had repeatedly emphasized that the Soviet Union, contrary to the view long held during the so-called "missile gap," was significantly weaker than the United States in strategic nuclear striking forces. The Soviets, who two years earlier had boasted that the "balance of forces" had shifted decisively in their favor, were either silent or defensive in estimating who was "ahead" in the military competition. Since their claims to superiority had been exposed, their minimum requirement now was at least an appearance of equality. Had it been successful, the Cuban operation would have dramatized Soviet capability and will to redress the military balance. Whether the numbers of missiles capable of hitting the United States would then have approximated the number of US missiles capable of striking the USSR is beside the point. The Soviets would have demonstrated, as they had in launching Sputnik, that for political purposes they were an equal contender in the arms race. Thus, Khrushchev's explanation of the missile deployment—prevention of a US invasion of Cuba—may, in a special sense, be the correct one. The Soviets wished to prevent a US initiative that they feared, not by firing off missiles from Cuba, which would have been unnecessary, but by reasserting in a particularly dramatic way the point that they themselves constituted a major nuclear threat.

The Russians have been particularly sensitive to the fact that the objectives of the arms race are primarily political. Both sides accumulate and deploy weapons as symbols of national power to secure national objectives. The number of weapons on both sides has already reached a point at which additional increments have only marginal military significance. The mere accumulation of weapons of mass destruction does not result in an increase of power, i.e., the capability to bring about a significantly different result. The antagonists are not impressed that a significant change has occurred when overkill capabilities are increased or politically meaningless strategic options are multiplied.

On the other hand, a dramatic shift in deployment can symbolize a posture which, in political and psychological terms, can do more to intimidate and impress an adversary than a massive speed-up in weapons production, although in purely military terms, an arms build-up could represent greater destructive power. Thus, the missiles that went to Cuba had presumably been trained on US troops in Europe and on the principal cities of our allies for years and had prompted no crisis. It was only when they were introduced into an area from which the US felt it had the right and the power to exclude them that a confrontation developed.

Thus, in the absence of arms control, shifts in deployment rather than the stockpiling of weapons may well become the principal focus of the arms race. By deployment we refer not only to the physical location of weapons but to the circumstances of their control, for the two considerations are intimately related. The Soviets resented the US intermediate-range missiles in Turkey not only because they were physically present near their borders, but also because legal ownership of them had passed to the Turks. While the Turks were under legal restraint not to use the weapons without the assent of the United States, some risk existed that they might fire without authorization. Similarly, one of the principal risks attached to Khrushchev's Cuban adventure was that the weapons, despite the chairman's assurances to the contrary, would somehow fall into Cuban hands.

The location and control of nuclear weapons are two aspects of what has come to be known as the "nth country problem"—the proliferation of nuclear weapons to an indeterminate but increasingly significant number of states that now do not have them. The Cuban crisis revealed an important aspect of this problem. The placing of nuclear weapons in Cuba added one more issue to the list of political controversies that the parties have threatened to decide with nuclear weapons. If the missiles had remained, they would have served notice to the United States that it could not take action against Cuba without taking into account the possibility of nuclear war. Whether the Soviets would ever have used them to counter an invasion we shall never know, but the risk that nuclear weapons would be used was undeniably increased. A new "nuclear" issue had been created.

The willingness to introduce nuclear weapons into new political situations as well as new geographical areas is the essence of the nth country problem and the Cuban experience is but one of a series of events suggesting that this problem will increase unless it is specifically controlled. The French desire for an independent nuclear force stems from their belief that there are political issues that in terms of their interests are "nuclear" but that in terms of US interests are not. The development of nuclear weapons in the Middle East will ensure the introduction of nuclear weapons into a series of quarrels in which such weapons now play no role. The emergence of Communist China as a nuclear power will intensify the danger of nuclear war, less because of the additional "hands on the trigger," but due to the additional ambitions and grievances for which nuclear weapons will become relevant.

The Cuban crisis also demonstrated another danger of the arms race. The fact that the Soviets in Cuba actually did "the unthinkable" dramatizes the likelihood of political miscalculation. Clearly the United States was not the only power surprised by the turn of events in the Caribbean. Either Khrushchev never anticipated that the US would act strongly to secure the withdrawal of the missiles (clearly a grave misreading of the American political temper) or he refused to face the consequences until the crisis was actually upon him. Either explanation demonstrates the danger of misreading the intentions of the adversary.

Moreover, it appears that the chances of such miscalculation will increase. As the military confrontation comes to assume more and more the character of a stalemate, and additions to military establishments on both sides produce little effect on the power balance, the pressure to try for breakthroughs will mount. Weapons will be produced and deployed chiefly for their psychological or political effect, for only dramatic military developments will be translatable into political power. Such moves are designed to produce reactions from the adversary such as terror, docility, or panic. But, as the Cuban episode suggests, they can produce quite different reactions, and it is the surprise reaction to the surprise threat that holds the greatest danger of unintended war.

IMPLICATIONS FOR DISARMAMENT NEGOTIATIONS

If these observations on the probable direction of the arms race are correct, they suggest the area in which controls should be most zealously sought. At present one or the other of the great powers is legally free to deploy its weapons on the territory of third countries provided only that the third countries acquiesce. Considerations of power politics, not law, have dictated the circumstances under which one side undertakes deployment arrangements likely to be viewed as provocative by the other. Thus the United States could safely place missiles in Turkey because a mild Soviet reaction was reasonably anticipated. By the same token, the Soviets could not have counted on a similarly weak reaction had they chosen to send strategic weapons to Guatemala during the rule of the pro-Communist Arbenz government. In these situations the Soviets lacked the power either to frustrate a deployment arrangement viewed as provocative or to secure one which might be used to political advantage.

The Cuban crisis suggests that, since this system of

tacit agreements has broken down, a system of explicit agreements based on law is needed to take its place. Even assuming that a good legal case can be made under existing international law for distinguishing between the legality of the missile deployments in Turkey and the missile deployments in Cuba, such distinctions[1] do not provide adequate guidelines for future action. More precise legal criteria than these are needed to prevent future crises. Not only do restrictions on deployment pose relatively fewer technical problems of verification, but they have potentially greater political impact than all but the most far-reaching disarmament agreements. Since unrestricted deployment is of greater concern than unrestricted arms production, these measures are likely to produce significant changes in the political and military environment. Such agreements would be relatively easy to verify since the deployment of modern weapons is difficult to conceal for very long. Moreover, the very reasons that would impel a nation to deploy weapons abroad, principally for deterrence or intimidation, would encourage it to publicize the deployment. For these reasons, bans on arms shipments, denuclearization of designated geographical areas, and other deployment restrictions appear to be particularly promising techniques for controlling the arms race. The major problem—but also the major opportunity—that they present is that they are not likely to be acceptable unless accompanied by some related practical settlement. For example, many deployment measures to

[1] The distinctions suggested have rested on such considerations as whether or not the missiles were deployed pursuant to a defensive alliance, whether a majority of the states in the adjacent area were opposed to the deployment, whether or not the deployments were overt or clandestine, or whether or not they were precipitously arranged or drawn out over a protracted period.

RICHARD J. BARNET

reduce the intensity of the military confrontation in Central Europe have been proposed during the postwar period. All have been rejected up to now largely because they were judged to upset the political status quo. Thus the Federal Republic has opposed disengagement because of its fear that any US-Soviet agreement relating to the use of German territory would keep Germany permanently subject to Great Power control. Only in the context of an agreement in which major German political demands were met would the Bonn government be willing to negotiate seriously on deployment restrictions.

IMPLICATIONS FOR INSPECTION

The Cuban episode also provides useful insights into the ways in which an inspection system might work under a disarmament agreement and points up some of the problems that might be encountered. While the Soviet introduction of missiles into Cuba was not an explicit violation of a bilateral agreement, it directly contravened a number of pledges publicly and privately given on which the United States placed considerable reliance. Whether the United States was reasonable in relying on a unilateral pledge when it was under no similar obligation itself is beside the point here. The United States expected that the Soviets would observe the prohibition on deployment of missiles. The US had said that it would insist upon it, and the Soviets, on military grounds alone, seemed unlikely to challenge it. Thus there existed an arms limitation analogous to a disarmament agreement but resting on a basis other than explicit consent.

The Soviet violation of the prohibition was treated by the United States in the President's words as a "definite threat to the peace" which called for drastic response. In order to gain support for that response, the United States undertook a strenuous campaign to convince the world that the violation had in fact taken place. The evidence consisted chiefly of aerial reconnaissance photographs obtained exclusively by the government of the United States. It was not surprising that the evidence should have been wholeheartedly accepted by the political leaders and the general public in this country. However, it was remarkable that the validity of this evidence was immediately accepted by allies and usually skeptical neutrals. While in a few quarters the immediate reaction to the President's charges was incredulity, these murmurs of disbelief were stilled when the pictures were produced.

The fact that the evidence presented by the United States was not seriously challenged on the ground that it was procured entirely by one of the parties in interest in the controversy and had not been authenticated by any neutral or international body has important implications for inspection in disarmament. One of the principal arguments raised in the case against the system of so-called adversary inspection—in which there is no international or central inspectorate but each side inspects the other— is that evidence developed by adversaries will not be credible to third parties. The Cuban experience suggests that this is not necessarily so.

There were of course special circumstances that contributed to the credibility of the evidence offered by the United States. In the first place, the United States acted as if it believed it. Nothing was more impressive in conveying the mood of seriousness in Washington than the combination of military, political, and psychological preparations the United States carried out upon learning that the intermediate-range missiles were in Cuba. Second, the

Soviets did not make serious efforts to deny that the missiles were there. Their rejoinder was the justification that they had a "defensive" purpose. Third, the United States had had time to stage a careful campaign which included the dispatch of high-level emissaries to various world leaders before it made its charges public.

Some of the advantages claimed for adversary inspection were borne out by the Cuban operation. Inspectors responsible solely to a national government can move more quickly than an international inspectorate in which decisions are subject to conflicting political pressures. For the foreseeable future the principal powers are likely to have inspection techniques, equipment, and personnel at their disposal that will be unavailable to an international body. Adversary inspection, which need not be based on explicit agreement, is often more acceptable to the inspected country than international inspection. Although Khrushchev had accepted international inspection for Castro, the Cuban premier had other ideas. He adamantly resisted territorial inspection in Cuba by the UN for reasons, to be considered shortly, that were wholly political. He has tolerated continued aerial surveillance, not because he lacked either the will or the means to shoot down the reconnaissance planes (he proved otherwise during the crisis), but because it was the least unacceptable technique for monitoring the untangling of the crisis. In political terms, it required the least concession; he did not need to recognize the legitimacy of the inspection or give it any kind of allegiance.

While it was easy for the United States to convince the world that the missiles were present in Cuba, it was far more difficult to persuade important segments of the US population that they had, in fact, been removed. Rumors and suspicions of deception ran so high long after the Soviets had ostensibly returned the missiles to the Soviet Union that the United States was forced to present a nation-wide television briefing in support of its own certification that Khrushchev had kept his promise. At the briefing the Secretary of Defense presented photographs showing far more detail than those that had been made public in connection with the crisis. The presentation of these photographs, it was admitted, required the disclosure of reconnaissance techniques which the United States would have preferred to keep secret. These were reluctantly revealed, however, because the situation demanded evidence of a higher quality than was required to convince the world that the missiles had been placed in Cuba.

The two inspections of Cuba—the one before the removal of the missiles and the other after—illustrate that there are at least two different functions of inspection: detection and reassurance. This means that in a disarmament arrangement inspection will have at least as important a role in convincing participants that a violation does not exist, or that if it did exist, it has been corrected, as in exposing violations. A disarmament arrangement with an inspection system inadequate for reassurance will collapse. Once a violation is discovered or a convincing accusation is made, the participants will lack the incentive to maintain the agreement unless they can be persuaded that the violation has been removed and that it is unlikely to recur. Since some violations or alleged violations are virtually certain to occur during the life of an agreement, some machinery for restoring the incentive to maintain the agreement is essential.

We have come increasingly to recognize that one of the principal purposes of inspection is to stimulate appropri-

RICHARD J. BARNET

ate responses. Thus, violations should be detected with sufficient promptness and accuracy to permit the "victim" nations to employ effective countermeasures, whether these take the form of sanctions, collective security, or abrogation of the agreement. The demand for a high level of inspection stems from a concern that without it warning will be insufficient either to prepare appropriate responses or to justify them before world opinion. The Cuban experience suggests the other side of the problem. Inspection has an equally important role in moderating the response, preventing overreaction and ultimately in restoring the incentive to maintain the agreement. It also suggests that while the adversary approach to inspection may be most appropriate for detection, a different approach may be indicated for reassurance. Particularly in the case where violations have been discovered and the violator has agreed to correct them—essentially the situation illustrated by the Cuban affair—self-disclosure can do more to provide reassurance than any other kind of inspection. In such a situation the objects of concern are known. The violator himself is in a unique position to convince the other parties to the agreement that the objects of concern no longer exist and that analogous violations are not occurring elsewhere. Since the violation has caused a special need for reassurance, the burden should be on the violator to provide it. It is never easy to prove a negative proposition but the side that has access to the necessary information should be expected to make the attempt.

The Cuban episode also reveals the political significance that nations attach to inspection. Although Castro refused to allow territorial inspection if Cuba were to be the only country subject to legalized international surveillance, he proposed that inspection take place in both Cuba and Florida. The United States refused to take Castro's proposal seriously. It is clear that Castro regarded the agreement implicit in the Kennedy-Khrushchev correspondence for international inspection in Cuba as a serious blow to his prestige. Similarly, the United States regarded Castro's proposal as an affront to its national dignity. For a government to agree to accept inspection implies not only an acceptance of constraints on the absolute freedom of action it likes to think it possesses but also an admission that the allegations of other governments that it may have engaged in deception are to be taken seriously. In purely strategic terms inspection in Florida in return for inspection of Cuba was an exchange that favored the United States. We had strong incentives to know what was going on in Cuba and difficulty in obtaining definitive information without territorial inspection. On the other hand, the United States is so vulnerable to foreign intelligence activities that the Cubans could obtain reasonably accurate information about possible military activities in Florida without any inspection. The United States refused inspection in Florida because it did not wish to admit the implication of Castro's demand, i.e., that there were activities in Florida affecting the security of Cuba which were of *legitimate* interest to the Cuban government. The experience suggests that we cannot insist upon inspection as a "substitute for trust" as we have called it, and at the same time expect not to be distrusted ourselves. But if our aim is to build institutions capable of restraining sovereign nations—friendly and unfriendly—from threatening the international community for the sake of national advantage, we should understand the distrust of others as well as our own and seek for ways to allay it.

PART TWO

THE PROTECTION OF STATES

IN DISARMAMENT

INTRODUCTION TO PART TWO

PART two examines the options open to nation-states under disarmament when some disturbance of the international order has occurred or is believed to have occurred. By "response" the authors mean the entire range of actions available to a decision-maker in a national state in the event the disarmament arrangement has broken down. The term includes resort to international sanctions, unilateral acts, both military and non-military, as well as the decision to do nothing.

Chapter IX offers a framework for analyzing violations. It is an attempt to distinguish various cases of violations and to provide a basis for determining what might be the appropriate responses. This is part of an effort to establish a reasonable relationship between the violations to be deterred or countered and the corrective action that might be taken by the victims of violations. Some of the thinking that has developed in nuclear deterrence strategy is applied to a disarmament situation where, it appears, notions of "flexible response" and "graduated deterrence" may actually be more feasible than they are in a world engaged in a nuclear arms race. Chapter X surveys a wide range of responses and evaluates how some of these have worked in the past.

The last five chapters take up two specific institutions for protecting the interests of states in disarmament: international law and an international police force. Chapter XI argues that a strong system of legal rules upon which all states, large and small, could rely is prerequisite for a disarmable world and would be an important instrument for stability in a disarmed world. This chapter also explores the problems of building respect for law in a world divided by political and ideological conflict. The last four chapters deal with some of the major problems associated with the classic means of response envisaged for disarmament agreements: the international police force. Chapter XII points to the special need for a range of responses in drastic disarmament by showing the limitations of inspection in a world of complete and general disarmament; Chapter XIII is concerned with the problem of how, at the same time, international police can control the conduct of governments, and governments can control the conduct of the international police; Chapter XIV suggests ways in which such a force might operate so as to maximize the prospects for "flexible response"; Chapter XV takes up the crucial question of assuring the impartiality of an international police force.

All of the papers in this section confront in one way or another the problems of predicting organized human behavior in an unprecedented political environment. Difficult as it is, the effort is essential if we are to build useful institutions for disarmament.

In chronological terms, inspection, of course, precedes the response. The process of enforcing security in disarmament begins at the point at which either compliance is verified or violations are detected. But logically the response is the starting point in the design of disarmament control arrangements, since the quality and quantity of information that an inspection system should develop depend directly on those uses that the information is to serve.

CHAPTER IX
VIOLATIONS OF DISARMAMENT
AGREEMENTS

BY RICHARD J. BARNET

WHAT IS A VIOLATION?
SUBSTANTIVE VIOLATIONS

THE classic problem of cheating under a disarmament agreement, which has been recognized and discussed by both the Soviet Union and the United States, is the spectre of the hidden nuclear weapons stockpile. A clandestine stockpile could result either from production antedating the disarmament agreement through a combination of under-declaration and imperfect inspection or from clandestine production carried on while the agreement was in force. Concealed nuclear weapons are not in themselves substantial threats without effective delivery systems, but concealment of some quantity of delivery vehicles also now appears feasible even under conditions of extensive inspection.

The treacherous attack that shatters the peace of a supposedly disarmed world and the sudden ultimatum backed by a dramatic revelation of a nuclear weapons cache are the two terrors to which disarmament discussions return again and again. It is to these nightmare situations that the mind first leaps when it contemplates a world substantially without legalized armaments. Most of the proposed disarmament inspection arrangements and sanction procedures have been addressed to these situations.

The possibility that violations would occur according

to the standard pattern can obviously not be discounted. However, it is imprudent to exaggerate their likelihood or to concentrate on them to the exclusion of other violations that appear more probable. Preoccupation with the extreme cases tends to inhibit the design of imaginative and appropriate responses for violations of a lesser order. Just as a penal code should not be oriented exclusively around murder, so rules for international behavior should not be obsessed with the desperate end of the spectrum of violations. Finally, it will not become necessary to find sanctions to deal with the extreme situations discussed above until long after the moment when appropriate responses to lesser violations must be devised, since these classic violations become possible only in a world of near-total disarmament.

Thus, while a satisfactory solution to the problems raised by the extreme examples must be found before complete and general disarmament can be realized, the search for such solutions should not distract us from the fact that there are at least two other possible models of substantive disarmament violations for which quite different responses are appropriate. One would be an overt, but less than all-out, challenge to the disarmament arrangement. Missile production might be resumed, a demilitarized zone might be reoccupied, or the schedule for weapons destruction might be delayed, but no attack would be launched and no ultimatum would be issued. The violations committed by both the Weimar and Hitler governments up to the time when the disarmament provisions of Versailles were completely repudiated were of this character. Each step in the rearmament process, including specifically the reoccupation of the Rhineland, was either a clumsily concealed or completely open probe of the determination of the World War I Allies to maintain the treaty. Nazi documents, which reveal that Hitler had given the order to retreat in the event of local French opposition, suggest what an appropriate response would have been in such a case. Breaches of the rearmament provisions of the Korean truce agreement were of the same character. The North Koreans had no way of keeping secret the introduction of prohibited military equipment into the truce area but were willing to risk whatever US action might follow detection.

A third category of substantive violations concerns real or alleged misinterpretations of the obligations themselves. It is the essense of the desperate cases considered above that the violator preserve surprise and make no prior attempt to justify his behavior. In the case of an overt minor challenge, the violator does not seek to defend his behavior on the basis of the agreement itself; but if he defends it at all, he is likely to do so on grounds outside the agreement as, for example, the "inherent" right of self-defense or the right to take countermeasures against actual or suspected violations of the other side. In other situations, however, a party to a disarmament agreement might take the position that its conduct is fully supported by the agreement despite the fact that other signatories will be likely to disagree and become apprehensive. The potential number of situations in which compliance with substantive disarmament provisions could become a disputed issue is virtually unlimited. Gaps in the agreement would be revealed after a period of operation. Whether a particular weapon was actually covered by the agreement, whether a certain object known to be possessed or manufactured was actually a "weapon" within the meaning of the agreement, whether a certain area was, in fact, intended to be included within the agreed demilitarized zone, and whether a missile was actually developed for "peaceful purposes" are typical examples.

Other disputes might concern questions of individual or national culpability. Is either an accidental failure to destroy prohibited weapons or an unauthorized entry into a demilitarized zone a "violation" and, if so, what kind of a response would be justified? Even if the agreement contained no explicit provisions regarding justification, some recognition of the concept would be necessary for the survival of the agreement, since an innocent violator would quickly become suspicious of the good faith of the other parties if they should choose to treat manifestly unintended acts as deliberate ones.

PROCEDURAL VIOLATIONS

The basis of most disputes early in the operation of disarmament agreements would be violations of procedural obligations. Thus, the rights and duties of inspectors, the interpretations of the meaning of such concepts as "free access" or "strict international control," the limitations on the right of search and seizure, the limitations on the right to conduct unannounced inspections, the timing of inspections, the types and quantities of permitted equipment, and the extent to which an inspection authority could develop its own rules for hiring, discharging, and transferring employees or for locating its facilities on the territory of signatory states are potential sources of friction that could come into issue at the very moment the disarmament system goes into operation.

No matter how sincere a government may be in wishing to comply with a disarmament agreement, it cannot help but regard the inspectors as adversaries. While the basic objectives of the inspectors and of the government wishing to comply may be identical in that both desire to assure the degree of disclosure that will develop a confidence on all sides that the acts prescribed by the agreement are being carried out and that the prohibited acts are being eschewed, the inspected country will not necessarily agree on what specific acts of inspection are needed to achieve that result. Moreover, the inspected country is likely to suspect the motives of the inspectorate, just as the well-meaning motorist who is stopped for speeding on the highway is more apt to ascribe his arrest to the police officer's overzealousness, bad temper, or corruption than to a commendable devotion to law enforcement. Suspicions will run particularly high at the beginning of any agreement in view of the past strained relations among the signatories. Thus, the natural desire of the inspectorate, and of states depending upon it for their security, to interpret inspection privileges as liberally as possible may be interpreted by the inspected country as a desire to harass or embarrass it or even to threaten its military security or social system. Since the inspected country and the inspectorate (or the other states, if an adversary inspection system is used) will each view its own conduct as justified by objective circumstances, the inspected country will be suspicious of attempts to extend inspection, and the other countries will be nervous about that country's efforts to resist inspection.

Another potential set of procedural questions concerns the operation of sanctions. Just as the performance of a state, with respect to its substantive disarmament obligations, may be grounds for suspicion, so the response of a state to a suspected violation may also transmit disturbing signals to the other parties. Too great an alacrity to abrogate the agreement, to take unjustified punitive action against the suspected violator, or to make premature denunciations of the motives of an accused state might indicate a desire to use the conduct of other states as a pretext for extricating itself from undesirable obligations. No violator has ever called his own conduct a "violation." It is always a "response."

Because procedural questions on inspection are likely to arise early in the disarmament process, the way in which such disputed events are handled will set the tone for the future operation of the disarmament system. For this reason, it would be desirable to have procedures for dealing with procedural violations built into the agreement or otherwise agreed upon in advance, so that threshold questions could be disposed of without immediately jeopardizing the substantive provisions of the agreement. It is likely to be easier to obtain agreement on procedures for dealing with procedural issues than on procedures for dealing with substantive issues, since the signatories will wish to preserve greater flexibility for unilateral action in the latter case.

VIOLATIONS OF OBLIGATIONS OUTSIDE
DISARMAMENT AGREEMENT

The third area in which the conduct of states would be relevant to compliance with disarmament obligations is the most difficult to delineate: the behavior of states with respect to obligations that transcend the letter of the disarmament agreement. The extreme cases are obvious. A state has violated a comprehensive disarmament agreement if it makes war upon another signatory whether or not the disarmament agreement or other international obligation explicitly includes an undertaking to refrain from making war. It is possible, of course, to envisage some arms control agreements that would survive a war, but these would relate to the conduct of the war itself, such as a rule against the first use of nuclear weapons, a restriction on the size or type of weapons to be employed, or agreements with respect to targets. On the other hand, an agreement to undertake significant reductions of armaments and any agreement for arms control that is intended to be followed by acts of further control are premised on the existence and continuation of a minimum condition of peace.

The definition of that minimum condition is the prime difficulty. As far as early stages are concerned, it would be politically unacceptable to outlaw the rights of self defense or collective security. Neither the US nor the Soviet disarmament proposal envisages dismantling self-characterized defensive alliances until an undisclosed point far down the disarmament road. "Defensive" military operations are not excluded under disarmament, although it is obvious that at least the adversary will regard any "defensive" military operation as "offensive" and "illegitimate" and will consider it a "violation." Thus, any military operation of the dimensions of the Korean battle would immediately raise the issue of the compatibility of the conflict with the disarmament agreement. Logically, it might make considerable sense to isolate such a conflict, to rearm only to the extent necessary to maintain forces actually needed for that operation, and to attempt to keep the rest of the agreement in force. If the actual Korean experience is an accurate guide, however, this is not likely to happen. When the Korean war broke out, the United States not only reinforced its Far East garrisons, but built up NATO, developed the hydrogen bomb, and tripled the defense budget. While efforts were made to limit that conflict, no time was lost in preparing for further conflicts. It is hard to see why the same psychological and political pressures would not operate in the early stages of a disarmament agreement. Indeed, they would probably be stronger, since the sense of outrage, disillusionment, and apprehension would be enhanced if a state launched a Korea-type war from a posture of negotiated disarmament on which other states had begun to base their security. On the other hand, if the disarmament agreement were otherwise operating to the satisfaction of the other signatories, there would be strong counterpressures, which were absent in 1950, to keep at least parts of the agreement in effect.

A Korea-type engagement represents the outer limits of a conflict compatible with a disarmament agreement, and, as I have indicated above, the maintenance of disarmament even at this level of conflict seems highly unlikely. However, the lower levels of conflict are inevitable with or without disarmament agreements, and the relationship between the conduct of states with respect to such low-level conflict and their disarmament obligations becomes exceedingly complicated. It has been stated that a disarmament agreement represents an attempt to conduct international conflict by outlawing irrational means. In this view, disarmament is a way of preserving the viability of international conflict now made obsolete by the abundance of nuclear weapons. While it would be rational to separate means of conflict into two classes—one being those weapons that can achieve political objectives that outweigh the damage done by the weapons and the second being those means that, if used, would destroy the political objective as well as the enemy—a number of political and psychological obstacles prevent such a neat dichotomy. Although it is a sensible notion that states should choose the means of conflict that will permit their survival and abjure those that will threaten their destruction, states, like individuals, do not like to foreclose options to pursue their interests by a variety of means. Thus, while a signatory might prefer to conduct conflict at lower levels of violence, it will in the early stages of disarmament preserve its capability to conduct it at higher levels. The mere existence of this capability represents a risk that it will be employed. At some point, obviously, the increased use of violence jeopardizes the agreement.

What that point is would seem to depend not only upon the nature of the agreement but upon the level of conflict existing when the agreement was negotiated, because that level would in large measure determine the expectations of the signatories. The agreement could probably not survive a marked increase in the intensity of violence present at the time when the agreement was reached. Thus, if guerrilla activity of the kind presently being conducted in Viet Nam were continuing when the agreement went into force, the spread of similar activities to other areas in which the interests of the rival blocs were roughly comparable would probably be tolerated. One of the tacit ground rules of the disarmament system would be its compatibility with the program of guerrilla activities supported by one bloc or another. Whether or not the agreement contained general prohibitions against "indirect aggression," such activities would in practice be accepted as part of the game, assuming that one or more of the signatories had not been led to believe that the activities would cease upon the signing of the agreement. In practice, guerrilla operations at this level would be regarded as unregulated conduct not giving rise to a "violation." Similarly, counterinsurgency support for the government challenged by the guerrillas would not be regarded as a violation by the bloc interested in supporting the guerrillas.

It is readily apparent that the line between such permissible conflict and a conflict that one side or the other would regard as a violation is extremely hazy. A series of conspicuous victories or defeats, the extension of guerrilla activities to other lands, and changed perceptions as to their interests in such areas on the part of the signatories might lead one nation or another to revise its view as to what constitutes an acceptable level of conflict. Whether or not expressly stated as a premise, the character and the dimensions of the conflict at the time the agreement was negotiated would serve as the base point for the principal signatories in assessing the utility of the disarmament program. Therefore, if one signatory believed that the conflict was going against it and that one or more of the arms restraints to which it had agreed was contributing to its loss of position, it would probably hold either that the other side had violated the agreement or that it was justified in freeing itself of all or part of its disarmament obligations on grounds of *rebus sic stantibus.* The conditions under which the agreement had been made would, in the view of the disadvantaged nation, no longer be in effect, and hence it would be free either to abandon the agreement or to demand its renegotiation. This motion has been explicitly written into the partial test ban agreement concluded by the US, Britain, and the Soviet Union. The treaty provides for a right of withdrawal in the event that "extraordinary events related to the subject matter of this treaty have jeopardized the supreme interests" of a signatory.

A frustration of expectations may be more likely to occur where the disarmament agreement is accompanied by explicit political settlements. The signatories would be likely to adopt more optimistic expectations and thus to set higher standards for their adversaries, if, at the same time as the disarmament agreement were concluded, a Berlin settlement or a cease-fire in Viet Nam were also reached. The outbreak of new conflicts or the resurgence of old ones would be regarded as especially disappointing and threatening if the disarmament program were viewed by the participants as being linked to the maintenance of a specific détente.

DETERMINATION OF THE SIGNIFICANCE OF VIOLATIONS

The detection of a violation is important to the other signatories primarily because it is a signal of the intentions of the violator that enables them to take action to remove the violation and to forestall others. Only in the exceptional case will a violation result in immediate physical injury to the other parties. But whenever violations occur, potential victims are placed in some degree of apprehension whether or not the violator attempts to exploit the fruits of the violation.

The chief function of a disarmament verification system is to provide information in such a way that an appropriate level of apprehension is created when violations occur. It serves as a stimulus for evoking appropriate responses. The appropriateness of the response depends upon many factors. Many of these concern the purpose of the response, i.e., whether it is designed to deter further violations, to restore the physical situation to an approximation of what it was before the violation was committed,

167

or to satisfy the psychological demands of the government or population for retribution. Responses should be judged in the light of the purpose that they are designed to serve.

It is possible, although improbable, that a violator might, without any warning whatever, present a total challenge to the disarmament system and, in effect, call for the capitulation of the other powers. A nation might follow such a course if it believed that it was the only way to extricate itself from a disadvantageous agreement without sacrificing its political objectives or subjecting itself to the risk of punitive measures. The obvious responses to such a challenge would be primarily military. The exact nature of these would depend upon the level of armaments remaining to the victim nations, the composition and strength of an international police force, if any, and the determination of the threatened populations to resist. As regards the latter factor, it would seem that the incentive to defy the violator would be very powerful. His actions would amount to an unambiguous attack on the status quo and would indicate the worthlessness of his obligations. The violator would be in a poor position to offer peace on any terms short of total surrender, since no nation would trust him to observe a negotiated armistice. Unless the violation were on such a scale as to guarantee the overwhelming destruction of its population, the prudent course for the victim nation would be to reject demands for unconditional surrender.

A bid for victory through the use or threat of military power is thus the most dangerous motivation for disarmament violations. In the usual case, however, motivations would be more tentative. A deliberate violation or a series of violations might be designed to test the strength of the disarmament arrangement in order to determine which provisions would actually be enforced. In other words, a violator might have neither a timetable nor even a fixed intention to overthrow the agreement but might wish to determine the extent to which the technical limitations of the inspection system or the irresolution of the other signatories would permit him to whittle away his obligations and resolutions. Such a probe would be analogous to Hitler's reoccupation of the Rhineland. The chief functions of responses in such a situation would be to let the violator know that he could not carry out the proscribed act with impunity and to restore the military balance. This could be done either by commensurate rearmament of the other powers or by the exertion of pressure on the violator to undo the violation. An example of the latter course, which would involve less danger of escalation than rearmament, would be confiscation of the fruits of clandestine production. Whether additional penalties should be demanded would depend upon the circumstances. If the violation represented a first offense, a prompt, vigorous action to restore the status quo might be a sufficient deterrent to future violations. On the other hand, if a pattern of violations were established, additional penalties would be exacted not only to provide additional deterrence but to assure the participants who comply that a violator, if caught, will end up in a worse position than a non-violator.

A third class of violations might involve negligent acts or omissions. An official could misread the agreement or misinterpret it. Armaments might be left off an inventory by mistake. A pilot might violate an agreed deployment pattern for his vessel or aircraft through error.

This sort of violation should be relatively easy to deal with. The response should be of such a nature as to assure other participants that the contravention of the disarmament rule was, in fact, accidental. It should also serve to assure the violator that the other participants do not intend to take advantage of his unintentional violation in order to alter or abrogate the agreement. In such a situation, the violator nation should itself initiate corrective action. It might discipline persons responsible for the mistake, take the necessary measures to prevent a repetition of the accidental violation, invite the other participants or the international inspectorate to make a special investigation to verify that the mistake had been rectified, and make a report of its actions to interested parties. Whether or not such action was specifically prescribed in the agreement, the other participants could suggest it upon discovering the accidental violation.

The Soviets have taken the position in the disarmament negotiations that most violations, if they occur at all, will be of this type, i.e., that the source of the violation will not be the highest level of government. They argue that since violations will contravene the policy of the violator nation, that nation itself has the incentive necessary to deal effectively with them. Clearly, in terms of power and access to the individual wrong-doers concerned, the responsible government is in the best position to dispose of the case. The difficulty with this position is that it assumes that the government is innocent of either complicity or sympathy with the violator except perhaps in the rare or unimportant case. The US assumption, which is supported by the evidence of German rearmament and the "violation" of the Washington Naval Armaments Limitation Treaty of 1922, is that the probabilities are reversed. The dangerous case for which a system of adequate responses must be developed is the government-directed violation.

Nevertheless, the assumption often made in the West that the only likely violations will be government-inspired also seems unwarranted in view of the wide range of possible degrees of governmental involvement. Where an ambiguous case exists, the government of the violator state should be given the benefit of the doubt. Thus, it should be encouraged to cooperate with the other participants in removing a common danger rather than be forced to defend its honor. In some cases, a useful fiction might develop whereby both violator and victim would treat the prohibited act as accidental, even though the violator government knew and the victim government strongly suspected that the act had been government-inspired. Espionage has traditionally been treated as an "accidental" violation of the rules of international conduct in that the violator government does not admit responsibility for an apprehended spy and the victim government does not attempt to fasten responsibility on it. Individual cases are disposed of by taking action against the spy. The advantage of this fiction is that the prestige and integrity of governments are not called into question in every case of espionage. The governments concerned can respond in whatever way they consider prudent: they can increase or decrease their espionage or counterespionage activities, but they do not have to challenge or defend national honor.

Treating an ambiguous violation as unintentional offers a violator a way of reversing his course without having to lose face. Instead of accepting the humiliation of judgment and punishment, the violator government could restore itself to good graces by making further com-

171

mitments to the disarmament program either by punishing responsible individuals or by establishing internal procedures to ensure against a repetition of the violation. When the violation is discovered, the violator has a choice of correcting it by such means or, in effect, of condoning it. Choice of the latter course would raise suspicions that a basic challenge to the disarmament system was intended, and the other states would then probably treat the violation as intentional. A series of accidental violations that formed a pattern of behavior could also be treated as intentional.

Unauthorized conduct might constitute a fourth class of violations. When the unauthorized act is committed by an individual or small group, the problems presented are essentially the same as in the case of accidental violations. Thus, while the individual who commits the act may intend the consequences, he is acting in defiance of the government whose interests he believes he is serving. The man who fired at President Truman to achieve independence for Puerto Rico is an example from recent history. The SAC general who destroys a Soviet city as a personal contribution to US security is an example from current fiction. In such cases, the response should be pressure upon the violator government to deal appropriately with both the individual violator and the results of the violation.

A somewhat different problem arises when the unauthorized conduct is carried out by a larger group, particularly, where the legitimate government has lost a measure of control of its territory. Thus, an organization similar to the OAS in Algeria might attempt to sabotage the disarmament agreement. The responses would depend upon a number of considerations, including the feasibility or desirability of giving aid to the legitimate government, the existence of international military forces, the strength of the dissident forces, and the likelihood that they would overthrow the agreement if they achieved power. In some cases, it might be necessary to anticipate the overthrow of the legitimate government and to react as if the dissident group had already gained power.

Another class of prohibited acts might consist of a series of minor, covert discrepancies. Such "creeping violations" might be designed as insurance to improve the military position of the violator should the agreement break down. Thus, a nation might be quite willing to live with the agreement, have no intention either of probing its outer limits or of posing a more fundamental challenge, and yet desire to hedge against an uncertain future. The psychology that impels nations in an environment without arms control to increase armaments levels in order to gain increased security, despite a growing belief in the negative correlation between arms and security, could also operate under a disarmament agreement. Responses to creeping violations would be designed to correct significant discrepancies and to develop additional deterrents to repeated violations. Thus, the other participants might demand the right to conduct additional inspections on the territory of the violator on the grounds that the existing level of inspection had not been sufficient either to deter the creeping violations or to expose them with adequate promptness. Perhaps the violator could be invited to arrange a program of self-disclosure that would provide increased assurance that the violations would not continue. While the motivation for the violations in this class would be different from the class of "accidental" violations, they would probably appear almost indistinguishable to the other participants, since in both cases the discrepancies would be of small military significance and the intentions of the government would be uncertain. Thus, in this situation, too, it might as a general rule be preferable to assume mistakes rather than bad faith and to invite the offending government to cooperate in restoring the status quo.

Other motivations might induce a nation to commit creeping violations. It might genuinely regard its own deviation from the rules not as a violation but as a response, i.e., might actually believe that other parties to the agreement were not living up to their obligations and that therefore its own prohibited acts were justified. Retaliatory violations would probably be overt, since one of their principal purposes would be to deter further supposed violations of the other side. Since reciprocal violations would be rooted in divergent factual and juridical interpretations of disarmament obligations, violations of this type might be more susceptible to being treated as disputes than most others. It is conceivable, therefore, that the adversary nations in a reciprocal violation situation might be willing to submit the disputed facts either to third-party arbitration or to adjudication. An alternative might be the exchange of investigating teams.

Finally, a nation might deviate from certain disarmament rules while respecting the remainder of the obligations in order to effect a de facto renegotiation of the agreement. The most conspicuous example from recent history of a selective violation is the erection of the Berlin wall. The appearance of the wall changed the status of the city in only one respect: it virtually eliminated intracity interaction. But this was the one aspect of the Berlin status the Soviets considered it most urgent to alter in view of the refugee flow. After the violation was committed, the Soviets went to some lengths to assure the West that they were posing no immediate challenge to the rest of the Four Power agreements on Berlin.

A nation that came to believe it had struck a bad bargain might similarly attempt to revise some aspects of the agreement, while seeking to preserve the arrangement as a whole. The traditional method of renegotiating treaties is unilateral denunciation. A signatory that wanted to change some aspects of the agreement would have three basic options. First, it could abrogate the agreement altogether. This option and the responses the other signatories might make are discussed above. Second, it could call for a renegotiation. Unless the idea of periodic renegotiation were built into the agreement, the prospects for removing disadvantageous provisions through this route would not be good. Third, it could abrogate the agreement only with respect to the objectionable provisions. If it regarded the agreement as otherwise advantageous, this would be the preferable option.

Reciprocal non-compliance is the obvious response for the other signatories. The reaction of the US to the introduction of military equipment into North Korea prohibited by the truce was to bring prohibited equipment into South Korea. It is true that reciprocal non-compliance is an irrational response. If the disarmament rule was worth instituting in the first place, it should be worth preserving. Throwing out the law because the criminal has violated it does not promote order. Nevertheless, the prospect of reciprocal non-compliance might be necessary to deter selective violations. If a violator is made to realize that once he changes the agreement through unilateral action it may be changed further by other parties in ways not to his liking, he will presumably be more cautious about tampering with it at all. It is true that threats to raise the level of non-compliance run the risk of destroying the agreement. Nevertheless, they are such natural responses that they cannot be ruled out and, in some cases, may be an effective means of preserving the agreement. A signatory should be aware, however, that reciprocal non-compliance, even with respect to a minor obligation, is an extreme response in view of the principle involved. More moderate responses should be considered first.

One response that should be considered in such cases is an offer of renegotiation. While the line between renegotiation and "appeasement" in any particular case is a subjective one, it seems clear that disarmament obligations accepted at a single point in time cannot be immutable. A viable agreement must contemplate some machinery for revising obligations in the light of changed circumstance. Revision of one-sided provisions to make the agreement fair is in the interests of all the signatories, since it is the perception by each signatory of the self-interest to be served by disarmament that is chiefly responsible for sustaining the arrangement. A power could take advantage of renegotiation provisions and press for a series of unwarranted concessions, but this could be made difficult if the circumstances under which renegotiation could be demanded were reasonably specific and limited. Of course, any such provisions are subject to abuse by a nation determined to force a revision of the agreement on its own terms.

It should be remembered that any discussion of compliance with disarmament agreements that concentrates on violations necessarily gives a somewhat distorted view of the disarmament process. Ultimately, it will be the positive incentives to maintain the agreement rather than the machinery for discouraging violations that will determine whether we can evolve toward a disarmed world. As this evolutionary process takes place, the whole question of compliance will take on a different appearance to the participants, since, it disarmament succeeds as a political process, it will help bring about profound changes in existing relationships among states and peoples.

CHAPTER X
RESPONSES TO VIOLATIONS:
A GENERAL SURVEY

BY LOUIS B. SOHN

R ESPONSES to violations of a disarmament treaty may be designed to serve one or more of the following purposes: to punish the violator, to remove the violation, to restore the balance, or to deter a violation. The last one is probably the most important; if a violation has been deterred, other aspects of the response problem are avoided. From this point of view, deterrence merges with inducement. The prospective violator is induced to abandon his scheme by the prospective unfavorable consequences of the violation. In legal terminology, these consequences are usually called sanctions. The classical definition of sanctions by Austin speaks of "The evil which will probably be incurred . . . in case a duty be broken."[1] Similarly, in modern literature, the meaning of sanctions is extended "to comprehend all the means by which law observance is induced or enforced."[2] It is often pointed out that it is not the action of the other parties or of some international authority that constitutes sanctions but the fear of such action.[3] Once the threatened

[1] John Austin, *The Province of Jurisprudence Determined* (London, 1832), p. 8.
[2] Payson S. Wild, Jr., *Sanctions and Treaty Enforcement* (Cambridge, Mass., 1934), p. 58. See also F. Blaine Sloan, "Comparative International and Municipal Law Sanctions," 27 *Nebraska Law Review* (1947), p. 1, at 2.
[3] "In one sense we may well enough say that there is no law without a sanction. . . . Now what is felt to be wrong is felt to call for redress. This may be direct or indirect, swift or tardy; but in the

sanction has failed to deter, other responses have to be considered. But even those responses frequently contain an element of deterrence; if the present violator does not benefit from his violation, he and others will hesitate to commit a violation in the future. Some violations are merely tentative explorations of the character of the response. If the response is quick and firm, the violator is likely to call it a mistake and to abandon his further evil plan.[4] On the other hand, if there is either no response or a weak response, this encourages the violator to proceed more boldly and to pile one violation on top of another until the whole system of restrictions breaks down.

At the same time, it is necessary to remember that a response should fit the violation. There should be some proportionality between the response and the violation. If the response overcompensates for the violation, the violator might be forced to counterrespond, and a vicious circle could easily be started.

Finally, it may be pointed out that at various stages of disarmament different responses might have to be used. In particular, in the early stages it would be necessary to rely to a large extent on unilateral measures, while in the later stages international institutions might play a bigger role. Though national security would not be significantly endangered in the early stages by even major violations, it

---

mere sense and apprehension of redress to come, however remote and improbable it may seem, and however uncertain in manner it may be, we have already some kind of sanction, and not the less a sanction because its effect may be precarious." Sir Frederick Pollock, *A First Book of Jurisprudence* (London, 1896), pp. 24-25.

[4] For instance, the German generals considered the seizure of the Rhineland in 1936 as Hitler's gamble and were willing to retreat and to overthrow Hitler if the Allied Powers should resort to military countermeasures. William L. Shirer, *The Rise and Fall of the Third Reich* (New York, 1960), pp. 291-293.

is quite likely that there would be in those stages a tendency to respond very strongly regardless of the actual importance of the violation. On the other hand, it is probable that in later stages the desire to prevent an interruption of the disarmament process might be so powerful that it might prove difficult to respond adequately even to dangerous violations.

Taking these factors into account, a survey might be made of the various methods developed in international law over the last 300 years for dealing with violations of international agreements. Most of them could be applied easily in case of a violation of a disarmament treaty.

In general, one can divide these methods into two groups. In the first group, enforcement would be delegated to national authorities subject to international supervision, while in the second group the response would be exclusively in the hands of an international authority. In certain situations, the first methods might be feasible; in others, direct international action would be necessary. In the first group, individuals would be the main objects of sanctions, while in the second, sanctions would be directed chiefly against states or governments. However, international proceedings against individuals are also possible.

ENFORCEMENT THROUGH NATIONAL CHANNELS
ENACTMENT OF NATIONAL LEGISLATION

The disarmament treaty might oblige the parties to enact legislation prohibiting treaty violations in their territories or by their nationals. Such legislation would enumerate all the activities that would be prohibited and would specify the penalty for each violation. While some uniformity might be necessary, the legislation in each country would have to fit into the system of its criminal law, and both the definitions of crimes and the penalties for violations would have to be adapted to local customs. Nevertheless, minimum international standards would have to be established, and an international authority would have to check on compliance. Thus, copies of all relevant national laws and supplementary regulations would have to be sent regularly to the international authority. The staff of that authority would scrutinize the texts and would verify their conformity with the international minimum standards. On the basis of the staff report, the international authority would decide either that a particular national law conformed with the standards or that it did not. In the latter case, it would request the nation to modify its law and might suggest what modifications would be necessary to achieve the required conformity.[5] If the request was not complied with, this fact might be considered as an early indication that the non-conforming nation did not intend to take its obligations under the disarmament treaty sufficiently seriously.

REPORTING OF VIOLATIONS

Assuming that we had gone over this hurdle successfully and that all problems of the adequacy of national legislation had been ironed out, we would be interested in the arrangements made by each nation for actually enforcing its law against the violation of the disarmament

[5] A procedure of this kind has been developed by the International Labor Organization to ensure uniform application of international labor conventions. See, e.g., E. A. Landy, "The Effective Application of International Labour Standards," 68 *International Labour Review* (1953), pp. 346-363; C. Wilfred Jenks, "The Interpretation of International Labour Conventions by the International Labour Office," 20 *British Year Book of International Law* (1939), pp. 123-141.

treaty. Some such arrangements might have purely psycho-logical effect. For instance, the head of government would make radio and television broadcasts urging all citizens to comply, making it clear that it is the government's policy to ensure compliance, and ordering all persons who have any information on any suspicious activities that might constitute violations to report on them immediately to proper authorities. Such an exhortation could be backed up by legal sanctions, and the basic legislation would in-clude a provision subjecting to punishment any person who, though possessing information about a possible violation, has not submitted the required report. At the same time, rewards might be given to informers who sub-mitted a report leading to the discovery of a violation.[6]

NATIONAL INVESTIGATIONS

While all national enforcement officers (federal, state, and local) would be responsible for the discovery of violations and the apprehension of violators, it might also be desirable to establish a special investigation serv-ice that would have as its sole purpose the discovery of any activities prohibited by the disarmament treaty. A cooperating system of such national networks might be developed, similar to Interpol, with a minimum of inter-national supervision.[7]

It would be the duty of national investigators to check all the reports of the informants, to investigate rumors, to

[6] Lewis C. Bohn, "Non-Physical Inspection Techniques," in Donald G. Brennan (ed.), *Arms Control, Disarmament and National Security* (New York, 1961), p. 347, at 349.

[7] With respect to the work of the International Criminal Police Organization (Interpol) in the field of suppression of illicit traffic in narcotic drugs, see "The United Nations and Narcotic Drugs," 6 *United Nations Review* (1959), No. 6, p. 47, at 56.

conduct inspections of facilities in which prohibited activities might be conducted, and, in some cases of actual violations, to arrest the violator in accordance with local procedures (e.g., on the basis of a court warrant or, in special circumstances, without it). Each national service would submit annual reports and, in an emergency, special reports to an international authority, giving all relevant details about the investigated cases and the problems encountered in its activities. The staff of the international authority would analyze those reports, point out their deficiencies, request explanations, and, in turn, submit a report to the board of the authority for final action. Such action might involve requests for additional information, for improvement of the local service, or even for additional action. In case of refusal, international action might be required to remedy the situation.

NATIONAL TRIBUNALS

When the national investigators uncovered a violation, the violator (an individual, a corporation, or other legal person) would be brought before a national tribunal for the determination of his guilt and punishment. A local prosecutor would handle the case, and local judges would make the decision. Either the prosecutor or the accused violator might appeal from the decision to a higher tribunal and, if necessary, from that one to a supreme court, to the extent authorized by local law. The international authority might only have observers in the local courts reporting to it on the performance of the local judges.[8] Going one step further, it might participate in

[8] Analogous procedure has been developed, for instance, under the NATO Status of Forces Agreement of June 19, 1951 (199 UN Treaty Series, p. 67), and United States observers are usually present

the proceedings as "a friend of the court," in order to comment on questions of interpretation of the disarmament treaty that might be involved in the proceedings. The international authority could also be given an independent right of appeal to higher national courts in cases where it deems that the treaty or the local law has been misinterpreted or that the punishment meted out is inadequate.

More difficult problems would arise if the treaty should envisage either an additional right of appeal to an international tribunal or a right to submit the case to an international tribunal for further consideration. Under some constitutional systems, it might be impossible to empower an international tribunal to reverse the decision of a national supreme court. Some international treaties provide that in such a case the international tribunal might grant the injured party "equitable satisfaction," such as payment of monetary compensation for the violation.[9] This solution might not be entirely satisfactory in case of a violation of the disarmament treaty, but some methods might be devised for compensating other parties to the treaty for the fact that a particular person was not properly punished for his violation.

Even where proper punishment has been decreed by a local court, the problem does not necessarily end there. Through a lenient interpretation of local provisions or by means of an executive pardon, the person might be released from jail prematurely and the whole punishment

---

at trials of US military personnel by foreign courts. Joseph M. Snee and Kenneth A. Pye, *Status of Forces Agreements and Criminal Jurisdiction* (New York, 1957), pp. 114-116.

[9] See, for instance, the Revised Geneva General Act for the Pacific Settlement of Disputes of April 28, 1949, Article 32; 71 UN Treaty Series, p. 101, at 118.

184

process might become a mockery.[10] The international authority must, therefore, continue to keep an eye on the execution of the penal sentence, and, in case of a violation of the letter or spirit of the disarmament agreement, it must have the right to take some remedial action.

ADVANTAGES AND DISADVANTAGES

The basic advantage of the system outlined above is that it does not require a complicated international machinery and could be introduced, therefore, very early in the disarmament process. This system has worked fairly well in areas of common international concern, such as abolition of slavery, international traffic in women and children, and international control of narcotic drugs. To the extent that the individual involved in a violation can be considered as the enemy of the human race, the detection of his violation by national investigators and his punishment by local tribunals acting in accordance with local laws might prove quite effective. An inventor trying to develop a new device to destroy mankind, a "doomsday machine," might be properly punished by any country. Perhaps the common revulsion against bacteriological warfare might be strong enough to ensure that any person caught producing dangerous bacteria would not escape punishment. It is also possible to conceive of instances in which some clandestine activities are conducted either without the knowledge of the government or of some of its members or under orders of a prior government with which the new one disagrees. There might also be cases

[10] For an account of the "tragi-comedy" of the Leipzig trials of German war criminals after World War I, see Sheldon Glueck, *War Criminals: Their Prosecution and Punishment* (New York, 1944), pp. 19-34.

in which a government, having found out that the international inspectorate or the intelligence service of some other party to the treaty has discovered or is about to discover a violation, would anticipate the accusation and would sacrifice the individuals involved by bringing them before a national tribunal for punishment. In other cases, where the state concerned considers itself unjustly accused, it might welcome the trial of the suspected persons before a local tribunal in order to prove its innocence. In some circumstances, the government might adopt the attitude, now prevailing with respect to spies, of disowning any violator who is apprehended. Finally, the national system of reporting suspicious activities and of investigating them might work so well that activities that were supposed to be immune to it would be discovered, and the government would be unable to stop further action with respect to their punishment.

It is quite conceivable that, for these various reasons, the national detection and punishment system might work quite effectively in many countries, especially in the democratic ones. Disobedience to secret orders of the government might be more difficult in Communist countries, and action against the guilty persons would be possible there only if the lower echelons were actually convinced that their leaders really meant it when they proclaimed loudly and repeatedly that they did not approve of any clandestine rearmament activities.

A distinction might also be made between local detection and local punishment. It is more difficult to expect a local detection service to flush out a violator than to have a local tribunal adequately punish a discovered violator. This would be especially true if the local trials were conducted in the glare of world publicity, and it would become important to establish the reputation of local tribunals as impartial and unbiased. Because of the nature of the judicial system, it might be easier also to establish international remedies against abuses and to provide for an adequate international review of improper decisions.[11]

In general, however, only limited reliance can be placed on any national system of enforcement. It might be better than nothing and it might work in some cases, but in the long run it does not offer sufficient guarantees against large-scale violations. It might be useful as a supplement to an international system, but it is not a substitute for it.[12]

[11] A list of cases in which decisions of the Supreme Court of the United States have been reviewed by international tribunals is printed in *US Foreign Relations*, 1910, p. 600.

[12] In the Genocide Convention of December 9, 1948, Article VI provides that "Persons charged with genocide or any of the other acts enumerated in article III shall be tried by a competent tribunal of the State in the territory of which the act was committed, or by such international penal tribunal as may have jurisdiction with respect to those Contracting Parties which shall have accepted its jurisdiction" (78 UN Treaty Series, p. 277, at 280-282). In the Soviet "Draft Convention to Prohibit the Production and Employment of Weapons Based on the Use of Atomic Energy for the Purpose of Mass Destruction" of June 19, 1946, the only provisions on sanctions were a declaration that any violation of the Convention "is a most serious international crime against humanity" and an obligation to "pass legislation providing severe penalties for violators" of the Convention. UN Doc. AEC/8; US Department of State, *Documents on Disarmament, 1945-1959*, I (1960), 21. Similarly, the Soviet draft "Treaty of General and Complete Disarmament under Strict International Control" of September 24, 1962, speaks only of national criminal sanctions. For instance, in paragraph 3 of Article 22, it is provided that "Each State party to the Treaty shall, in accordance with its constitutional procedures, enact legislation completely prohibiting nuclear weapons and making any attempt by individuals or organizations to reconstitute such weapons a criminal offence" (UN Doc. A/C.1/867, p. 18). There is an analogous provision in the US "Outline of Basic Provisions of a Treaty on General and Complete Disarmament in a Peaceful World" of April 18, 1962. According to that draft, in Stage II the "Parties

187

INTERNATIONAL ENFORCEMENT AGAINST INDIVIDUALS

Since the First World War, there have been many discussions of international responsibility of individuals for violations of international law. The Treaty of Versailles provided for the trial of Kaiser Wilhelm, but the Netherlands refused to extradite him.[13] After the Second World War, most of the defendants in Nuremberg and Tokyo trials were punished not only for war crimes but also for waging an aggressive war.[14] The International Law Commission of the United Nations in 1954 prepared a "Draft Code of Offenses Against the Peace and Security of Mankind" for which "the responsible individuals shall be punished." This Draft Code includes, among other offenses, as punishable acts: "Acts by the authorities of a State in violation of its obligations under a treaty which is designed to ensure international peace and security by means of restrictions or limitations on armaments, or on military training, or on fortifications, or of other restrictions of the same character."[15]

Another special committee of the United Nations prepared in 1953 a "Draft Statute for an International Criminal Court" for the purpose of trying "natural persons accused of crimes generally recognized under inter-

---

to the Treaty which had not already done so would, in accordance with their constitutional processes, enact national legislation in support of the Treaty imposing legal obligations on individuals and organizations under their jurisdiction and providing appropriate penalties for noncompliance." US Arms Control and Disarmament Agency, *Blueprint for the Peace Race* (1962), p. 28.

[13] See Sheldon Glueck, *op.cit.*, pp. 20-21.

[14] John A. Appleman, *Military Tribunals and International Crimes* (Indianapolis, 1954); C. A. Pompe, *Aggressive War: An International Crime* (The Hague, 1953).

[15] General Assembly, Official Records, 9th Session, Suppl. 9 (UN Doc. A/2693), pp. 11-12.

national law."[16] No final action has been taken by the United Nations with respect to either the Draft Code or the Court, since the matter got mixed up with the question of the definition of aggression. Due to the United States opposition to such a definition, all three documents were referred to a new committee that is supposed to decide on the proper moment to discuss them. The committee has met a few times, but it still considers that the time for a substantive discussion has not yet arrived.[17]

In the area of disarmament, punishment of individuals for a violation of the disarmament treaty has been considered from time to time.[18] The main reason given is that it might be easier to proceed against individuals rather than states. As mentioned in Section I, there might be cases in which a government would prefer to have an individual punished rather than to have action taken against the government itself or the state. The accused individual might be found abroad and then be extradited to the international authority. Or, as in the Eichmann case or in the case of the rescue of Mussolini by Skorzenny and his paratroopers, a person might be snatched away without the knowledge of the government concerned. Finally, the government might change and the members of the old government might be surrendered for trial by the new one, sometimes not only without difficulty but even with pleasure.[19]

[16] *Idem*, Suppl. 12 (UN Doc. A/2645), pp. 23-26.

[17] See UN Docs. A/AC.91/SR.8, pp. 4-5, and A/AC.91/3 (1962).

[18] See, for instance, the outline prepared by the UN Atomic Energy Commission in 1947, which included the "Examination of the nature of direct international jurisdiction over individuals and the principles governing the application of individual punishments." UN Atomic Energy Commission, Official Records, 2d Year, Special Suppl., Second Report to the Security Council (UN Doc. AEC/26), pp. 6-8.

[19] Similar arguments were made in connection with the discussion

Analogies from domestic law are often brought up. In the Federalist Papers, a strong argument was made for individual punishment rather than for sanctions against the state members of the federal union.[20] In criminal law, punishment of the responsible individual is considered a more effective sanction than punishment of the legal person involved.[21] In an antitrust case, imprisoning the officers of a corporation could be more efficacious than fining the corporation.[22] Where states cannot be sued, methods have been developed for bringing a case against a government official, and at least declaratory judgments can be obtained ascertaining whether or not action is illegal.[23]

Similarly, in disarmament cases it might be possible to have two types of cases, civil and criminal (or penal) suits. In the first place, states might not object to cases before an international tribunal in which one of their officials is sued for having violated the disarmament treaty either through his own action or by ordering or condoning action of others. The purpose of such a case would be to obtain an injunction prohibiting further activity, an order requiring certain action (e.g., prosecution of violators in accordance with local law), or a decision requiring removal of a violation e.g., the destruction of a clandestine

---

of the general question of the establishment of an international criminal court. See General Assembly, Official Records, 7th Session, Annexes, Agenda Item 52 (UN Doc. A/2275) (1952), pp. 20-23.

[20] *The Federalist*, Nos. xv, xvi, and xx (John C. Hamilton's edn., Philadelphia, 1868), pp. 141-152, 176-177.

[21] Nathaniel F. Cantor, *Crime and Society* (New York, 1939), pp. 366-371.

[22] This was done in the General Electric Case in 1960-1961.

[23] Cf. James Brown Scott, *Judicial Settlement of Controversies between the States of the American Union* (Oxford, 1919), pp. 63-90; Roger Fisher, "Internal Enforcement of International Rules," in Seymour Melman (ed.) *Disarmament: Its Politics and Economics* (Boston, 1962), p. 99, at 105-106.

production facility).[24] While for all practical purposes this would be indistinguishable from an action against a state, the psychological effect would possibly be different. Though a state might strongly oppose any attempt to declare it guilty of a violation, it might find it easier to explain to its population and to other nations that the whole affair was not a premeditated act of the government but the result of a misguided conspiracy that it was glad to have discovered.

A government might be willing to take a similar attitude in a criminal case, though the stigma of penal condemnation would seem more difficult for it to accept. In addition, influential members of a government who do not mind being ordered to take some action would feel quite differently about being put in jail or subjected to capital punishment. In such a case, they are likely to use all their power to obstruct the prosecution of the suit against them, even if it might bring disaster upon their country. It is considered, therefore, quite impractical to expect that in most cases the guilty persons would be surrendered for an international trial; and the argument is made that this fact would soon discredit the whole procedure.[25] On the other side, it is contended that there might be cases in which, as mentioned above, this method might work and that a few successful cases would establish sufficient threat of possible punishment to constitute a powerful inducement to compliance.[26] On balance, it would seem that this

[24] An injunction against causing damage through dangerous fumes was granted, for instance, by an arbitral tribunal in the Trail Smelter Case in 1941. UN, Reports of International Arbitral Awards, III (1949), p. 1938, at 1966.
[25] See the letter from the Foreign Office of the United Kingdom of June 5, 1952 (UN Doc. A/2186, pp. 35-48).
[26] See the report of the Sixth Committee of the General Assembly

method, like that of national enforcement, cannot be considered an adequate guarantee against large-scale violations but might supplement other, more efficacious procedures.

The establishment of a system of international punishment of persons responsible for a violation of a disarmament treaty might require special personnel and apparatus.

AN INTERNATIONAL INVESTIGATION SERVICE

Such a service might form a part of the international inspectorate or be separate from it. While the inspectorate would simply determine that a violation had occurred, it would be the duty of the investigation service to determine what person was responsible for the violation. On the basis of such an investigation, the person or persons concerned would be, if necessary, arrested and brought before a competent international tribunal.

INTERNATIONAL PROSECUTORS

The preparation of the case for presentation before an international tribunal and the actual prosecution would be in the hands of an international prosecutor (district attorney). He would also make the decision whether the accused should be arrested and whether he should be taken outside his own country.

INTERNATIONAL TRIBUNALS

It might be enough at the beginning to have one international tribunal, which might be modelled on the International Criminal Court proposed by the United

---

of December 3, 1954, pars. 6-9, General Assembly, Official Records, 9th Session, Agenda Item 50 (UN Doc. A/2827), p. 2.

Nations.[27] That tribunal might travel on circuit and hear the cases in the country where the violation has been committed or in a neighboring country, to which the accused and the necessary witnesses would easily be brought. If there should be many violations of a minor character requiring trials all around the globe, it might prove necessary to establish a system of regional tribunals for the trials of violators. In the latter case, in order to provide the necessary uniformity of interpretation, it would be useful to have an appeals court to which appeal could be made on important questions of law.

A BILL OF RIGHTS

To safeguard the rights of the accused against malicious prosecution or unfair trial, a bill of rights could be enacted to protect the individual against abuse by the international authority. The authority enforcing the rule of law in the world should not itself be immune from it. In proper cases, the authority might be required to pay compensation for trampling on the rights of an individual.[28]

It can easily be seen that if one should wish to proceed along this road, there would be many complications along the way. Some of the legal problems involved might be similar to those resulting from trials of foreign soldiers under the status of foreign forces agreements, such as the trials of Americans in NATO countries and Japan. Other questions might be resolved along the lines of the trial of war criminals at Nuremberg and Tokyo. In many areas,

[27] General Assembly, Official Records, 9th Session, Suppl. 12 (UN Doc. A/2645), pp. 23-26.

[28] A provision for compensation was contained in the Second Report of the UN Atomic Energy Commission of September 11, 1947. See UN Atomic Energy Commission, Official Records, Second

however, new paths might have to be trodden for which only inadequate analogies exist in national legal systems. Whether one should accept this approach would depend on the alternatives that might be available. If governments should find national enforcement inadequate and should shrink away from sanctions against nations, the middle road of international action against the responsible individual might prove to be the only available solution. It might work in some types of situations where the discovered violations were not clearly of governmental origin and where both the violating party and the other parties might prefer to dispose of the matter on this lower level rather than to make an intergovernmental issue out of it.

UNILATERAL RESPONSES BY GOVERNMENTS

Most discussions of the problem of responses to a violation of a disarmament agreement have been concerned with unilateral responses. An important violation of an agreement by one party might justify the abrogation of the agreement by the other parties, in whole or in part.[29] This might involve the right of the complying parties to make up for the violation by starting to produce prohibited weapons or by engaging on a crash basis in research and development activities.

In such responses, there is always the danger of over compensation and of a chain reaction of recriminations

---

Year, Special Suppl., p. 64; US Department of State, Documents of Disarmament, 1945-1959, I (1960), p. 93, at 143.

[29] An express affirmation of "the inherent right of a party to withdraw and be relieved of obligations," if the provisions of the treaty "are not being fulfilled and observed," was contained in the United States proposals of June 27, 1960 (Controlling Principles, No. 5). US Department of State, Documents on Disarmament (1960), p. 126, at 127.

and counterviolations. To the extent that each state is its own judge as to the danger of a particular violation and the need and magnitude of its response, the matter can easily get out of control. On the other hand, if a nation should feel that it cannot rely on the responsiveness of an international system and on the willingness of noncommitted nations to participate in an adequate system of responses, the right to take unilateral measures would have to be safeguarded in a disarmament treaty either explicitly or implicitly.

INTERNATIONAL RESPONSES

The modern method of channeling responses to an important violation of international law is through an international organization. Both the League of Nations and the United Nations were given authority to take steps against violations of basic principles of the League Covenant and the UN Charter.[30] The sanction provisions in the Covenant were considered inadequate by the United Nations, and a special effort was made at the Dumbarton Oaks and San Francisco Conferences to fill in the gaps.[31] There is no longer a question of legal insufficiency; there is only lack of will to use the available means. The United States wanted to ensure that it would not be obliged to take part in any enforcement measures without its consent, and the Soviet Union wanted to protect itself against the possibility that the new organization would take measures against it. Consequently, they agreed to give the Security Council the primary responsibility for the mainte-

[30] Article 16 of the Covenant of the League of Nations and Chapter VII of the Charter of the United Nations.

[31] See the report by Mr. Paul-Boncour to the San Francisco Conference, June 10, 1945. United Nations Conference on International Organization, Documents, XII (1945), 502-513.

nance of peace only on condition that no enforcement action would be taken without consent of all five permanent members of the Security Council. Should such consent be given, the United Nations can take action that is legally binding on all its members to enforce the decisions of the Security Council by diplomatic, economic, and military sanctions. Without the consent of the Big Five, no binding action can be taken. Nevertheless, under the Uniting for Peace Resolution of 1950, the General Assembly asserted its secondary responsibility for the maintenance of peace and its power to recommend collective measures in the case of a breach of the peace or an act of aggression if the Security Council, because of lack of unanimity of the permanent members, fails to exercise its primary responsibility.[32] While such recommendations of the General Assembly are not binding on member states, any action taken pursuant to them could not be considered a violation of the Charter injunction against use of force in any manner inconsistent with the purposes of the United Nations. Whether any action would be taken in any particular case would depend on the willingness of member states to adopt a strong decision in the first place and to execute it in the second place.

Economic sanctions taken against Italy after her attack on Ethiopia failed, but that test was not meaningful, since the sanctions were in effect only for a short time and since they did not include the two measures that might have brought Mussolini down—embargo on export of petroleum products to Italy and closure of the Suez Canal.[33] While

[32] General Assembly, Resolution 377A (V), of November 3, 1950. General Assembly, Official Records, 5th Session, Suppl. 20 (A/1775), pp. 10-12.
[33] For the text of the measures taken against Italy, see the documents of the Co-ordination Committee, reprinted in the League of

the reason given for not taking these measures was that Mussolini might have considered them a cause for war, it is not likely that he would have compounded his difficulties by declaring war on all the members of the League who were participating in sanctions against him. There were also some indications that even the limited economic and financial sanctions taken against Italy might have led to her economic collapse if they were continued for a few more months.

The United Nations General Assembly recommended an embargo on shipments of war materials to Communist China in 1951, after her "volunteers" joined in the Korean War.[84] In view of the limited economic relations of China with non-Communist nations, this measure did not prove significant. The Soviet bloc considered this recommendation as invalid because the General Assembly was allegedly not authorized by the Charter to adopt such a recommendation and because the members of that bloc continued to maintain the fiction that the original attack came from South Korea and that the United Nations was supporting an aggressor in violation of the Charter.[85]

Despite this unsatisfactory record, it is frequently insisted that the United Nations should be responsible for taking enforcement action against a violator of the disarmament treaty, either in accordance with the present Charter or on the basis of new rules embodied in the dis-

---

Nations Official Journal, Special Suppl. 150 (1936), pp. 1-12. See also Albert E. Highley, "The First Sanctions Experiment," 9 Geneva Studies (1938), No. 4; M. J. Bonn, "How Sanctions Failed," 15 Foreign Affairs (1937), pp. 350-361.

[84] General Assembly, Resolution 500 (V), May 18, 1961. General Assembly, Official Records, 5th Session, Suppl. 20A (UN Doc. A/1775/Add. 1), p. 2.

[85] Security Council, Official Records, 5th Year, No. 24 (482nd Meeting), pp. 3-10.

LOUIS B. SOHN

armament treaty itself. It might be useful to canvass the possibilities for international enforcement measures that might be made available in a disarmament treaty.

REMOVAL OF THE VIOLATION

In many cases it might be sufficient to order the violating state to remove a violation. If the fact of a violation has been properly ascertained and if any dispute about the question whether a particular activity really constituted a violation has been resolved by procedures provided for in the disarmament treaty, the violating nation might admit that it was mistaken in regarding the activity as a legal one and would be willing to remove the violation by destroying prohibited weapons or by dismantling an illegal production facility. It might be desirable to accept this action as closing the incident rather than to insist on further punishment of the state concerned.

Should a state refuse, however, to comply with a request to remove the violation, in some cases it might be possible to remove it through international action. The international authority might authorize a party to the treaty to send a mission to the territory of the violating state to destroy the arms depot or the illegal factory. After a proper warning had been given to the civilian population in the neighborhood, a single plane dropping ordinary explosives might accomplish this task. The violating state might, of course, complicate the matter by forcing its population to stay in the danger area, and, in such a case, a further decision by the international authority might be necessary before any action could be taken that would endanger the lives of many people. Should the violating state oppose the international mission, for instance, by trying

198

to shoot down the plane, this would be considered an additional violation subject to further penalty.

If in later stages of the disarmament process an international armed force should come into being, it might be authorized to remove the violation by the military means at its disposal. In some cases, specially trained sabotage agents might be employed to execute the decision without involving a large-scale use of force.

IMPOSING A FINE ON THE VIOLATOR

In cases of minor or medium-size violations, a fine might be imposed on a state. If it should refuse to pay, this would constitute an additional violation. Some suggestions have also been made for ensuring that the fine would be collected. For instance, each country might be obliged to deposit a certain amount of gold or of convertible currency in an international or a Swiss bank at the time of ratification of the disarmament treaty; if a fine should be imposed on a country, an appropriate part of its deposit might be transferred to the international authority. Alternatively, it might be agreed that existing rules of international law about sovereign immunity and protection of foreign governmental and private assets against seizure should be relaxed sufficiently to enable the collection of the fine through seizure of the violating state's funds in foreign banks and its other assets abroad and even perhaps through seizure of the foreign assets of its nationals.[86]

ECONOMIC SANCTIONS

Both in the late 1930's, as a result of the Ethiopian

[86] Oscar Schachter, "The Enforcement of International Judicial and Arbitral Decisions," 54 *American Journal of International Law* (1960), p. 1, at 7-14.

experience, and in the 1950's, in consequence of the Korean War, detailed studies have been made of economic sanctions. Relevant experience has been provided also by measures of economic warfare during the Second World War. The United Nations Collective Measures Committee prepared several reports suggesting improvements in the machinery of economic sanctions. In particular, it would be desirable for states to enact national legislation permitting immediate imposition of an embargo when ordered by an international authority. A list of items that should be subject to an embargo has been prepared, and steps might be taken to ensure uniform application of that list by all concerned. Finally, proper procedures are necessary to ensure that the burden of economic sanctions would not fall unevenly on a few nations having extensive commercial relations with the violator and that nations making special sacrifices would receive compensatory assistance from other, more fortunate nations.[37]

In general, economic sanctions might prove effective against some smaller nations not supported by one of the major powers. A few nations are so strong that it is not likely that they would be affected by such sanctions unless all their friends should desert them. No nation is entirely self-sufficient, and a complete boycott would play such havoc with its economy that it would probably not be willing to pay that price except in a case where national survival was considered to be at stake. On the other hand, as long as only a few nations are completely on their own and

[37] For the reports of the Collective Measures Committee, see General Assembly, Official Records, 6th Session, Suppl. 13 (UN Doc. A/1891); idem, 7th Session, Suppl. 17 (UN Doc. A/2215); and idem, 9th Session, Annexes, Agenda Item 19 (UN Doc. A/2713), pp. 1-4.

most nations belong to strongly knit blocs, it is quite unlikely that economic measures would be effective against
big blocs that had weathered the storms of the "cold
war" and the economic pressures exerted by opposing
groups of nations. Nevertheless, there is considerable
evidence that the West German government has been able
to curb harassments to West Berlin by threatening to
curtail interzonal trade, on which East Germany depends
to a significant degree.

MILITARY SANCTIONS

Both the Charter and the Uniting for Peace Resolution provide for military sanctions to be executed by
national contingents put at the disposal of the United
Nations. Because of a dispute about the size of the contingents to be made available to the Security Council, no
agreements for such contingents have been reached.[38]
Similarly, only insignificant forces were volunteered when
the General Assembly asked in 1950 that nations maintain
within their national forces special contingents that would
be made available for service as United Nations units upon
recommendation of the Security Council or the General
Assembly.[39] Nevertheless, sufficient forces were made
available in the Suez and Congo crises to police the danger
areas.[40]

It has been suggested that an agreement of disarmament should be coupled with an agreement on a United

[38] See the report of the Military Staff Committee of April 30,
1947, Security Council, Official Records, 2nd Year, Special Suppl.
1, pp. 1-12.

[39] William R. Frye, A United Nations Peace Force (New York,
1957), pp. 57-61.

[40] See the reports of the Secretary-General of October 9, 1958,
and July 18, 1960 (UN Docs. A/3943 and S/4389).

Nations Peace Force, and the official US Proposals of April 18, 1962, lay great stress on the establishment of such a force. While the Soviet Union agreed in September 1961 that an international police force should be strong enough "to deter or suppress any threat or use of arms in violation of the purposes and principles of the United Nations," it has since retreated from that position, and its current proposals do not envisage such an effective force. Should it be decided, nevertheless, that such a force should be established, difficult problems of controlling the force would have to be solved. It is generally agreed that this difficulty need not stand in the way of early stages of disarmament and that considerable disarmament measures might be put into effect prior to the solution of the problem of an international peace force. But it is doubtful that general and complete disarmament would be possible without such a force. At some point, a nation would not be able to rely any longer on its own deterrent power; at that point, an international force would have to provide an additional element of security, without which further disarmament would not be feasible.

Once such an international force is established, it could be used for military sanctions against a violator of the disarmament treaty. Until that moment, only national forces would be available for such sanctions. In some cases international control or even command of such forces might be possible. In any event it might be desirable to establish clear international standards for the employment of such forces; otherwise, self-help might lead to retaliation and such reciprocal escalatory use of forces might eventually result in a nuclear war.

Conclusions

A large variety of responses, unilateral and multilateral, is available. In some cases, it might prove both possible and desirable to proceed against the individual responsible for the violation rather than to challenge a government. There might be situations in which national enforcement machinery, properly supervised by an international authority, might be used for action against individuals. In other situations, an international enforcement system might be preferable, with its own investigators, prosecutors, and tribunals.

Where the responses have to be directed to governments, they can be tailored to the gravity of the violation. Some responses, such as the destruction of an arms depot or of a clandestine production facility, might be directed toward the removal of the violation. Other responses might be punitive in character. In some cases economic or military sanctions would be necessary to coerce a state to agree to abide again by its obligations.

Some responses, especially unilateral ones, are based on general rules and need not be mentioned in the disarmament treaty. Others, however, would involve either a grant of new powers to existing international institutions or the creation of new institutions or procedures, and it would be necessary to specify them in the treaty.

CHAPTER XI

RESPECT FOR INTERNATIONAL LAW AND
CONFIDENCE IN DISARMAMENT

BY RICHARD A. FALK

Tʜɪs chapter considers the relevance of the law habit in world affairs to security during disarmament. It proceeds from the assumption that an increase in respect for the obligations of international law has much to do with creating confidence in disarmament as an undertaking consistent with national security. I wish to emphasize, especially, the importance of prevailing attitudes toward international legal obligations; for it is the direction of these attitudes rather than the elaboration of legal forms and conventions that determines more than anything else the extent of confidence in law as a basis of public order.

Likewise, resort to a somewhat unfamiliar phrase like "the law habit" expresses my belief that what is most important is to establish a characteristic way of acting in international affairs, the distinctive feature of which is a virtually automatic acceptance of legal constraints as a limitation upon the national process of choosing among options in foreign affairs.

Within an international environment in which the law habit has come to prevail it is much easier to envisage a commitment by states to comprehensive disarmament. The possession of military strength would not be perceived as crucial to the protection of vital national interests, since the most signal demonstration of the existence of the law habit is the renunciation of unilateralism, especially with regard to the threat or use of force. Law is above all a system of reconciliation, of reliance upon persuasion rather than coercion, and of acceptance of community procedures of review and judgment.[1]

The disarmament literature has given surprisingly little attention to the extent to which security during disarmament is dependent upon the growth of respect for the methods and procedures of international law. Vague assertions are frequently made about the necessity of establishing "the rule of law" in world affairs. To the extent that these assertions are spelled out, they have tended to produce either schemes for the expansion of the jurisdiction of the World Court or pleas for an increasing reliance upon international adjudicative techniques. Such advocacy has tended to disguise the problem by making its solution depend upon the growth of third-party settlement procedures. These procedures are often not appropriate for resolving international disputes, especially if the conflict between states cannot be formulated as a justiciable issue or if a stable solution requires a new standard of legality (a legislative solution) or a new regime of order.

The failure of international law to foster confidence is much less a consequence of its inadequate institutional forms than it is a result of the attitude of states toward the legal forms that are presently available. Furthermore, the basic image of international law is created in the course of state-to-state relations rather than by the dealings of states with supranational legal institutions. In this inter-nation setting, the structures and processes of

[1] See, e.g., David E. Apter, "Political Religion in the New States," in Clifford Geertz (ed.), *Old Societies and New States* (Glencoe: The Free Press, 1963), pp. 57, 73-77; and Myres S. McDougal and Florentino P. Feliciano, *Law and Minimum World Public Order* (New Haven: Yale University Press, 1961), pp. 261-283.

legal authority are subject to self-interpretation, but they also permit a state that so aspires to demonstrate its increasing seriousness about acquiring the law habit of constraint, of reasonable explanation, and of persuasive bargaining. This law endeavor, not institution-building, is more likely to foster the kind of confidence that could create an atmosphere propitious for negotiations about comprehensive disarmament.

It is helpful to realize that our sense of personal security in domestic society is largely attributable to confidence in the prevalence of the law habit, rather than to the absence of law-breakers. A realization that we may risk becoming the victim of a crime does not undermine our security or even lead us very often to take such steps in the direction of self-reliance as the acquisition of a gun. It is this confidence in the law habit that is needed, not any necessary assurance (which in any event is impossible to achieve) that a harmful violation will never occur. The idea of building confidence in international law has often been distorted in the past by the rather naïve assumption that the development of international sanctions would provide a satisfactory substitute for present systems of national security. Neither can sanctions assure effective law in any social system nor are they always needed to produce confidence in the effectiveness of law. We acquire the wrong mental set as long as we identify security during disarmament with the development of an inspection system that can assure the detection and neutralization of a violation before it can do harm. No inspection system can promise this, nor do we expect nearly such a firm guarantee in the current system of security based on military self-reliance. Loopholes in the operation of inspection can always be found. Therefore, we must

develop an orientation toward security in which the persistence of these loopholes is understood not to matter
as much as the benefits of disarmament. In addition, at
some point the burdens of a perfected inspection and enforcement system—in terms of intrusion and complexity—
will seem to be more undesirable than will the risks of a
less comprehensive system. Most of us prefer to take
our chances with crime rather than to pay for and endure
several policemen on every city block.

One can summarize the discussion to this point by ob-
serving that an increasing respect for international law
is among those conditions that must evolve if comprehensive disarmament is to become a realistic objective.
The implication is that modifications must take place in
international society not only in the course of disarmament itself, but prior to its commencement as well. This
is part of a wider need to develop a strategy to promote
the transition from the present arms-controlled world to
a disarmable world. This provides an appropriate focus
for a consideration of the role of international law in the
promotion of global security and in the preparation for
comprehensive disarmament.

The emphasis upon attitudes toward law is intentional.
The security needs of states reflect their image of the
world, including the extent to which their voluntary compliance with governing norms is characteristic behavior.
This image, much more than empirical proofs of compliance, defines the requirements for security in a disarming world. As long as distrust prevails and a cynical
view of law endures, no rational alternative to military
strength and a posture of self-reliance seems to exist as
a basis of national security. However, if an attitude of
seriousness about the reality of legal constraints can be

introduced into governmental decision-making processes, then there is likely to arise an increasing willingness to perceive security as resting more on the qualities of good citizenship than on the apparatus of law enforcement. A social system that is dependent upon enforcement to provide security is very primitive, probably too primitive to induce its members voluntarily to give up habits and capabilities of self-reliance in exchange for a bolder undertaking by the organized community to protect the rights and interests of its members. This is precisely the transformation that disarmament entails: states must give up self-reliant postures to attain security through community procedures. But, to overcome the inertia of the existing system, it is essential to dramatize the deficiencies of the present order and to demonstrate the feasibility of the proposed new order. This is not primarily a matter of blueprinting security arrangements or of strengthening specific legal procedures or institutions. It requires, rather, that a revolution be staged in the political consciousness of mankind. Our contention here is that the growth of habits of respect for law may contribute significantly to this revolution and may allow it to take place peacefully rather than traumatically.

The modification of attitudes toward international law involves a complex and difficult process. At the present stage, we can do little more than give our reasons for the recommended reorientation. This involves several steps: first, to indicate the reasons why a growth in the respect of states for international law is a prerequisite to a disarmable world; second, to make evident the failure of leading states to manifest the requisite seriousness in their current behavior; third, to illustrate the somewhat contrary demonstration that despite the deficiency in present attitudes there is no occasion for despair or cynicism about the role and future of legal restraints in world politics; and, fourth, to argue that national objectives in the contemporary world are more definitively advanced by conforming national behavior to the constraints set by international law than by pursuing policies that flaunt law in order to maximize national power, wealth, and prestige. Part of this argument is based on the view that obedience to law need not contradict reasonable requirements of national security. A prime function of international law is to satisfy the reasonable security needs of states; and law is able to adapt itself to shifting security requirements as they arise.[2]

*

On the basis of this introductory statement, our case should now be documented somewhat by a reference to prevailing patterns of national behavior. States participating in world affairs do not now express the requisite attitudes of respect for international law. The most obvious example is the challenge directed at international legal order by the Communist states and by the modernizing states of Latin America, Asia, and Africa. Both groups of states justify their disrespect for international law by arguing that it is a legal system created to serve the interests of capitalism and colonialism. This allegation, although false when overgeneralized, is true enough to warrant a revision of international law to take account of the divergent interests and attitudes of the modernizing states. The participation of these countries in the reconstruction of international law may contribute more to their acquisition of the law habit than will specific

[2] McDougal and Feliciano, *op.cit.*, pp. 1-96.

substantive reforms in their favor. Part of the task is to make the more sensitive of the statesmen from the new states feel that they have a stake in upholding the legal system, that it is not something alien, but rather is receptive to their initiative.

Of course, it is also important to eliminate legal standards that are designed to support only the interests of the foreign-investing states. International law can hardly appeal to the Afro-Asian states unless it is seen as reconciling their interests in economic development and modernization with the obligations imposed. Thus the international norms governing such subject matter as the expropriation of alien property must be revised to compromise the divergent interests of capital-exporting and capital-importing states.

The West has begun to appreciate the need to reconstruct international law upon the basis of common and reciprocal interests of the leading groups of states. Such an endeavor will itself, if successful, help foster confidence in law as a source of order and welfare in international life. It is most important that the new states do not insist upon a legal order that is extremely unfavorable to the rich and industrialized states. The developing states have an interest in encouraging the flow of private and public capital across boundaries; this interest is denied if the foreign investor is denied all legal protection.

The legitimate complaints made by the new states about the unfair rules of traditional international law are endangered by increasing evidence of a growing nihilism on the part of certain leading Afro-Asian states. This nihilism is a product of irresponsible behavior; it creates a widespread sense of insecurity in international relations that handicaps the efforts of the Great Powers to reach settlements of their differences.

India contributed one prominent example of international nihilism that undermined confidence in the acceptance of the prime norm of minimum world order—the renunciation of aggressive force as a means to settle international disputes. As elsewhere in international affairs, the image of law is tarnished less by conduct than by a callous style of justification. Thus India's invasion of Goa was explained by Indian statesmen in a manner that unnecessarily undermined confidence in India's renunciation of force in international affairs. India could have attained the same objective less disruptively had it claimed that the use of force against Goa was a matter of domestic politics, as an enclave lacks international personality and is, therefore, not protected by the restraints imposed on the use of force by international law. In fact, India could have used the occasion to affirm her adherence to these standards, a display that might have had a certain benefit when later India appealed to the world for protection against China's use of force in their border dispute.

There are many other examples of a startling disregard of the fundamental prohibition upon force in the diplomacy of the new states. For instance, the frequent threats by Egypt and other Middle Eastern states against Israel's independence and Indonesia's preparations for war against Malaysia are flagrant repudiations of the basis of world peace that is incorporated in the Charter of the United Nations. Such instances of coercive diplomacy are damaging to any effort to improve the quality of world order, whether by a strengthening of the role of law, by disarmament, or by other means.

If we turn now to consider the extent to which the well-established and rich states have acquired the law habit, we are confronted by further discouraging evidence. These states often act and talk in a way that unnecessarily destroys confidence in the capacity of law to keep order in world affairs. I refer, especially, to the tendency of these states to abandon legal restraints when they interfere with the pursuit of traditional national interests. Such an attitude reinforces the common view that international law will be respected only so long as the issue is not vital.

Thus one must conclude that the law habit is disturbingly weak, even among states that pride themselves upon a tradition based on government according to law. This contention can be considered by referring to United States practice in recent years. It must be emphasized that the United States, more than any other state, has argued that law and force are mutually exclusive alternatives in world affairs and that the development of a peace system presupposes the existence of a reliable law system. Also, the United States has a great domestic tradition of respect for legal constraint, which predisposes it to believe that just and stable order must always rest upon law. Nevertheless, in the course of its struggles to promote national goals in world politics, the United States recently has not been willing and/or able to manifest an image of respect for international law. This failure in practice is matched by a continuing tradition of oratory declaiming the virtues of the world rule of law. The discrepancy between Machiavellian behavior and Wilsonian language fosters the cynical view that international law is an insubstantial influence upon national behavior and that its advocacy is not to be taken very seriously. Considerable evidence of this disregard for international law by the United States

in its recent history is unfortunately available, and a few examples can be furnished.

The disregard for international law occurs most dramatically in the context of strategic world conflict. Some questions help to frame the issue. To what extent should United States strategy and conduct in the cold war be influenced by patterns of legal constraint? How should the illegality of U-2 flights, for instance, have influenced decision-making in the United States before and after the crisis of May 1960? How should this persisting illegality influence responses to complaints by China and Cuba? These questions suggest another. When should the United States disobey applicable legal rules and disregard the negative effect of its policies upon the growth of world legal order? Any legal violation manifests an attitude of lawlessness that affects the behavior characteristic of a social system. The impact of a violation is especially pronounced in international society where the claims of law are not clearly established and where the means to vindicate breached law are visibly defective.

As we have argued, it appears fanciful to think that, although law is subject to strategic and subjective manipulation in the predisarmament world, it could suddenly become an effective regulator of national behavior once disarmament commenced. The maintenance of international legal commitments requires a firm national disposition to respect law. Thus, planning for disarmament discloses the importance of building law-oriented national dispositions in the predisarmament world. Such an assertion does not argue that a rule of law is or can be an *absolute* restraint but only that it is a *significant* source of restraint; and thus a violation should be justified in the most responsible manner possible. It is important to

213

appreciate that it is not only obedience to the law that counts; the law habit is manifest when a state explains its behavior in the light of legal norms and discloses an effort to pursue its policy by as close an approximation as possible to these norms.

Cold war pressure and strategy have led the United States to adopt several lines of conduct that are incompatible with the growth of a world order based upon legal restraint. Four categories of illegal conduct can be distinguished:

1. Direct violations of applicable legal rules. Illustrations: U-2 overflights of the Soviet Union and other protesting countries, American participation in the April 1961 invasion of Cuba at the Bay of Pigs.

2. Politicalization of emerging legal institutions. Illustrations: insisting that the Republic of China retain a permanent place on the Security Council of the United Nations, retention of the Connally Reservation to its acceptance of the Compulsory Jurisdiction of the International Court of Justice.

3. Irresponsible assertion of novel unilateral claims to act in an area previously unregulated by legal rules, despite protests by other affected nations. Illustrations: hydrogen bomb tests on the high seas, use of space satellites to perform military intelligence and reconnaissance functions over foreign states.

4. Advocacy of policy proposals without evident consideration of applicable legal restraints. Illustrations: a series of plans favoring various kinds of military intervention by the United States in the internal affairs of foreign states in order to offset either Sino-Soviet indirect aggression and subversion or indigenous Communist movements.

A detailed discussion of these illustrations is beyond the scope of this essay. In each instance, an attitude of disrespect for law is manifest; as well, a preferment of interests other than that of promoting the growth of legal order is evident. This attitude is expressed not only in the behavior itself but also in the refusal to offer explanations that might serve as a partial justification. Instead, the tendency is to issue unconvincing denials, which fail to demonstrate that the challenged activity was in some sense essential to the maintenance of security. The question may also be asked, of course, why should the strongest state in the world feel itself entitled to do more than any other state to guard its security? The memory of Pearl Harbor lingers to torment us. But today we have a military capability that is sufficiently indestructible to deprive potential aggressors of illusions.

How does action by an adversary reasonably imperil our security? On what basis can we justify flying U-2 planes over mainland China or Cuba? Of course, we can claim that our global commitment to resist the expansion of Communism requires that we have information about what is going on in these states. But is this rationale very convincing? Have we felt a declining sense of security since we were persuaded to discontinue U-2 flights over the Soviet Union? And yet the Soviet Union is the only state in the world that has the capability to challenge us directly on a military basis.

Have we felt less secure since 1960, when the Bay of Pigs invasion failed? In what sense is Castro a menace to our national security? It is true that Castro has tried to spread Communism to other Latin American countries by illegal means. But does this authorize our recourse to an armed attack in violation of the Charter of the

United Nations? The major premise of world legal order is that national force can only be used for purposes of individual and collective self-defense. Certainly Castro does not directly threaten our military security. Is it not odd that by far the strongest state in the Western hemisphere seems to be the one that is most menaced by the unfriendly presence of the Castro government? These questions point to an insistence by the United States upon a grandiose conception of national security that authorizes it to do whatever it deems prudent, whether legal or not, to advance its interests at the expense of its rivals. Nevertheless, the question can be asked, is this not the way the game of international politics has always been played? Although the answer is "yes," it is nevertheless unsatisfactory, as there exists widespread agreement, that includes the United States, that the game should be discontinued or revised because of its excessive danger to the players. The whole notion of disarmament is taken seriously only because the absence of effective restraints upon the pursuit of national objectives leads to wars that are more and more mutually destructive. Therefore, the proper appraisal of the reasonableness of American "illegality" depends, in part, on what methods should be used to change the old game and what action should be taken in the meantime, that is, in the interval between the time the old game is rejected and the rules for the new one are agreed upon and established. From this perspective, confidence in the effectiveness of the legal system becomes imperative. At the minimum, this requires that a nation must make a very clear showing that a specific decision to violate the law or to shun the law habit was predicated upon a very imminent and substantial threat to national security. With the possible exception of the testing of nuclear weapons on the high seas, no such showing was attempted or made by the United States. Rather, old habits of subordinating legal restraints to political considerations have been retained, and no operational account has been taken of the new and negative realities brought into being by the evolving technology of warfare. No attempt has been made to correlate a habit of obedience to law with the creation of a system of order that might be able to sustain peace more reliably, if not more permanently.

The effectiveness of any legal system, as has been said, depends much more upon habits of obedience and patterns of spontaneous adherence than it does upon police techniques and sanctioning processes. This is especially true for a social order that lacks both strong central institutions and a common culture. The network of rights and duties in the international society emanates from a social order that is quite decentralized in comparison with the highly organized domestic societies. This does not mean that effective international law does not or cannot be made to exist, but it does emphasize the importance of specifying the distinctive conditions required for effective international law. The fundamental basis of international obligations is a generalized preference among nations for order, reinforced in particular situations by reciprocal interests in compliance, by bureaucratic tendencies to obey rules of law in the normal course of governmental operations, by the association between ideas of fairness and respect for law, by the wide discretion of national officials to retaliate and disrupt order in the event of a serious violation by others, and by a sense of mutual convenience arising from a confidence in the fulfillment of those international transactions that are based on law.

The underlying idea is that nation X will not act in a *prohibited* way in context A because it has a greater overall interest in inducing nations Y, Z . . . n to act in the *prescribed* way in contexts B, C . . . n. That is, the violation of a particular rule is rarely worth an attendant impairment of the system of order. The effectiveness of this form of legal order is enhanced if officials acting on behalf of a nation perceive that the stability of international relations is related to the protection of legal interests. This issue is timely because government policies are often formed with evident disregard for the national obligation to plan policy within the constraints of international law. An exception in this respect is the administration's attempt to offer a legal explanation for the quarantine imposed on foreign shipping during the 1962 Cuban missile crisis. This illustrates an appreciation by the government of the United States of the duty to respect international law at least to the extent of presenting legal arguments in defense of its position. This response is quite different, however, from that of choosing a position compatible with the applicable rules of law as they might be determined by an impartial observer. The most guilty man can hire a lawyer to generate a plausible argument that bends the facts or the law or both. But this capacity to argue one's case in legal rhetoric is not the most essential attribute of a law-abiding citizen. The individual who is considered law-abiding is the one who guides his conduct in such a manner that most impartial observers would conclude that he was acting in accord with law. And thus it is with states. The net result of the balance between the arguments for and against a challenged conduct is the proper way to appraise legality. Government officials and legal scholars have a serious obligation to make clear the differences in their roles when they are acting as counsels to the United States, as legal experts, and as citizens.

But perhaps the adversary use of law to bolster a national policy of dubious legality is less disruptive than the tendency to embark on conduct with the attitude that international law neither matters nor even exists. So long as law is kept relevant to the policy process in government, it can at least play a moderating role. Legal advisers can influence the choices that political officers make about the means to be used for the achievement of certain ends, such as the prevention of missile emplacements on Cuban soil; this legal advice may narrow the claim asserted, minimize the violence used or threatened, and least infringe the relevant legal rules. The legal adviser expected to justify his nation's conduct will often be able to persuade his government that his job can be more usefully done if applicable rules are not too blatantly affronted. Thus, law, even if not allowed to be a parameter for government action, can act as a moderative influence. If law is not made explicitly relevant to official acts, however, then vague and undisclosed considerations of prudence are the only restraints that operate to control national egoism, and no progress is made toward the goal of increasing confidence in legal restraint.

The United States asserted its intentions to use observation satellites to gather military information during its overflights of foreign countries. Nowhere in the various controversies about the Samos-Midas program is there evidence that the United States was concerned that its claim might initiate a potentially destabilizing pattern:

219

namely, that a claim by nation X would authorize a similar or equivalent claim by nation Y and that a unilateral initiation of a military use of outer space by the United States would authorize a corresponding use by the Soviet Union or by any other future space power. This pattern of unilateral claim generating unilateral response is exceedingly destabilizing in the military arena. The benefit of self-restraint, the negotiation of permissive restraints, and the invocation of broad community supervision seem to be important, yet neglected, aspects of the endeavor to improve world order. These factors also reflect the kind of national behavior that is essential for the atmosphere of disarmament. The Samos-Midas program illustrates the problems of achieving national restraint in an area in which prohibitive legal rules are absent; this suggests the importance of generating permissive rules rather than of allowing order to develop by the unregulated and shortsighted processes of unilateral claim and counterclaim. Such an evolutionary process, characteristic of the earlier development of the law of the high seas, is no longer appropriate for an arena as interdependent and as militarily significant as outer space. Responsible national behavior requires a greater deference either to the will of the world community or to negotiated techniques of authorization when a proposed pattern of national conduct is protested by other nations. It is dangerous to allow nations to establish legal rights by the mere assertion of unilateral claims to act in areas of human activity that remain unregulated by formal rule. A permissive basis for national action is needed once such action has been challenged by a state that alleges an injury as a consequence of the claim. The United States, as the leader of states seeking stable peace, has a responsibility to acknowledge this problem and to work for its solution. Moreover, it can be pointed out that the growth of confidence in international law is a stated objective of United States policy. To attain this objective, certain facilitative means must be adopted. The record of non-compliance by the United States with international law does not disclose a sufficient sensitivity to the need for confidence-building in international relations.

*

Is it not reasonable to inquire why the United States should exercise self-restraint in international affairs when its main political rivals flaunt their disrespect for rules of international law and for procedures of international order? Does not international law depend for its validity upon a widespread demonstration of respect for its constraints? Why, in short, should the United States and its allies honor the constraints if the Soviet Union and its allies do not? These questions suggest a sharp contrast in Soviet-American attitudes toward respect for international law that is unsupported by evolving Soviet practice and doctrine.

In fact, there is reason to be encouraged about the prospects for increasing global respect for international law. The Soviet Union has demonstrated an increasing awareness of the relevance of international law to the satisfaction of its own national and ideological objectives. The Soviet Union's diplomacy often now relies upon principles of international law; Soviet international lawyers are active in the International Law Association and in other serious groups that have been formed to promote the growth of international law. There is no evidence of a persistent and flagrant disregard of legal rules by the Soviet

221

Union. Soviet education includes teaching respect for international law, and the ideology of the Communist Party now associates the welfare of the world with the strengthening of international law. Of course, this formal advocacy of international law is contradicted by sporadic Soviet disregard of world community judgments about what constitutes permissible action—most notably, the suppression of the Hungarian uprising of 1956 and the resumption of nuclear testing during the moratorium. Nevertheless, on balance there is nothing irreconcilable about the current behavior and objectives of the Soviet Union and the progressive improvement of law habits in world politics. We must not assess the Soviet attitude toward international law by examining their discarded dogmas about law as an instrument of class domination, dogmas that according to the evidence no longer influence Soviet policy or action in the world.

Part of this increasing acceptance of international law by the Soviet Union is attributable to a mellowing of the revolution, and part can be attributed to a sense of concern about the consequences of a breakdown in minimum world order. Functional considerations alone dictate that patterns of threat and conflict be supplanted by systems of competition and reconciliation. Above all, the recent history of the Soviet Union indicates a real sensitivity, perhaps exceeding our own, to the horrors of modern warfare. This sensitivity leads to a universal commitment to the avoidance of nuclear war that solicits the participation of all states, regardless of political orientation, in a common struggle to improve the quality of world order.

In view of this situation, the United States has an important role to play by setting an example of law-oriented behavior in world politics, since the behavior of the United

States establishes the tone for the entire system. It is understandable, but undesirable, for the United States to adopt a cynical attitude toward law as a consequence of being confronted by a serious revolutionary challenge from the Communist world. But it must take stock of the fact that, although revolutionary states manifest a temporary refusal to be bound by the rules of international law, there is a post-revolutionary realization that interaction with non-revolutionary states is desirable and can only proceed within a framework of minimum reliability. This framework is created and maintained by international law. The United States concern with the attainment of international stability should take account of the time needed to assimilate revolutionary states into pre-existing patterns of legal order. It is more in our interest to tolerate some non-compliance by our political enemies than to imitate it. At the minimum, the United States should be ready to acknowledge the Soviet Union's increasing compliance with the rules and processes of international law and must act to encourage this trend. Although the present Soviet tendency to seek order in world affairs does not imply a repudiation of revolutionary objectives, it may lead gradually to a renunciation of revolutionary methods. These remarks apply equally to mainland China.

*

The alternative to legal order in world affairs is international anarchy. Toleration of anarchy does not seem rational today, if it ever was. Therefore, the United States should display respect for the rules of international law if it is to demonstrate constructive leadership in world politics. If its disrespect for international law is met by disrespect on the part of other nations, the United States may suffer certain political defeats. The acceptance of the constraints of law naturally diminishes the freedom of a government to pursue its objectives. But the more worthwhile policy is one that tries to establish a system of constraint as a matter of common interest in survival and welfare. The risk of political defeat is generally outweighed by the need for world order. The growth of law is itself a national interest that may, on occasion, require the sacrifice of other national interests.

The recognition of this possible need to sacrifice one thing to obtain another is especially relevant to the acceptance of disarmament. Unless national actors are prepared to accept certain legal constraints upon national policy, there is little hope for order in a disarming world. The habits of law observance must be part of the governing framework of action for all states. If states pursue their ends by disregarding legal rules, then conflict is almost certain to involve violence. And political violence in international relations seems incompatible with a program of disarmament that proposes a new international society in which states are stripped of their capability to wage wars of either defense or aggression. If the habits of peaceful settlement and law abidance are instilled *prior* to disarmament, then disarmament risks should begin to seem plausible to powerful states. The time has come for the United States to demonstrate its commitment to legal order as a part of its serious preparation for disarmament. A recognition of the connection between law and disarmament also helps to establish the proposition that new standards of international behavior are as important to the success of disarmament as are rules about throwing weapons away. War and military strength arose in an international society of a certain character; their elimination through disarmament requires a new international society. A reappraisal of the national commitment to maintain a government according to international law (rather than according to men or policy) can help to clarify the wider implications of disarmament, as well as to create an atmosphere that is more favorable to the acceptance of disarmament risks. This injunction does not urge the adoption of a new legalism. Law is not a set of rules inscribed on tablets. Rather, it is basically a way of acting, a consciousness of community standards, a deference to community expectations, a reluctance to resort to coercion or its threat, a constant search for procedures and formulas of reconciliation, and a posture of respect for the law habit that emphasizes explanations for challenged conduct. This kind of orientation toward law must form a central part of the transition strategy needed for the great effort to create a disarmable world.

CHAPTER XII

THE LIMITATIONS OF INSPECTION
FOR DRASTIC DISARMAMENT

BY RICHARD A. FALK

A CONDITION of drastic disarmament can be said to exist when *no* state in the world can feel assured that it retains the military capability to inflict intolerable damage upon an aggressor. This view of the nature of drastic disarmament assumes that the most crucial impact of disarmament upon present security arrangements is the gradual erosion, and eventual disappearance, of deterrence on an internation level. It may well be that peace still rests in part on a deterrent system, but the capability will have been supranationalized and thus placed at the disposal of international institutions rather than nation-states. A few nuclear weapons may be allowed to remain under national control, as a residual deterrent, until the end of disarmament, but not enough to be confident that a diligent and determined aggressor would be deterred by their presence.

Any conception of drastic disarmament is almost necessarily vague since its character depends upon a multitude of virtually unpredictable features of the social, military, economic, and scientific environment. Nevertheless, I regard it as a sufficiently useful model to warrant attention. Part of its value is that it compels one to define the nature of the various problems pertaining to the different stages of any comprehensive disarmament process, by distinguishing between conditions of trivial, moderate, and drastic disarmament.

Such a conception is needed for several reasons. First, it shatters the illusion that security during disarmament is an undifferentiated quest to repress violations. An examination of the conditions of drastic disarmament suggest, if nothing else, that the security problems at the beginning of the disarmament process are very different from those toward the end. In the initial stages, concern about compliance is restricted to a demand for reassurance about the behavior of present political adversaries. Toward the end of disarmament, if the end ever comes about, political rivalries will almost certainly have changed their patterns, and the dangers of violations to the security of disarming states will arise from the activities of a far wider group of states.

Second, thought about drastic disarmament suggests sharply that an early violation is not likely to endanger the military security of the complying state, except possibly to the extent of inducing an abrogation of the disarmament agreement and a renewal, under circumstances of embitterment, of the arms race. This observation is based upon an interpretation of the existing military situation. One way to identify drastic disarmament would be to suggest that a violating state might reasonably foresee decisive advantages accruing from a surprise use or threat to use weapons illegally produced or retained. So long as relatively invulnerable missile systems exist on land and sea and so long as no active defense system promises to shield a state from retaliation, it seems implausible that a state would be tempted to violate a disarmament agreement, except perhaps to strengthen its position in a resumed arms race in the event that disarmament fails.

Third, even a sketchy series of speculations about a drastically disarmed world calls into most serious question the centrality given to inspection in our search for security during disarmament. For if there is little temptation to violate early in the process, then unilateral detection facilities, even if modestly bolstered by the disarmament process, would give states protection against large violations, that is, against the only violations that might conceivably be relevant to security. There would be almost no incentive to commit trivial violations—what purpose would they serve? And there is no security need to know about them. It is rather foolish to insist upon an inspection system able to detect violations that no one is likely to commit and that, even if someone did commit, do not endanger security interests. However, to acquire confidence about identifying such trivial violations, one needs an elaborate inspection setup at the outset. If we could learn to ask for only the inspection that we need against security—relevant violations—then many of our explicit differences with the Russians on the inspection issue would be eliminated. Such a learning process must allow us eventually to be able to say that we don't care whether someone cheats or not in certain situations. We can agree with the Russians or even with the Chinese, I suppose, on adopting a common set of maritime signals on the high seas without introducing concern about distrust. Why? Because the agreement would rest on common interests, on the absence of any incentive to violate, on a unilateral detection capability, and on the fact that no serious impairment of interests would result in the unlikely event of violation. I wish to contend that the early phases of comprehensive disarmament also contain many of these security-reinforcing attributes that make an insistence on inspection both unnecessary and inappropriate.

And, fourth, the vulnerability of states to violations late in the process of the disarmament is so considerable that it requires modifications of international life more fundamental than the development of an inspection system and the creation of a world police force. At the least, there must be created a sense of community in international affairs so that nations do not perceive their own participation predominantly in the idiom of conflict and competition. This community cannot be brought into being by pious rhetoric. It requires a conscious effort to develop common interests among all states in the peaceful persistence of international society. However, these common interests are unlikely to emerge unless the gap between rich nations and poor nations is gradually closed and unless the organized community of states makes a serious effort to eliminate human misery wherever it is found. Security during drastic disarmament is, I submit, primarily a matter of fostering a world community based upon this proposed reallocation of the world's wealth and income, and only secondarily a matter both of seeking an inspection system that is good enough to catch a violator in time to permit a response and of creating a police force strong enough to punish a violator.

Given this view of drastic disarmament, it seems worthwhile to examine in some detail the supposed connection between security and inspection. This connection usually rests upon two premises, both of which are unsound. One premise is that the appropriate kind of inspection system can provide states with reasonable security against cheating at all stages of disarmament. The other is that the major security problems late in disarmament involve only the continuing supervision of the nuclear and nuclear-capable powers. The purpose of this chapter is to discuss these unsound premises and to consider certain implications of their rejection.

Little attention has been given to the relationship between an inspection system and the various levels of disarmament that exceed Stage I. The Wiesner Curve, as well as conventional thinking, assumes that an inspection scheme, if aptly designed and activated, can provide security at each and every stage of disarmament. As disarmament proceeds, the risks that attend a violation increase because military vulnerability increases. However, this growing risk can be offset, it is usually said, by an increasingly reliable and elaborate system of inspection to deter violations, to give the parties confidence in the soundness of the arrangement, and, in the unlikely event that violations occur, to make information available in time for an adequate response.

If one assumes a reasonably constant political environment, then the difficulties of obtaining security toward the end of a contemplated process of disarmament are much more complicated than at the beginning. The reasons for this are not primarily related to the persistence of bipolar rivalry; in fact, it is difficult to imagine a willingness to initiate a disarmament process at all, or at least to go very far with disarmament, if international relations continue to be dominated by the paramount pattern of conflict we now identify as the cold war. The more general grounds for concern about the final stage of disarmament are related to the character of international society rather than to the presence of a particularly troublesome antagonism within it.

First, in the third stage of disarmament, a diligent violator could probably gain important, perhaps even decisive, advantages by surprise attack. Once perceived, this danger would incline states to overrespond or to underrespond to suspicious information. In either event, the stability of international relations would be gravely impaired. Second, certain militarily significant violations in Stage III are virtually uninspectable. Early in disarmament, violations of this character can normally be nullified by retained weapons.

Third, many nations, not only the two nuclear super-states, have the capability, and some may have the incentive as well, to commit uninspectable violations in a disarming world. Unless disarmament is accompanied by a worldwide revolution that transforms social attitudes and that establishes a global welfare state, there is no realistic prospect that conflict and aggression will disappear in a disarming world. Formidable problems of poverty, disease, underdevelopment, overpopulation, political instability, racial enmity, and irresponsible national leadership are virtually certain to remain. Thus, late in disarmament, certain secondary and tertiary nations, by then equipped with weapons of mass destruction, might be inclined to embark on a course of regional, if not global, aggression.

Disarmament can proceed quite far without overcoming the dependence of international society for order upon the force at the disposal of its most powerful nations. However, when these nations begin to lose their preponderance in international society, an entirely different international security system will emerge. This new system will probably have to depend upon international institutions possessing a preponderance of force and operating on behalf of the general interests of the global community. But these institutions are not usually contemplated as possessing a capability comparable to the strong states prior to disarmament. Therefore, a violating state would not necessarily need very much strength to emerge as a powerful actor in regional or world affairs. Of course, powerful states have rearmament capabilities, but there would be serious dangers involved in, and constraints upon, an initiation of a rearmament race.

Poor, weak, troubled, ambitious states have increasing influence in, if not actual control over, the political organs of the United Nations. In a disarming world, this influence and control could be used to reorganize international society to serve the interests of the disadvantaged states. If the powerful states should transfer preponderant power to global institutions, then it might be that coercion could be used to their increasing detriment in a disarming world. So long as grave social and economic problems exist, there will remain in the world a political incentive to use force to overcome them, or at least to distract domestic public opinion from their existence. Thus a more centralized world society would not necessarily protect all states during disarmament, nor would an inspection system designed mainly to detect violations by the powerful states contribute much to this end.

These comments suggest that in the advanced stages of disarmament the environment would be complicated by a variety of political and military risks. But how could these risks be eliminated, or sufficiently reduced, by the design of a proper inspection system? An alternative idea is to consider that the requirements of international security make it necessary to precede Stage III by a radical revision in international society involving both its structure and its dominant attitudes. One can reasonably suppose that the United States and the Soviet Union could develop trust for one another in a disarming world, each becoming more prosperous and stable as the years passed. But what of the many national societies struggling to achieve modernization against overwhelming domestic and international odds? There is no basis to suppose that the rich nations will grow willing to make more than token contributions to the success of this process. History not only furnishes few examples of powerful states making enlightened sacrifices to satisfy the enormous needs of the poor, but also contains many examples of weak nations resorting under pressure to wild schemes of adventure and violence to cure their ills. Inspection, however augmented, offers small solace for, but causes great distraction from, these fundamental difficulties of obtaining security during the advanced stages of disarmament.

The focus of the United States and the Soviet Union upon a bilateral conception of disarmament is partly responsible for oversimplifying the security problems in a disarming world. The gravest challenge to peace and security is as likely to come from the most disadvantaged states as from the main political rivals in the predisarmament world. When the military supremacy of the Great Powers has been dissipated, then these disadvantaged states would be in a better position to seize control of the machinery of international institutions, as well as to improve their relative situation by imperial conquest. The potentialities and characteristics of biological and chemical weapons and their manufacture underscore the seriousness of the basic global instability caused by the wide disparity between rich and poor nations. These weapons can be developed, produced, and delivered by states willing and able to make only modest sacrifices in the pursuit of their other domestic goals. Such a capability may not create global dangers, but it could certainly influence decisively regional balances of power and thereby threaten the total world equilibrium. The production and storage of these weapons could be made almost undetectable and thus placed safely beyond the reach of even a large corps of inspectors.

A reliance upon inspection recognizes the likelihood that conflict and hostility will continue to be attributes of a disarming world. This reliance reflects the conventional attitude that inspection well serves as a substitute for trust. The correlation between increasing military vulnerability and increasing inspection rests on the assumption that it is possible to deter and detect violations throughout the disarmament process. But suppose both the deterrent impact of retained weapons and the detection prospect of the inspection system fall off sharply in the projected environment of Stage III? In such circumstances, what help would it be to request more and more inspection in exchange for a pledge to disarm all the way? The evidence available suggests that these are rhetorical questions, since inspection is not a reliable basis for security against an unscrupulous violator late in disarmament.

There is reason to fear that the prohibition upon the possession and manufacture of biological and chemical weapons is virtually uninspectable. The relevant activities are so easy to hide that no manageable inspection system could give reasonable confidence to the participants in disarmament. Advocates of total disarmament too blandly push aside the potential instability and damage that could be caused by biological and chemical weapons (BWCW) in a disarming world. There is no persuasive reason to suppose that a potential aggressor who was willing to use nuclear weapons of mass destruction would be decisively inhibited by the taboos or prohibitions associated with BWCW. If distrust dictates inspection in order to assure compliance with the obligations of nuclear disarmament, then BWCW must be assimilated into this logic. Such a requirement would all but preclude a transition to Stage III by a security-conscious or apprehensive state. Inspection cannot serve as a substitute for trust when a potential aggressor might be willing to use (or threaten) non-nuclear weapons of mass destruction to achieve political expansion. It should be obvious that the talk about maximizing the inspection capability in Stage III disguises rather than overcomes the military vulnerability of a disarming state, insofar as potential threats arise from uninspectable dangers. No inspection system, however grandiose, can assure parties that a violation will very probably be discovered in time for an adequate response.

This disguise functions as part of the inspection myth that dominates much of the current thinking in the West about disarmament. The myth glorifies inspection, implying that if inspection is sufficient there is no other serious barrier to disarmament at any stage. This idea is a myth because it overstates the relevance of inspection to security for all stages of disarmament, even for Stage I. I would reverse the central reliance upon inspection by contending that at the outset of disarmament we do not really need much, if any, formal inspection to be secure militarily, whereas at the end of disarmament our military security can never be protected by inspection, however extensive and reliable the system may be. Thus, an irrational insistence upon inspection as the key to the acceptability of disarmament, especially when added to the irrational intensity of Soviet opposition to it, acts as a covert way both to repudiate disarmament altogether and, ironically, at the same time, to obscure the real and the most serious security objections to advanced disarmament. Either the inability to find a practicable inspection scheme capable of detecting violations will forever block disarmament, or inspection must cease to operate as a perceived substitute for trust at some stage in the disarmament process. The most likely time for this to happen is the period during which the military balance among rival states is no longer regarded as resting upon a strategy of mutual deterrence.

The role of inspection as a source of security during disarmament has been greatly exaggerated. This does not deny the necessity and usefulness of inspection to meet certain security needs and to give parties the confidence to initiate a disarming world. It is essential to have a formal verification system in order to make a disarmament agreement acceptable to domestic institutions and public opinion in the United States, to increase confidence in the feasibility of disarmament, to give marginal compliance incentives to a nation contemplating gross violations, to verify certain disarmament provisions amenable to inspection, and to provide a nation with a way to vindicate to itself and to other nations a hostile response that it makes to offset the effects of a violation. In other words, inspection can valuably fulfill some of the *specific* political and military requirements that are created by an acceptance of disarmament, but it cannot persuasively function, in general, as a substitute for active distrust. If the postulate of distrust is accurate, then the policy of the United States should be to seek and maintain a system based upon minimum stable balanced nuclear deterrence;

the balanced deterrent does operate as a substitute for trust and, if kept at a minimum level, reduces many of the hazards of the arms race. If, on the other hand, we wish to pursue the goals of general and complete disarmament, then it is necessary to reconceive our security requirements so that they are more in accord with reality. In this context, institutional schemes and inspection arrangements, no matter how comprehensive, are the paraphernalia of a magician. Unfortunately, reliable disarmament requires a universal and mutual reorientation of political consciousness and a radical repudiation of the settled habits of relying upon unilateral defense establishments to achieve military security. Even the distrust inspired by the cold war is only a symptom that prevents study of the deeper, more intractable syndrome arising from an aggressive and egocentric human nature and a disposition of social groups to fight against one another. The preconditions for disarmament include "not only the invention and establishment of institutionalized sanctioning practices—the authority structures and procedures—appropriate to varying contexts, *but also, and more fundamentally, the creation and fostering of the necessary predispositions in effective decision-makers to put such structures and procedures into operation.*"[1] The keys to the locked portals are to be found primarily in the consciousness of mankind, not in the discovery of diplomatic formulas that promise to calm the political rivalries of the day and certainly not in the proposal of ingenious institutional devices that claim the ability to guard the innocent against the greed of the guilty. This characterization of the disarmament

[1] Myres S. McDougal and Florentino P. Feliciano, *Law and Minimum World Public Order* (1961), p. 263 (emphasis supplied).

tangle is quite pessimistic. It assumes that a commitment to general and complete disarmament entails not only the virtual disappearance of rivalries among great nation-states, but also both a willingness by the rich states to give the poorer states a far larger share of the world's wealth and a demonstration of a human capacity to shift dominant political loyalties from the nation-state to the world community. In effect, the risk of complete disarmament will only be undertaken, it is argued, in an atmosphere of international harmony that has never yet been experienced. Inspection can neither create this requisite harmony nor operate as a substitute for it.

The insistence that inspection is the main barrier to disarmament rests, of course, on a variety of considerations. A habit of mind has now grown up in the United States that associates security during disarmament with the inspection process. This habit is reinforced by the Soviet Union's dogmatic opposition to any form of inspection that confers sovereign powers upon foreign or international inspectors physically present within the Soviet Union. The Soviet position is perceived to be a part of a total strategy designed to advance the world revolution at the expense of the non-Communist states. As such, Soviet opposition to inspection seems to confirm the correctness and reasonableness of United States demands. "Why else," it is asked, "has the Soviet Union been so adamant about the inspection issue?" As a consequence of this background, which has been given shape and history by protracted negotiations and annual legislative hearings, the political acceptability of a disarmament scheme has been made to rest quite falsely upon the adequacy of its inspection machinery.

As a first step on the long road leading to complete

disarmament, this chapter argues for a keener awareness of the obstacles that are most difficult to remove. The hazard of the clandestine manufacture and possession of biological and chemical weapons is a dramatic example of a disarmament risk that continues to attract little attention. Another related example concerns the coordination of disarmament with the traumas of modernization that are expected to occur in many countries during the remainder of the century, giving disadvantaged states incentives to use or threaten force to revise the international status quo in their own favor. Security for drastic disarmament must be construed in light of these considerations When this is done, one might expect a shift from the present emphasis upon inspection toward a new concern with the ways of creating a new international society, a society in which members would have neither the incentive nor the temptation to cheat because the interests of all would depend, and would be perceived to depend, upon the successful continuation of disarmament. We need to make a conscious effort to give all states, not only the richest and most powerful, a stake in the outcome of disarmament. In this manner, the idea of cooperation can be made to replace the idea of conflict as the basis of participation in world affairs. Without this development of a higher idea, there will be no security in drastic disarmament even in the unlikely event that it comes about. The pursuit of a cooperative system of international relations is intimately dependent upon a readjustment of the material relations between rich and poor states so that the disparity gradually lessens and so that the stark reality of human misery is eliminated as a matter of common endeavor by an aroused and mobilized world community.

CHAPTER XIII

INTERNATIONAL POLICE: A SEQUENTIAL
APPROACH TO EFFECTIVENESS
AND CONTROL

BY ROGER FISHER

THERE are at least three quite distinct functions that an international police force might perform: it might seek to enforce the provisions of a disarmament or arms control agreement; it might seek to restore and maintain law and order in a place like the Congo where effective government has broken down; or an international police force might be used to establish and maintain a cease-fire between opposing military forces. This paper is directed to the first function, although much of the discussion may be relevant to other problems as well. It is concerned with the double-edged problem of how, at the same time, international police can control the conduct of governments, and governments can control the conduct of the international police. The paper does not propose the composition and structure of a particular international force, but rather it explores a general theory by which such reciprocal controls might be applied and identifies some of the variables involved.

Assumptions. The assumed factual context for the kind of police force here considered is a world perhaps ten years in the future. Some international agreements have been reached establishing substantive rules of conduct limiting the manufacture, possession, and deployment of arms. Some governments may not have accepted these rules, but the United States, the Soviet Union, and some other governments have. Several countries retain substantial armed forces. This latter assumption seems essential to maintain a degree of realism in the problem being considered. Even in a state of complete disarmament, the domestic police forces that a large country like China, the Soviet Union, or the United States would retain for the purpose of maintaining internal order would be of sufficient size to cause a major problem if deployed in opposition to an international police force. It is assumed that nations remain highly organized and independent units; there is no world government. How might an international police force work in such a world?

Freedom for Whom? At the outset, there is a question about how effective a force one might want. Many of us in the United States think that we would like a strong international police force. We have tended to assume that it is to our interests to have the police force as "effective" as possible and that the critical limitation in this regard is going to be the reluctance of the Soviet Union or of other countries to accept the kind of police force we want. This thinking may stem from the period when the United Nations was dominated by Western powers. Or it may derive from our concern with how to be sure that the Soviet Union is complying with a nuclear test ban. It may also reflect our lack of concern with how such a ban would be enforced against us. More recently, doubts have been expressed from some quarters within the United States. United Nations operations in Katanga have caused many to wonder for the first time just how strong and independent an international police force we do want.

One must recognize that the choice may be between freedom for a country and freedom for the international police. Greater freedom for one may mean less freedom for the other. If a country wishes to reduce the risk of other countries' misbehaving, it may have to give up to the international police some of its own freedom of action. In considering the effective strength of an international police force, the United States is faced with as much of a problem as is the Soviet Union or any other country. In fact, the traditions of the United States, even more than those of the Soviet Union, are opposed to giving too much freedom to the police. While the Soviet Union has tended to emphasize the importance of freedom for the government and for the police to take appropriate action for the good of the people, the United States has tended to emphasize freedom from the government and from the police so that the people can take appropriate action for themselves.

When we consider police at the international level, we should be able to understand the ambivalent desires of ourselves and others. The police force should have a chance to be effective, but it should be sufficiently hobbled so that it does not create much danger either for the legitimate freedoms of the Soviet or any other government or for the legitimate freedoms of the American or any other people.

Two Problems, Not One. There are two basic control problems with respect to an international police force. One is the problem of control *by* the police, the problem of how an international police force will exert its authority and power in a manner that tends to produce compliance. The second is the problem of control *of* the police, the problem of defining the limited authority of an international police force and confining their actual activities within those bounds. The two problems obviously go hand in hand. It is difficult to consider the task of confining a police force to the activities in which it ought to engage without first identifying what those activities are. The reason for having an international police force is to control governmental conduct. How a police force is expected to accomplish that task needs to be understood before one turns to the problem of how to keep the police from doing more or doing less. If an international police force were expected to compel adherence to international law through the use of a hair-triggered thermonuclear deterrent, the problem of political control would be quite different than it would be if the police were the international equivalent to unarmed English bobbies.

CONTROL BY THE POLICE

General Approach
Action Rather Than Threat

As suggested, one technique by which an international police force might seek to cause compliance with a disarmament agreement would be through a threat of massive retaliation. The international police might possess a score of nuclear submarines armed with thermonuclear missiles and tell the world to behave "or else." Such a technique has serious disadvantages. The inappropriateness of nuclear punishment in many cases, because it was disproportionate to the offense, because the circumstances were unclear, or because the punishment would, in fact, fall on innocent people, would tend to make its imposition unlikely. The threat would probably be ineffective except as a deterrent to the most extreme and drastic violations. Should the threat ever have to be carried out, the international community would suffer moral as well as extensive physical damage. A nuclear deterrent, as the United States has discovered, requires that the constitutional restraints that we have imposed on a declaration of war be by-passed and that a single man be given enormous power. It seems most unlikely that the countries of the world could agree on the centralization of power required for such a single international deterrent. The experience within NATO, a single military alliance, indicates the extreme difficulties involved in devising international political control for a quick-reacting nuclear force. Finally, even were international police to have a nuclear deterrent, it would also need to have other means for dealing with minor, ambiguous, or creeping violations.

It is possible that a few simple and basic rules of international conduct, such as prohibitions of surprise nuclear attack or outright invasion, could be enforced by a deterrent that would never have to be exercised. Under more complicated disarmament schemes, containing not only many more substantive rules but various procedural arrangements for verification, there are bound to be ambiguous circumstances that appear to some as violations. In such circumstances we do not want a police force faced with the choice of doing nothing or of using nuclear weapons.

Rather than starting with the idea of the threats that a police force should make and then turning to the question of what it should do if those threats are ineffective, it seems more useful to start with the latter question. The answer then tends to shift from a single response to a process of responding over time and from a massive measure to an accumulation of smaller ones. Rather than further explore problems of deterrence—where the enforcement technique has already failed its purpose if it ever has to be carried out—this paper explores in a preliminary way the process of control that consists of a sequence of steps designed not merely to be threatened but actually to be undertaken by an international police force.

When one speaks of a police force of limited power, he is not speaking of the total quantity of fire-power available to the police in the last resort but rather of the procedural hurdles that must be overcome by the police, step by step, as they impinge upon the liberty of others. The critical element that distinguishes a "police state" is not the number of policemen or the size of the weapons they carry, but their rights. A handful of police with unlimited rights—including, for example, the right to execute any public official without charge and without trial—would be extremely dangerous. On the other hand, most of the hundreds of thousands of police now in the United States, possessing the limited rights that they do, are accepted as creating little danger to our freedoms. These police have limited powers, meaning that they "must" proceed in certain ways toward the enforcement of the law. If they proceed, step by step, in accordance with the pre-existing rules, getting the needed authority from the proper bodies at the appropriate times, there is no limit on the physical amount of force that can ultimately be brought to bear. The last resort, however, is rarely if ever reached.

It is often thought that since the most dangerous situation is a large-scale war, an international police force should be designed primarily with that problem in mind—

245

that we must create institutions capable of controlling the worst outbreaks. But no police force can be designed to meet all contingencies, for among such contingencies are various kinds of disloyalties and insurrections within the police force. As with medicine, the most promising avenue seems to lie in devising means of dealing with problems before they reach epidemic proportions. Just as vaccination cannot stop a fully developed disease, so no police force can stop a nuclear bomb as it falls.

A police force should be designed to postpone and avoid a maximum confrontation, not to handle it. It is to deal with disorder in an orderly way, hopefully, one that dampens the disorder rather than inflames it. No one would think of designing a federal law enforcement agency in this country to meet the possibility that the Army refused to obey the Secretary of Defense. We design a police force to meet more likely and less drastic possibilities, and, should the worst arise, we will expect the individuals in it to proceed in as nearly the routine way as circumstances permit—and hope for the best.

A "SECOND-STRIKE-ONLY" POLICE FORCE

Conceivably, a police force might operate by taking the initiative and telling people what to do, much the way a police officer directs traffic at an intersection. It might seek to prevent the production of prohibited weapons by affirmatively telling all factories what to produce; it might seek to control the deployment of forces and weapons by affirmatively deciding where they should be located. While the international licensing of nuclear or other facilities may be desirable, it is clear that the world is far from desiring a world "police state" in which affirmative responsibility for what goes on is given to the police. On the contrary, what is contemplated is a "nega-tive" police force, a force that is merely prepared and on the lookout for the bad and does something about it, rather than telling people and countries what to do that is good. The general principle we wish to follow is one of freedom of action for people and governments, in which the police come into play only when there is some in-dication that someone has stepped over a line.

The international police may be working full time, inspecting, investigating, probing, and patrolling, but they are not to start taking what we would consider en-forcement action until there is some evidence or complaint of a violation. In rare cases, there may be disclosure of an intended future violation, but even here this will usually involve evidence of something wrong that has already happened, something that indicates even worse things to come. If we do not want the police to be running things, the general position will be that they may look around but that they should not start to act against anyone un-less there is evidence that somebody has done something wrong. The primary rules of conduct established by a disarmament treaty or otherwise thus form a kind of trip-wire that brings the police into action.

The most significant consequence of precluding the police from telling people what to do in the first in-stance is that, although the police are being asked to enforce the law, they are not allowed to do anything until, in one sense, it is too late. They are to wait until there is a violation and then—after the milk has been spilled—they are supposed to do something about it. If we do not want the police to engage in preventive deten-tion or in other police-state tactics, they must act only after a violation has occurred. Deterrence aside, it is clear that perfect enforcement would thus never lead to perfect compliance. Enforcement is only to take effect after there is evidence of non-compliance.

To a large extent, the police force should at that time be self-starting. If any police officer uncovers evidence of non-compliance, he should have the right and duty to initiate enforcement action. The only real question as to the initiation of action is over the extent to which those outside the police should be able to initiate enforcement action and, if so, of what kind. In this country, an individual may turn over evidence to the police and may swear out a warrant or a complaint, but he cannot require the police to prosecute a case if the police do not want to. It may well be that governments in general, and perhaps individuals too, should have power to press an enforcement action or at least to get it started and into public view. The extent to which people outside the enforcement agency could initiate action might have important consequences in preventing the police force from doing less than its duty but would apparently have little bearing on the problem of preventing the police force from doing more than it should.

Successive Determinations of What Ought to Be Done Next

Once there is an indication that the trip-wire has been crossed, that some government or individual has engaged in prohibited conduct, the question is: what should be done now? All enforcement activities are future oriented. Past conduct is relevant only to the extent that it has a bearing on what someone should do in the future. Public attention may well be directed toward the past, toward whether there was or was not a violation, toward whether or not someone was guilty, and toward resolving disputed facts or disputed interpretations of a treaty. None of this has any importance except to the extent that it will affect what happens in the future.

The police establishment (including the police themselves and related authorities) has two tasks in coping with violations: to decide what ought to happen and to make it happen. The theory here being explored is that there is to be not a single response but rather a sequence of responses depending upon the circumstances and upon what happens. If the police system is to be this flexible, there will have to be someone with the right and duty to make decisions. These decisions will have three ends in view: (1) to stop any continuing wrongful conduct; (2) to undo the damage done; and (3) to deter future violations. In addition, there will be some interim and procedural goals in order to accomplish the foregoing. Any imposition of punishment would presumably be for the purpose of deterring future violations. (Punishment might conceivably fall under item 2 if considered as retribution, imposed for the purpose of removing emotional handicaps resulting from pent-up antagonism on one side or a sense of unrequited guilt on the other.)

An illustrative sequence of determinations as to what ought to be done in a particular case might include: orders to investigate, the granting of search warrants, temporary restraining orders pending hearing, orders to destroy designated equipment (or perhaps, orders not to interfere with its destruction by international police), permanent injunctions, orders to show cause why one should not be held in contempt, warrants for arrests, and the imposition of a fine. Such orders cannot follow automatically from a predetermined list. There will have to be a series of decisions as to what, in view of all the circumstances, ought to be done next. The police establishment taken as a whole will have to be capable of producing a sequence of commands, and it is toward compliance with such commands that its future-oriented enforcement efforts will be directed.

CAUSING SECOND-ORDER COMPLIANCE
THE TASK: TURNING FIRST-ORDER VIOLATIONS INTO SECOND-ORDER COMPLIANCE

It seems useful to distinguish between primary rules of international conduct, established by a disarmament treaty or otherwise, and the subsequent commands or orders of international police, international courts, or other law enforcement bodies; it seems useful to distinguish between first-order compliance, compliance with the general standing rules, and second-order compliance, compliance with the particular orders and commands of courts and police. Even in a well-functioning legal system, we must continue to expect a substantial amount of non-compliance with the basic rules. If it requires an apparent violation of such a rule before the police move into action, every enforcement case will involve a case of first-order non-compliance. This should not trouble us too much so long as the general standing rules of conduct are placed far enough back from the precipice of war so that we can afford instances of non-compliance. Disarmament itself is such a precautionary or trip-wire rule. A violation of a disarmament rule in itself is unlikely to cause any immediate or serious injury, but it is a proper basis for police action.

Even where a violation of a standing rule does cause immediate injury, we must apparently expect a fair amount

250

of first-order non-compliance, at least where a government is involved. Within the United States, no rules seem more basic than those contained in the Bill of Rights, and often when those rights are violated someone suffers immediate injury. Yet we do not have a high degree of first-order compliance with the Constitution. Congress has often adopted unconstitutional statutes; on hundreds if not thousands of occasions, the Federal and State governments have violated the rights of individuals guaranteed by the Constitution. In untold ways, officials have exceeded their legal authority. There are perhaps many more established cases of illegal governmental behavior in this country than in the Soviet Union, since the very concept of government under law involves the idea of a government submitting itself to an authoritative determination that it has behaved in an illegal fashion and being called to account. As unfortunate as it may be to have governments that violate the law, it does not indicate that law enforcement has broken down. A crisis is involved only when we have an instance of second-order non-compliance, when an official fails to comply with the explicit command of a court or a law enforcement official.

A government usually seeks to justify any instances of first-order non-compliance. In fact, there seems to be something intrinsic to a government that requires it not to engage in open defiance of admittedly binding law. Perhaps the fact that a government's own existence depends upon continued respect for law explains a government's unwillingness publicly to set an example of law defiance. Whatever the reason, this tendency of governments to justify their conduct means that most if not all violations of primary, standing rules will first appear as disputes. The government whose conduct is in question may dispute the facts, it may dispute the interpretation or validity of the rule, or it may contend that despite the rule its conduct is justified because of some higher rule, a prior violation by others, changed conditions, or some special circumstance. For this reason, there will usually be a period of time during which it is unclear whether or not there has been first-order non-compliance. In fact, until an ambiguous rule has been authoritatively interpreted, an objective concept of compliance can hardly be said to exist. During this period, and even after the question has been resolved, the enforcement agency is extremely interested in second-order compliance—compliance with any interim judicial or police commands and compliance with the ultimate decree of the body that settles the original dispute.

In view of the experience within the United States, it appears that first-order compliance by governments and government officials is rarely brought about through direct use of the criminal law or other deterrents. The laws that tell Federal, State, and local officials what they should and should not do in their governmental capacities rarely carry with them criminal penalties. The Congressman who helps pass an unconstitutional statute or the administrative official who exceeds his statutory authority is not sent to jail or fined when he is found to have acted illegally. The basic way in which we deal with the problem of first-order non-compliance by governments is to obtain a high degree of second-order compliance. We wish to encourage officials to use their discretion. There is great tolerance for the official who acts contrary to the rule where the rule is vague or ambiguous. We almost never punish an official for having acted contrary to a general rule, even where the rule is clear.

When, however, there is a specific judicial or police command running directly to a designated official, he is expected to comply with it or to risk criminal penalties. Second-order compliance is exacted through deterrence. The threatened punishment may not be great, but it is exceedingly probable. In a functioning law-enforcement system, the punishment for clear defiance of an authorized police or judicial command is almost automatic.

Although the police have force at their disposal, it appears that, in most cases of enforcing laws against public officials, the force remains in the background and is not actually used. The problem of bringing superior force to bear on a town official or a recalcitrant governor is quite different from that of capturing a fleeing bank robber. In the case of a government official, we are trying to obtain second-order compliance from an individual who has failed to observe first-order compliance. We hope to operate on his mind so that he will be persuaded now to do what he is being ordered to do, even though a short time back he decided to act contrary to law. So long as nothing changes, it is unlikely that he will weigh the pros and cons differently. It is unlikely that simply being told that he was bad will now cause him to be good. The enforcement process consists rather in changing the situation from what it was before so that, whatever was a sensible decision with regard to first-order compliance, the sensible choice now is overwhelmingly in favor of second-order compliance. The process of enforcing the law consists of getting the defendant or defendants involved in the enforcement procedure and then of proceeding step by step to change the question from what it was before, to convert the vague and debatable primary command into an explicit and direct secondary command, and while doing so to change the anticipated advantages of non-compliance.

CHANGING THE QUESTION

Although we are dealing with the problem of having an international police force enforce rules against governments, we are trying to control human behavior. The purpose of the police force at any given time is to get some person to do something. An important way of changing the question from the rule of international conduct with which the government failed to comply to a command with which there will be compliance is to shift the focus from the government to the individual whose conduct is actually desired. The first-order rule ran to the government, much the way the Fourteenth Amendment runs to the states. The second-order command will be directed to a particular official.

It appears that an international police force should at all times operate on the assumption that it is enforcing the conduct of individuals rather than of governments. It should be established on the premise that the international rules that it is to enforce have been adopted by the governments or accepted by them and are as binding on the individuals within the various nations as the United States Constitution is binding on the individuals and officers of the various states.

It has sometimes been suggested that a police force should distinguish between the accidental, inadvertent, or unauthorized violation, where the responsible individual should be dealt with, and the intentional, willful, governmental violation, where the police force should recognize that it is a government that is involved and apply sanctions to the government as such. The contrary

254

position seems wiser. In view of such cases of governmental defiance as that of the State of Mississippi to the integration of its public schools, it appears that superior force will have its optimum chance of being effective if it looks through the government entity and deals with the particular individuals who are standing in the way. This would seem to be even more true when dealing with a foreign nation where it may be less clear that the police, in fact, have superior force. In essence, the notion is one of divide and conquer. If the police force is proceeding against the nation as such, all of its supporters will tend to rally to its defense. On the other hand, if the police force is proceeding against merely a few designated individuals, the government may or may not back them up. Even if it does, an individual in the front lines withstanding the police may weaken, finding that if he resists he will be treated as a criminal rather than a soldier.

A critical difference between law enforcement and war lies in this element of not recognizing the legitimacy of illegal commands to subordinates. In war, a soldier who is carrying out superior orders is treated with respect as a prisoner of war who is not responsible for the illegal or evil purposes of his superiors. In law-enforcement operations, the fact that a man is obeying superior orders is no defense to criminal responsibility. Law operates on the assumption of individual responsibility. And when the individual discovers that he is being held personally responsible, he becomes more responsible; he thinks about what he is doing and whether he wants to continue doing it.

One can perhaps visualize these alternative ways of proceeding by considering what might have happened at the time that Governor Barnett was interfering with the admission of James Meredith to the University of Mississippi. If the court had ordered the arrest of Governor Barnett and if he had called upon the state police to defend him from arrest, there would have been a head-on confrontation. One way to proceed would then have been for the Federal authorities to bring in sufficient superior force to conquer the state police in a battle and to capture the Governor. That would have been to proceed on a "war" theory, in which it was understood that the individual state policemen were not at fault but were simply obeying superior orders. An alternative and apparently far wiser way to proceed in such circumstances would have been on a law-enforcement theory in which sufficient superior force would be brought to bear to arrest the first state policeman who interfered with Federal officers in the carrying out of their duty. He would have been charged with the offense and faced with serious punishment. The same would be done with the second and third state policemen who interfered. They would be no more able to raise the defense that they were acting under orders of the Governor than it would be a defense for Chicago bank robbers to say that they were acting under orders from Al Capone. Such an approach would increase the pressure on the next state policeman to step aside rather than to subject himself to certain and personal criminal punishment.

In shifting an international rule so that it points to an individual rather than to a government, possible justification for non-compliance will be removed if the precise individual whose conduct is desired is identified in the order. Specifically designating the one or more individuals to whom the judicial or police command is directed improves the chances of compliance by making it increasingly likely that punishment may follow non-compliance. When the defendant is identified, there is less room for the argument that he did not know that *he* was supposed to do it. To maximize the chances of compliance, a command should also be as explicit as possible as to exactly what is or is not to be done.

Preferably, again to eliminate possible justifications for second-order non-compliance, the command should be in negative terms. In the first place, it is difficult to phrase an affirmative command that is sufficiently specific yet does not go too far by demanding that something be done in a particular way when other ways of doing it would be equally legal. An affirmative command thus often strikes the defendant as unjustified. There are always possible reasons why a person was properly unable to do something. He may have been ill, he may have been physically unable to accomplish the task, he may have been impeded by others, etc. Non-compliance with an order to refrain from doing something is much more difficult to justify. A command for affirmative action is also more difficult to back up with force. Force can often stop somebody from doing something or require him to do something simple, but it cannot be used physically to compel somebody to do something complicated. Further, a negative order has the advantage of lessening the importance of persuading the government as such to go along. An official who has been ordered by an international court to do something affirmative may feel that he needs the consent of his own government to do it and, in the absence of that consent, may be reluctant to proceed. On the other hand, an official who has been ordered *not* to do something may simply wait to see how the wind blows and do nothing, at least until his own government

257

orders him to act. In such circumstances, government decisions may be even more difficult to bring about than they usually are. In any event, governmental inertia is put on the side of compliance. Thus, if an international police force wishes certain property destroyed or removed, it should seek not an authoritative order to local personnel to destroy or remove the property but rather an order to the local personnel not to interfere with the destruction or removal of the property by the police.

In the process of whittling away grounds for non-compliance, it is exceedingly important that the enforcement machinery have the authority to hear and to decide upon all possible grounds for non-compliance with its commands. There should be a court that, no matter how limited its jurisdiction, has the authority to decide whether it has acted within its jurisdiction—at least until some other body has overruled it. Its orders should be understood to be binding even if erroneous, at least within certain broad limits. Surrounding its conceded central jurisdiction, there needs to be an authority, for example, to issue restraining orders that must be obeyed even if unjustified and to order the arrest of individuals who may be innocent.

The consequence of a step-by-step whittling away of the possible justifications for non-compliance and the increasing specificity of the command is to change the form of the question that confronted both the individual on the spot and his government. For each of them, the question will have been shifted from one of possible non-compliance to one of open defiance. During the process of changing the question, the police force should also devote its attention to shifting the consequences of the decision. The police action should be designed to affect both the advantages and disadvantages. Compliance should become less painful and, if possible, positive benefits provided. As non-compliance is turned into defiance, the anticipated gains should be reduced and the anticipated costs increased.

ALTERING THE ANTICIPATED CONSEQUENCES

Compliance: Reducing the Costs. Presumably a government would choose to engage in conduct that violated an international rule because it had found that the rule impeded it from doing important things that it wanted to do. The rule might have appeared to impose large and permanent restraints on governmental activity. If the cost of complying with the various police and judicial orders is to be significantly less, the orders must be narrower in scope than the primary rule. Directing the judicial or police command to an individual narrows the immediate impact of the rule upon the government in proportion to how far down in the hierarchy the individual is. The lower and more subordinate the official to whom the command is first directed, the greater freedom there is for other government officials. The lowest official whose conduct is in question might well be the respondent. Even though other officials are engaging in comparable conduct, it may be wise, at least where there is no emergency situation, to have the early orders impinge upon only one. Higher officials, whose actions tend to involve greater prestige, greater loss of face, and greater news value, should be left alone.

The very first orders should be so small and easy to comply with that the government readily goes along and begins to find itself enmeshed in the enforcement operation where one step leads to another and where no one

259

demand or order is sufficiently larger or more onerous than the last to justify a shift in policy from compliance to defiance. At every stage, the orders should tend to be narrow in scope, of limited significance, and of limited duration.

Compliance also tends to be easier if the action or inaction required is physical rather than juridical. The less one demands broad admissions, statements, and promises, the greater the chance of compliance. The broadest demand, one for unconditional surrender, is the hardest to obtain. And in asking for it, one is inevitably asking for more than he needs or wants. As soon as a man or a country "unconditionally surrenders," the victor restores to him, gratuitously, many of the rights that he required the vanquished to yield. Without these demands, the vanquished would have been more willing to yield.

The same principle dictates that the order not be seen as setting a principle or a precedent. The police officer's suggestion, "You'd better move along," speaks to a particular fact situation and is easy to comply with. A police officer's statement, "That kind of conduct is illegal; stop it," immediately raises the price of compliance, which may now connote acceptance of the general position.

Again, compliance will be more readily forthcoming if the order is one of short duration. A temporary restraining order that is effective only for a day or two is far less threatening, and far easier to comply with during those days, than would be a permanent injunction. The order to come down to the police station gets much less resistance than would an order to come to jail for a year. Even though a temporary order may be extended, the first bite is small and makes the order easier to take.

Finally, the fact that a demand is subject to being reviewed and upset makes compliance in the first instance easier. Most governments, like most people, tend to see a situation from their own point of view. They tend to judge their conduct by their own standards and to pay a great deal of attention to their own interests. This results in most governments and most individuals believing that they are right. We are usually so confident that we are in the right that we are convinced that fair and right-minded people will probably agree with us. The very fact of appellate litigation, let alone the quantity of it, attests to the optimism with which each side tends to view the outcome of an appeal. This optimistic view that one will eventually be vindicated is extremely helpful for compliance at the early stages of law enforcement. Knowing that one has a right of review, one may accept the adverse command for the time being. This hope can last through several stages of review. If one finally loses at a stage where there is no further review, this factor obviously disappears. But by that time, the possibility of losing has been with one so long that the original unacceptability of such a result may have worn off. Even so, it may be wise always to keep open the possibility of further review, reconsideration, pardon, habeas corpus, or whatever.

Compliance: Providing Rewards. Sometimes it may be possible for an international police force to arrange matters so that a complying official attains some public approbation or other political reward for having gone along with the international organization. Although a troublemaker may gain respect by being feared, there may on occasion be an even greater advantage flowing to the now friendly cooperator who is prepared to acquiesce. There is almost no reward for quietly being good and obeying a primary rule. But there may be political rewards for belated improvement. Khrushchev received some praise for removing his missiles from Cuba in October 1962; he had received none for not putting them there prior to his doing so.

Building up the prestige of an international police force by yielding to it and complying with its orders may also carry with it the possible future gain that may result from having the police force succeed and prosper. Each government benefits somewhat from a general improvement in international order. It also has the chance to gain specific benefits from future acts of the police force. The greater chance a government sees in using the international police force to its own advantage at a later date, the more it may be willing to see the police force succeed here, even at the expense of a subordinate official or interference with a particular activity.

Defiance: Reducing the Rewards. An elemental function of a police force is to see that a law violator does not "get away with it"—does not reap the fruits of his illegality. Force should be available to frustrate the law violation. When the police force moves into operation, it should be apparent that one had better comply with the enforcement measures since it now appears that in the long run one is not likely to get much out of this violation anyway.

In reviewing the kind of force and equipment needed by an international police force, one would want to consider the kinds of violations that might occur and the force needed to frustrate them. If there is to be a rule against constructing certain kinds of installations, how much would it take to destroy installations discovered? It should not take a great deal of force. This is particularly true today where so much of national defense is based on deterrence. An international police force should make clear in advance that it will not be deterred, that its responses are mandatory, legitimate, and fully authorized by the prior consent of the appropriate people concerned. If the police actions are limited to narrow and discrete objectives, threatening not the independence or political existence of a state but simply precluding one limited form of activity from which other nations are similarly being precluded, it becomes unlikely that an attempt to deter the international police force through use of nuclear weapons would ever be carried out. It is not clear, indeed, what kind of a threat a nation could use to attempt to deter an international police force.

If the police force is not to be deterred, the only way a nation could prevent the police from accomplishing their limited objective of, say, destroying a particular plant would be to defend the plant by military means. The general technological superiority of offensive weapons (which leads national military establishments to rely so heavily on deterrence) would make this a formidable task. Hopefully, no such contest would take place except in the minds of the government officials. For example, they might previously have decided that despite the disarmament treaty they would continue to keep in ready condition a factory for military aircraft. The benefits of doing so would have seemed large and the risks small. Now they have been ordered to convert the factory to other uses. The disadvantages of not doing so have increased, since, if they fail to convert the factory, there is a risk that it will be destroyed. In any event, there seems less to gain from defiance now than there appeared to be from non-compliance before enforcement machinery moved into action.

Defiance: Increasing the Costs. An international police force wants to confront both the individual at whom a command is directed and his government with a choice of either complying and doing the best they can within the system (by engaging in other acts that have not been prohibited, by seeking a reversal of the order, etc.) or defying the command and suffering high costs. The process of authoritatively considering and rejecting possible justifications for non-compliance works toward identifying the government's conduct as blatant defiance. This has some effect in raising the political cost to the government of its conduct.

The cost to a government of not complying with the orders of an international police force can be increased to the extent that such non-compliance can be assimilated to non-compliance with orders of the police of that country. One thing that a government is most reluctant to do is to teach contempt for its own governmental commands and police orders. If a government is going to urge mass disobedience to the orders of the international police, it will wish to have in the public's mind a clear and convincing distinction between orders of the international police and orders of the local police. If this distinction has been effectively blurred, a government will be reluctant to urge disobedience to the international police. An international police force may thus wish to have its status confirmed by local law. Perhaps, in addition to having international passes, each international police officer should carry a card signed by the local head of state, notifying all that they must obey the policeman. Local statutes and billboards could similarly establish the authority of the international police in a way that would increase the costs to a government of urging and engaging in non-compliance with the orders of the police.

Some of the political cost will be in terms of reputation and public opinion. The more significant political cost will tend to consist of the damage to the international community that such defiance may immediately cause or may lead to over a time. A country has a good deal to gain from ongoing international cooperation. Hopefully, the stake that each country has in the world community may increase over time as did the stake that each state of the United States had in the Union. The more limited is the judicial or police command, the greater is the likelihood that a country will risk less in complying with that order than it would risk losing in the disruption of the then-existing international community, however modest that latter might be.

Identifying the government's conduct as defiance, however, may well have less significance to the government by way of increasing the costs than it has by way of decreasing the chances of successful gains through continuing on that course of conduct. The more clearly unjustified is a government's conduct, the more willing and perhaps insistent will other governments be to see that it is frustrated. The effect on the government is likely to be less in terms of probable punishment than in terms of a decreasing chance of accomplishing anything affirmative, as discussed above.

Let us turn to the individual at whom the order is directed; here is an opportunity to increase markedly the costs. Here deterrence can play an important role. When a policeman says, "You'd better come along with me," the man to whom he speaks has a choice between going along quietly or making the problem serious indeed. Resisting arrest and assaulting a policeman are crimes for which serious punishment is meted out. Not only that, but the policeman is immediately authorized to use such force as appears reasonably necessary in order to subdue the prisoner. So long as the possible punishment that may await the defendant if he goes along with the police is less serious or less sure than the punishment for resisting arrest, he is likely to go along. In the same way, compliance by government officials with court orders is enforced by the threat of criminal contempt, even though no criminal punishment is threatened for most primary conduct in excess of the law. Similarly, an international police force should be able to threaten criminal punishment for second-order non-compliance.

In seeking to persuade an individual official who has failed to follow a general rule to comply with a specific police or judicial order, the effective pressure depends not upon the seriousness of the punishment with which he is now threatened but rather upon the *difference* between that and the punishment that he might receive for his first-order non-compliance. Assume, for example, that a disarmament treaty should make the manufacture of prohibited weapons an international crime for which any individual involved could be given life imprisonment. Assume also that the international police force could impose up to life imprisonment for defiance of court orders. In such circumstances, there would be little incentive for a guilty official to cooperate with the international police. If the possible punishment for his first-order non-compliance is great, he is already in a difficult situation. The threat of possible life imprisonment for defiance of the court order is likely to be ineffective because full cooperation may also lead to the same result.

It would seem wiser to provide no criminal penalties whatever for first-order non-compliance with most of the provisions of a disarmament treaty and to authorize criminal penalties for second-order non-compliance—for defiance of a court order. In these circumstances, an official involved in a treaty violation would be under far greater pressure to comply with judicial orders. By cooperating now with the international police, he can avoid all risk of punishment. The other choice, defiance of an explicit command directed to him personally, will be difficult to justify politically or morally and entails the risk of punishment.

Leo Szilard suggested a comparable discrepancy between first- and second-order violations in which both, however, would be treated as criminal. His suggestion was that an international court be empowered to impose fines and sentences of up to, say, two years in prison for violations of a disarmament treaty or for other international offenses. There would be one exception to this maximum sentence. Any defendant who with proper notice refused to come before the tribunal to answer charges could, after appropriate proceedings, be sentenced to death in absentia, the sentence to be carried out by anyone at any time. Again, under such a scheme, a named defendant would have strong reasons for coming and submitting himself to the court. If he appeared, he might win his case or he might receive only a reprimand or a modest fine. The worst that could possibly happen would be a year or two in jail. On the other hand, should he stay away, he might promptly be shot; in any event, for the rest of his days he would have to live in fear of being executed at any moment by some member or supporter of the international police.

In view of the general reluctance to punish officers for official acts that may not have been clearly understood to be contrary to the law, it would seem appropriate to have an international police force follow an enforcement method not unlike that used to enforce Section 5 of the Federal Trade Commission Act prohibiting unfair competition. Unfair competition is made unlawful, but no damages are allowed and no punishment is authorized except for defiance of an FTC order finding that a certain practice is unlawful and ordering that practice—carefully and explicitly defined—to cease. But if punishment is to be authorized for a first-order violation, it seems wise to provide markedly increased penalties for a second-order violation so as to increase the cost of defiance when the anticipated cost of first-order non-compliance has, by hypothesis, proved ineffective.

Such, in general, would be the theory underlying the sequential steps by which an international police force would seek to control the conduct of governments. Into such an operation must be geared the sequential steps by which the governments control the international police.

CONTROL OF THE POLICE

If there is not to be an infinite progression of police forces, each to be under the control of a higher one, it is patent that "the" international police force must be subject to some scheme of internal checks and balances. The solution is not going to lie in having a police force of given size, with certain kinds of weapons, equipment, and authorized functions. Rather it will lie in dividing the force into units, each of which has standing authority to do limited things. The structure should be such that with appropriate approval additional functions could be performed or additional men and equipment deployed, or both, and that with further approval still more functions could be performed and more force brought to bear, and so forth. The system should have no limit; with sufficient approval all international units and all national forces that were willing to respond for the particular purpose should be legally entitled if not required to do so. The problem of limiting an international police establishment is thus not one of determining the total manpower and equipment, the total powers, and the constituency of a body that will exercise total control. The problem rather is: (1) to divide the international staff into units of limited size and limited authority; (2) to strengthen the factors which tend to cause respect for the limits on their authority; and (3) to determine the constituency and procedures of the bodies which would augment (or restrict), by stages and depending upon circumstances, authorized activities of the various units.

LIMITED UNITS OF LIMITED AUTHORITY

Persons working in the international enforcement apparatus might conceivably be lumped together into one all-purpose category called, say, "UN Police." For purposes of controlling them, however, it would seem wise to divide them into a large number of different services. There might, for example, be narcotic inspectors, air inspectors, manufacturing inspectors, demolition officers, arresting officers, arms custodians, plain clothes detectives, military police units, and soldiers. Each of these categories of personnel could have distinctive duties and defined rights that were closely limited to those necessary for its particular duties. Some units might have no authority to use weapons but might have great freedom of movement. Other units might possess potent weapons but not be authorized to do anything in the absence of special orders from above. The officers and men in each unit of each service would have different channels and procedures by which they could expand their standing authority. The more fragmented the UN service, the greater would be the control over it; the less likely it would be to behave in an unauthorized fashion.

Causing Respect for the Limits on Authority
INTRA-UNIT RESTRAINTS

At any given time a unit of the international enforcement service will consist of a number of men who may possess a certain amount of military equipment and weapons. Such a unit, however, is not a fungible quantity of physical power on the loose. Like all other units of socially organized power it is "power for a purpose." It cannot be indiscriminately applied to whatever end its commanding officer may wish. First, of course, there are what may be considered as the physical limits on its ability to act; the number of men, their skills, and the amount and kind of military and logistical equipment. These physical limits will reflect the purposes for which the unit was organized, trained, and equipped. Regardless of the willingness of the individual members, a group of custom officers or a company of New York City policemen cannot be considered a unit of power that might be thrown into the fighting in South Viet Nam. They are neither equipped nor trained for that purpose. These physical limitations tend to keep the unit doing what it is supposed to do. The more specialized its function, the more it will be physically curtailed from engaging in activities different from those for which it was organized.

Beyond the physical limitations upon a unit there are limitations imposed by the willingness of the members of the unit to go along. Although the boundary here is far less clear, it nonetheless exists. There is a spectrum of possible activities; toward one end of the spectrum it becomes increasingly improbable that the men would will-ingly obey an order of their immediate commanding officer to engage in such activity. The probable obedience of the men corresponds closely with the perceived legitimacy of the activity. The legal limit on the authority of a unit thus tends to create an actual limit beyond which it becomes increasingly unlikely that that unit will go.

At the core of the purposes for which a unit is available are its standing duties. Here the men understand that they have continuing obligations. It is highly likely that men will obey a superior when his command is one which they understand he is obliged to give. Around these central activities there are others where the men understand that the commanding officer has discretion. He has the legal authority to order the men either way, to do it or not to do it. Here, again, it is highly likely that the men will respond to what they understand are the proper orders of their immediate superior.

When the commanding officer gives an order to the men which they believe he is not authorized to give, a problem arises. Each man now has a conflict between two duties. On the one hand, he has the duty to behave lawfully, and to honor his oath to uphold the constitution and laws of the government or institution which he serves. On the other hand, he has the duty to obey his commanding officer, who is present, who is telling him what to do, and who may use the balance of the unit (if they obey)

271

to impose prompt and effective punishment against anyone who disobeys. It seems likely that a subordinate,
faced with such a conflict, will give the benefit of any
doubt to the commanding officer and will comply with
an order which the subordinate personally believes to be
unauthorized. A commanding officer of a unit of force
thus has actual powers in excess of those to which by
law he is confined. Around the periphery of his lawful
authority he has penumbral powers to do things which
he is not allowed to do.

These penumbral powers are not, however, of unlimited scope. The more clearly it appears to his men that the
commanding officer is acting illegally the less probable
it becomes that they will respond and go along as a unit.
At some point members of the unit would feel too strongly
that they were being told to do something that they were
not supposed to do. Perhaps more relevant, at some point
a commanding officer would so fear disobedience, with the
consequent effects on his power, that he would not give
the order. The exact boundary on the purposes for which
a unit of force is available depends upon circumstances
and upon the perceptions of the members of the group.
The further outside the group's previously defined functions the proposed use is, the less likely it is that that
unit of men and equipment can be counted on as a force
available for that purpose. The task of rallying men to that
purpose will tend to resemble organizing and recruiting a
new force for a new purpose.

The extent of such internal restraint on the activities
of a unit of force depends upon many factors. The more
educated and knowledgeable the men are the more likely
they may be to think for themselves. Political indoctrina-
tion on matters of substance, in which certain countries or

people are understood to be good and others to be bad, may limit the flexibility with which the force may be used. A unit of foreign-legion-type mercenaries is presumably more readily available for some immoral tasks than would be a unit of college graduates in the Peace Corps, even apart from physical equipment and skills. The more clearly the men are informed of their standing authority and of the limits on the authority of their commanding officer the more likely they are to respect those limits. An authoritative pamphlet, prepared and signed by the highest authority, to be carried by each man at all times, saying what kind of orders he should obey and what kind he should not, could, for example, have a significant effect.

In establishing effective internal restraints on a police unit, two structural considerations stand out. The first of these relates to the horizontal division of functions among different kinds of services. The more different kinds of units there are, the more sharply limited can be the authorized functions of a given unit. The most effective kind of a legal limit on the authority of a unit will be clear-cut lines, which exclude whole categories of activities from the proper function of the service. Such limits might be in terms of territorial jurisdiction, in terms of the means to be used, in terms of the objectives for which the unit should act, or in terms of the personnel against which it should act. A Worcester health inspector is unlikely to obey an order to blow up a bridge in New York State, since he is not supposed to do anything in New York, and he is not supposed to blow up bridges even in Massachusetts.

A second significant structural consideration involved in keeping effective internal control on a unit lies in the formality and notoriety which must accompany the process by which superior officials or bodies augment standing authority. If each member of the unit understands that the standing authority of his commanding officer can be drastically increased by a chain of command of which he will have no knowledge, he is likely to accept the proposition that his commanding officer has been duly authorized to issue the order, at least in the absence of known contrary orders from above. In recent years detailed consideration has been given to the problem (highlighted in Peter Bryant's novel *Red Alert* and in its movie version, *Dr. Strangelove*) of the intermediate commanding officer who may have the ability to carry off a military strike without superior authority. Outside the military field, where secrecy is less critical, a subordinate is more likely to question the authority of his superior. The police officer may ask to see the warrant before he accepts an assignment to break and search a building. The Pure Food and Drug Inspector will not, upon the say-so of a superior, accept the fact that he now has all the duties and rights of a soldier and should join in a military raid against a foreign country. Although the government has the lawful right to broaden his duties from those of a good inspector to those of a soldier, such expansions are to be done publicly, through the draft, a new oath of office, and significant changes in official status.

The differences between a national army and a police force demonstrate these institutional means of political control. If great control is desired, in the sense of making it improbable that an international police force will act in an unauthorized way, it should more closely resemble a domestic police force than an army. An army unit will obey its commanding officer over a large range of activities without asking questions. There are no territorial limits on its jurisdiction, and no classes of persons against whom it will not act. A soldier is expected to do as he is told: "Theirs not to reason why. . . ." He is not expected to understand the relationship between what he is doing and a legitimate objective. A military unit is expected to destroy cities and kill people upon command, without asking whether it is a legal or an illegal attack. Presumably, however, there are some limits on the things an army unit will do and the purposes for which it will act. Orders to slaughter Congressmen or babies, to inflict torture, to bomb the White House, or even orders to pull a surprise attack on an unsuspecting ally might well prove to be ineffective; because of legal or moral limitations, some controls remain over military units in addition to our confidence in their commanding officers.

A police force usually has legally authorized functions which are sharply limited in contrast to those of an army. Normally its powers are limited geographically. Each unit of police is expected to perform its duties within designated political units or subunits. Although an individual police officer may in fact engage in a greater variety of activities than would a soldier, the policeman is expected both to respect legal limits and to understand why he is doing what. He is expected to review his own activities and to decide for himself not to do those things which he knows he ought not to do. A unit of such police is less likely to go off in unauthorized directions at the command of its superior than is a unit of well-disciplined soldiers.

EXTRA-UNIT RESTRAINTS

Even if all the members of a unit are willing to engage in unauthorized activity, they may be deterred or restrained from successfully doing so by others. Public understanding of the limited authority of the police may make their actions less effective than when they are acting legitimately. If not only the individual police officers but the public as well is fully informed and carries an authoritative pamphlet explaining the rights and duties of the police, police action in excess of their rights may encounter civil disobedience.

Other units of the international police may act against a unit which they, or their commanding officers or superior officials believe is acting improperly. The revolt under General Salan of the French army in Algeria suggests the difficulty which a military commander may have in successfully defying higher authority. Although other units of the same force may be reluctant to engage their compatriots in a battle, their active non-cooperation may frustrate the unauthorized military venture.

National police units would provide a further check against the unauthorized activities of a unit of an international force. An international unit of police which was seeking to exert its illegal will against a nation would have to rely far more upon physical force than it would when following the legitimate enforcement process described in the first part of this paper. The inability of such a unit to produce legitimate and authoritative commands of narrow scope would make it less able to undercut the organized strength of the national police.

A final way in which a unit of police could be controlled from the outside would be by the regular law enforcement process of the police force turned on itself. The dissident unit would be treated in the same way that the international police force would treat a dissident national unit. Where the international police unit had failed to comply with its first-order obligations, the enforcement mechanism would produce explicit and direct second-order commands to individuals, and an attempt would be made to get second-order compliance. So long as the misconduct or mutiny was modest, enough international apparatus would be left in existence to go forward in such a way. Such external international enforcement could not be the principal assurance against a major mutiny, the frustration of which would apparently have to rest on national resistance and upon the difficulty of organizing an illegal conspiracy among a large number of law enforcement officers.

CONTROLS DESIGNED TO PRODUCE ACTION RATHER THAN RESTRAINT

Up to this point attention has been directed to the negative task of preventing the police force from doing something which it had not been authorized to do. There is also the other side of the problem, the task of making sure that a police force does in fact do what it is supposed to do.

This seems a more difficult task, or at least one as to which the legal structure of the enforcement agency has less to contribute. To some extent, there is an unfortunate choice. The more a police force is structured so that it cannot exceed its lawful powers the greater the chance of built-in restraints which may cause the force to fall short of doing its duty. In an international police force as in a national one, legal and institutional restraints designed to prevent the police from going too far may act as a drag on law-enforcing activities.

The discretion of a policeman to look the other way is enormous. Internal devices against laxness can be estab-

277

lished. Two or three policemen can be required to travel together, with each given a duty to report any improper inaction by the others. Secret spot-checking on performance of duty can be established and in some instances, perhaps, mechanical aids like the watchman's time clock can stimulate proper police action. High motivation, training, discipline and unit morale would seem, however, to be more important for producing action than most devices which the law can produce.

It should be pointed out, however, that the sequential or step-by-step control system here considered should tend to minimize certain brakes on enforcement action. International organizations are apparently reluctant to force a crisis or to take a bold step. The system here discussed requires taking only small steps one at a time. If the consequence of finding that a particular government had violated a treaty was massive retaliation or criminal punishment of its officials, an international organization might be unwilling to reach such a conclusion, no matter how clear the facts were. On the other hand, if the only consequence of examination of past facts is to state what ought now to be done, some of the obstacles to international action have been removed. Thereafter if there is defiance of such an explicit, future-looking decision, further enforcement may be forthcoming. An international organization is likely to be more willing to decree punishment for an individual who has defied its own orders than to condemn a government which has trespassed on a general rule of international law.

No matter how easy enforcement action may be, the problem of possible inaction of the enforcement machinery appears serious. The institution cannot create the initiative, drive, and sustained concern which is likely to be essential. Perhaps the best that an institution can do by way of promoting affirmative law-enforcement action is to provide a way in which those who do have the concern and initiative can work through the law-enforcement machinery, obtaining the appropriate consent and authority as they proceed.

Augmenting Step By Step the Authority of the Police
KINDS OF ORDERS

At the time of a first-order violation of a disarmament rule the international policeman on the beat has extremely limited authority, both as to the kind of command which he can give to an individual and as to the kind of threat he can make if that command is not carried out. Perhaps he can ask to look inside a building. Perhaps the threat he can make in the event of non-compliance is that he will have to report the matter and get a search warrant. As the policeman proceeds to a higher officer or to another institution, the orders he seeks are of two general kinds. He seeks an order directed to one or more defendants or respondents requiring or enjoining particular action on their part. The policeman himself has only limited authority to create second-order obligations. Orders which are going to impinge more seriously upon the privacy or activities of citizens of any country will have to be issued by somebody else.

The policeman also seeks an order telling him and perhaps his colleagues what to do. Such an order may determine that the trip-wire has in fact been sprung, that the police are now entitled to use greater force, that they should make more explicit threats, or that they should arrest someone or physically prevent some action from

279

being undertaken or destroy some property. This second kind of order gives the police both a duty and an authority that they did not have before. The control of the police requires that they not have standing authority to do to anyone at any time that which, upon a proper showing and appropriate decision, they should do to some.

KINDS OF BODIES THAT GIVE ORDERS

Of the almost infinite kinds of offices and institutions that have been devised to play a role in defining secondary obligations of the public and in altering the rights and duties of police, three types stand out: (1) the chain-of-command superior, such as a lieutenant, a captain, or a chief of police; (2) persons or bodies exercising broader political or discretionary judgment, such as a commission, a prosecutor, a governor, or a president; and (3) judicial or quasi-judicial bodies that determine facts or interpret and apply legal standards, such as a grand jury, a magistrate, a jury, a judge, or a trial or appellate court. There need not, of course, be a clear-cut division between such offices and institutions. Single individuals or bodies may perform several functions, but the typical sort of division suggests one way of approaching the structure of an international law-enforcement agency.

If the substantive functions of the police force have been divided into separate services, each with different powers and duties, it is possible and probably desirable that different services have quite different solutions to the chain-of-command problem. A horizontal division of an international force means that those performing less sensitive functions, such as health inspectors or inspectors with limited geographic authority, may be given greater autonomy and a less cumbersome hierarchy than those performing tasks which give governments greater concern. Countries may be willing that a service of unarmed inspectors be under the command of a single chief inspector. Armed units of police may have quite a different hierarchy of control units, and straight military forces might be under still a third system of command.

The higher and more discretionary form of political judgment might best be made by the Security Council or the Secretary-General of the United Nations or by the council of an international disarmament organization. It may be appropriate that as increasing amounts of international force become involved there be an increasing consensus as a condition of going still further. There is obviously a wide open field of possible ways of defining the individuals, groups, and votes that should control on the various questions that would confront an international law-enforcement organization.

There need not be a body called a court. Certainly, however, within what is here considered as the police establishment, there must be some person or institution capable of resolving authoritatively such objections as may be raised to complying with specific commands. It may be a magistrate, finding whether or not there is cause for a search warrant or a warrant of arrest, or deciding whether the evidence justifies holding someone for trial. It may be a judge issuing a restraining order, releasing a man on bail, or deciding that particular conduct is not barred by a treaty. It may be a reviewing court, passing on the correctness of the decision of an inferior court. To a lawyer it is unthinkable that there could be law-enforcement machinery that did not have access to a court or other body performing a like function that could resolve all those cases where either the facts or the application of a rule was in dispute and issuing those limited and authoritative orders as to what should next be done. This seems particularly true where international rules are being enforced against government officials who undoubtedly will attempt to justify their conduct.

On the other hand, so long as someone does have the conceded authority to resolve such questions there is no necessity that he be called "judge" or that he behave in a judicial manner. There are virtues in the judicial process, particularly in the acceptability of its decisions, which appear to be, and often are, the impartial application by wise men of pre-existing and authoritative norms to the facts at hand. But comparable work can be done by administrators or politicians. Sometimes the acceptability of the decisions of politically responsible officials will exceed that of the decisions of old men deemed out of touch with reality. The task, however, needs to be done. Experience suggests that one or more bodies of the judicial type should be on hand to perform it. Here, again, the functions might well be divided and different bodies established to decide different questions. It may be appropriate, for example, to have one judicial technique applicable to temporary restraining orders, where speed is important and a decision is of no lasting effect, and another technique applicable to final and authoritative decisions, where just the reverse may be true.

A great deal of consideration has been given in the past to the composition of judicial bodies appropriate for international adjudication. To some extent the difficulty in defining a suitable court reflects not the feared biases of particular judges but rather the unwillingness to give to any judge questions of the kind which it is thought might come before an international court. This problem can be reduced by carefully defining and limiting the jurisdiction of the court. The problem may also be reduced by providing that access in the first instance shall be to the local courts. National courts might be given the right and duty to determine whether warrants should be issued or temporary stays granted. They might also conduct preliminary hearings or trials, subject to appeal or to trial *de novo* upon the application or decision of some other body or person.

However limited the jurisdiction given to judicial bodies, it would seem essential that each such body be given the legal right to decide whether it has or has not jurisdiction. Since the process of enforcement against a government involves removing justifications for non-compliance with judicial or police commands, a court will be quite powerless if it is left open to a defendant to say that the court acted outside its competence. Such a contention can plausibly excuse second-order non-compliance with one judicial order or any subsequent order. To be effective, a court must be given the legal right to decide the scope of its legal rights.

TECHNIQUES FOR ESTABLISHING INDEPENDENCE OR DEPENDENCE

Once an international police force has been divided horizontally and vertically, and the authority of each unit established, significant checks and balances will be built in. There remains the fundamental task of deciding how each slot in the table of organization should be filled, whether with an individual or with a group, how decisions shall be reached at each level, and the conditions under which the persons involved shall be appointed, serve, and be removed. These are problems as to which there is a

283

great deal of knowledge and experience in the fields of public administration and political science. It would be a mistake, however, to think that there is a single wise answer.

Techniques of political control are available. The question is where the community wishes to place its confidence, and how much. As to each place in the hierarchy a balance must be struck between independence and dependence. To what extent do we wish to induce a man to decide a question as he personally would decide it, paying a minimum of attention to the views of others? To what extent do we wish to induce him to reflect the wishes of others on the question? Responsible law enforcement, like responsible government, requires a balance between the virtues of democracy, in which the official must answer to the community for what he does, and the virtues of autonomy, in which the official is given sufficient authority and independence to do the job that he has been asked to do. There is little reason for dogmatism here. This government has had experience, both good and bad, with individuals and with commissions, with judges who were elected and with those who were appointed, with political appointees and with a civil service, with bodies like juries that require unanimity and with bodies like Congressional Committees or Communist front organizations where an energetic minority has effective power to do what it wants. Each position and institution should be examined with the variables in mind and with a mind open to accommodation between political control and independence.

Any particular function might be performed by an individual or by a group. A single man has greater responsibility thrust upon him; a larger group more accurately reflects the diverse points of view within the community. A man may be appointed, elected, or hired. He may have life tenure, serve for a term of years, be removable for cause or at will. Virginia has discovered that one of the most effective means of maintaining political control over a government is to have a small commission with the power of raising and lowering the pay of any state official at any time. Although an American court is freed from some forms of political control where the judges have life tenure, it is subjected to other forms of political control by being required to conduct open proceedings and to submit written opinions justifying its decision. A jury, on the other hand, has greater freedom by deliberating in secret and not being required to explain its action.

One general proposition might be asserted. In law enforcement a handful of officials should have the right to proceed in a particular case without first obtaining community consent. The officials should be responsible to the community for a course of conduct rather than having to seek community permission in advance to enforce the law. Even here, however, our own practice of giving any one of twelve representatives of the public the right to frustrate a criminal prosecution suggests the difficulty of generalizing.

Presumably the more that an international police force is restrained by internal checks and balances the less necessity there is that it be made politically responsible through the selection and removal of its officers.

CHAPTER XIV

THE ROLE OF POLICE FORCES IN
RESPONSE TO VIOLATIONS

BY WALTER MILLIS

THE present international order, as violent, inefficient and dangerous as it may be, is nevertheless an order. As such, it has a constitution—it is, in other words, a system for organizing the almost infinitely various and conflicting affairs of three billion individual human beings. It imposes a pattern of custom, law, and armed force that serves to regulate the whole. The pattern and its innumerable subpatterns are extraordinarily complex; and the net result may seem as unsatisfactory to us as, for example, did the pattern imposed by the constituted monarchy of the *ancien régime* to the French revolutionaries of 1793, or as the Articles of Confederation seemed to the American Federalists in 1798. It is still a constitution with which one is seeking to deal, and the problem posed by the political control of an international police is a problem of constitutional revision, not of statutory or technical tinkering.

It seems clear that the achievement of general and complete disarmament must imply dramatic revision of the existing global constitution. This is because general and complete disarmament proposes a fundamental change in the locus, the empowerment, and the control of legal coercive power within the international order; and, in any society, these are the factors that most clearly and strikingly determine the form of the constitution under which it lives. One cannot introduce important changes in the way a society organizes its legal coercive powers without introducing more or less radical change into the constitution itself and, usually, at least some modification in the power relationships of the groups, classes, economic interests, and geographic areas that live by it. Thus, it is in the first instance *constitutional* change that is proposed by the goal of general and complete disarmament. And the nature of this change, it is here submitted, can be rather simply stated. It is the transformation of the present world system from its existing police-cum-military organization of legal coercive force into a wholly police-type organization of legal coercion.

The existing global constitution rests upon a wide variety of armed, coercive forces, both legal and illegal. Forces such as those deployed in cases of mob violence or armed rebellion are, of course, illegal; they have no sanction in any form of law, yet they have often proved indispensable in effecting necessary social and political change. They thus remain as a potentially significant element in the present world order, and—since any constitution must make adequate provision for necessary change—they probably cannot be wholly excluded from a new one. This point was recognized in a curious way in the Second Amendment to the American Constitution, which guarantees the right to bear arms. This did not, obviously, establish a constitutional right to rebellion; it did, however, establish the individual's *legal* right to maintain the instruments of popular rebellion. For legal and technological reasons, the amendment is no longer of constitutional significance; but it was not unimportant to the rather subtle balances of armed power achieved in 1789, and it may be presumed that the constitution of a demilitarized

287

world will have to make at least tacit allowances for something like its equivalent.

The coercive forces that are legal under the existing international order are of two kinds: the police and the military. The soldier, of course, has as much legal standing within the present order as does the policeman. In battle, the soldier acts, or is supposed to act, in accordance with "the laws of war"; and it is as legitimate for him to mow down an enemy with a machine gun as it is for a policeman to fire into an otherwise uncontrollable mob. Both the policeman and the soldier are custodians of their government's monopoly of legal coercive force. Yet there is a basic difference in function between the two and in the political and social consequences of their actions.

Perhaps the difference can be most simply expressed by saying that in any social order the policeman enforces the observance of laws that it is no business of his to make; the soldier makes, or tries to make, laws that it will not be his business to enforce. Any system of "law and order" must, it would seem, contain three basic elements: (1) a generally accepted body of law, that is, general rules governing the rights, duties, and allowed behavior of all those subject to it; (2) a judicial system of some kind to interpret and apply the general rules to the specific cases of conflict that may arise; and (3) a coercive power somewhere in the background to ensure that the general rules are normally observed and that the specific decisions are accepted and carried out with a minimum of unacceptable violence. These are the essentials of any system of law and order. It may be noted that for such a system to operate it is not necessary that the laws be just, that the courts be impartial, or that the enforced order be non-violent.

Though the system is likely to gain in efficiency and permanence to the extent to which these ideals are approximated, it is still a system of "law and order," however turbulent the "order" may be in practice or however biased the legal system may be in favor of particular interests or groups. In all such systems, good or bad, just or unjust, it is the reserve *police power* that secures observance of accepted law; it is the *military power* that, through threat or action, endeavors to impose new law upon relationships or in areas where it does not exist or is insufficient.

The police are the legal coercive agents within a generally accepted system of law; the military are the legal coercive agents employed by various conflicting systems in the effort to make law. A police is a law-enforcing body; an army is (or hopes to be) a law-making body. Savage and destructive though their operations may be, armies are never deployed in the name of anarchy or destruction. Invariably they fight in the name of law and order; invariably the goal, whether of the aggressor or of the defender, is a "new order" of permanent peace in which the army's law-making function will once and for all have been fulfilled and in which police enforcement of the new law will meet all the new order's requirements for coercive force. Both the policeman and the soldier are custodians of legally recognized coercive force within the organized community, but they perform basically different social functions. It is true, of course, that the soldiery have often been called out to fulfill the police function of enforcing domestic law, while police organizations have at times usurped the military function of law-making. In the former case, the soldiers become policemen for the time being; in the latter, the police become (like the Roman Praetorian Guard) an army, making the law of its own country as an invading foreign soldiery would do. The military and the police functions remain, however, sociologically, politically, and legally distinct.

Any order (or constitution in the larger sense) must rest ultimately on coercive force of some kind. The present world order relies for its coercive force upon a mixture of the legal police powers and the legal military powers of the hundred-odd sovereign states. Within the great, stable, and developed states, the police maintain domestic law and order with a high degree of efficiency and a minimum of violence; it is in only a few of the most disorganized nations that bloodshed constitutes a serious problem in the day-to-day life of the world community. By assisting one another in the policing of international agreements of many kinds, the national police forces contribute materially to international order as well. In those areas of international conflict that are beyond the competence of the national police forces, the world community must rely upon the national military establishments for its coercive force.

It is these that must independently try to make the law defining the respective rights and duties of the states. Normally, they try to do so through the threat of military action rather than through actual resort to it. Until this threat system breaks down in major war, it is the mere presence of these military establishments that supplies the necessary coercive element in the international world, just as the policeman enforces far more law by his presence than he ever does through making arrests or issuing summons. Unfortunately, the breakdown of a threat system of this kind seems sooner or later inevitable, but in the intervals between such occurrences the present international system actually operates with a higher degree of law and order and with a lesser amount of violence than mankind as a whole has ever known. The present international constitution, distributing the available legal coercive force through the hundred-odd national police and national military systems, has great triumphs as well as great disasters to its credit and might well seem tolerable except for one thing. That is the rapidly increasing frightfulness of the disasters that it threatens.

The constitutional revision implicit in the proposal of general and complete disarmament involves the transformation of the remaining military element of coercion into police-type coercion. The demilitarization of the world means simply that legal coercive force will be wholly converted from a military to a police form. The element of military coercion remaining in our global constitution becomes daily more staggering in its current, and even more in its potential, costs, while it seems more and more superfluous to the successful functioning of a world order. The idea of general and complete disarmament implies the idea, held consciously or unconsciously, that the global constitution can get rid of this element and reduce all legal coercive force to police forces, whose function is to secure observance of existing law rather than to attempt to make new laws.

The constitutional problem that this poses is in some ways not unlike that which confronted the youngish men whom Americans now call the Founding Fathers. To create their "more perfect union," they had to demilitarize thirteen armed and sovereign states, containing a variety of organized military and police forces. They were aware that it was quite impracticable, under the circumstances, simply to disarm the lot and create an all-powerful Federal police force to keep them all in order. A considerably more subtle balance of coercive forces was demanded. Their solutions are not directly applicable today, since the circumstances surrounding the goal of a demilitarized globe are different from those surrounding the problem of demilitarizing thirteen weak states in a hostile world. But their care and caution are instructive. We cannot hope, either, simply to disarm everybody and set up an international police force to take care of all remaining problems. A good deal more thought than is usually given to the subject is demanded, concerning the role of coercion in the demilitarized order, the nature of the police function, the laws for which the police will secure observance, how the police will be empowered, and, finally, how the political control of the international police will be organized.

The National Police Forces

In a demilitarized world, coercive force will remain, as apparently it must remain in any presently foreseeable system of human organization; and it will remain in a variety of forms—legal or illegal, organized or chaotic. Even though all major military weapons are successfully eliminated, there will, plainly, remain a large amount of weaponry. The several national police forces will have to be weaponed, probably with more than nightsticks or revolvers. The manufacture of police weapons, which may well include such things as tanks and machine-guns as well as side- and shoulder-arms, will continue. Inevitably, these weapons will "leak" through illegitimate channels to the general populace. American gunmen today seem to have no difficulty in acquiring pistols, though in most

American states the sale and distribution of firearms is very closely controlled. Any police force, moreover, is always open to subversion; it may place itself or its weapons at the disposal of rebellious or otherwise illegal elements. The instruments of violence will be widely dispersed, in one way or another, through the demilitarized world; and unless one contemplates a completely and permanently rigidified global social and political system, it would seem that the new constitution must (at least tacitly) accept something equivalent to the Second Amendment. It need not establish a legal right to revolution, as the Russian insistence upon excluding "wars of national liberation" from the ban upon war in general would seem to do. But it must accept as a fact a probably wide distribution of the instruments of insurrection and disorder and the likelihood that they will be used in insurrectionary or guerrilla war situations.

There is at least a partial truth in the hackneyed argument that if all greater weapons of war were abolished, men would still fight one another with "bows and arrows, or sticks and stones." The aim of general and complete disarmament cannot be the elimination of all violent conflict from the world. The police in even the best-ordered of states never fully achieve this; and a police-type organization of coercive force in the world as a whole is unlikely to bring all violence to an end. It is not the elimination of all violent conflict that must be the object of demilitarization but its reorganization or devolution into less lethal and catastrophic systems than those that have now developed. While it is doubtless true that men will continue to destroy one another on occasion with "sticks and stones" when no more efficient weapons are available, it is still unnecessary if not indeed impossible to picture stick-and-stone warfare organized on the vast scale and self-perpetuating intricacy of modern military institutions.

The most that a police-type constitution for a disarmed world can hope to do is to organize the residual violence into less destructive patterns. And its main reliance for this purpose—a point that it is believed deserves much more emphasis than is usually given it—must be the existing national police of the six-score or so nation-states, which now actually carry the main burden of maintaining "law and order" throughout the world and will continue to do so. If it is to succeed at all, the role of the contemplated international police must, it is here argued, be severely limited.

One can see coercive force in a demilitarized world organized in a kind of pyramid of power. At the bottom will be the general power of men to combine and rise in furtherance of their own group interests; basically, this is the power of revolution, and the world cannot be denuded either of the weapons or of the ideas that make revolution possible. Revolution is, of course, an exercise of coercive power. Whether armed with plastic bombs or paving blocks, the revolutionary takes to the streets to enforce, by armed coercion, a new system of law and order upon the old. Normally, he is suppressed by the police, as he must be in a well-ordered social system; and one may expect that revolutionary coercion will continue to fall into disuse, as it has been doing over increasingly large areas of the globe, with the advancing integration of the world society. Yet a world in which a possibility of revolutionary violence did not exist would be repugnant to most Western ideas of freedom and perhaps even to Communist freedom as well. Today the right of revolution is hardly more than a tactic in the rivalry between the Communist and the non-Communist worlds. The West insists upon a right of revolution against Communist totalitarianism, and the Communists upon a right of revolution against "capitalist imperialism." Neither would project the right so far as to include revolution against a successful establishment of its own form of legitimacy. In a world system that is demilitarized, stabilized, and increasingly integrated, it is not impossible that the right of revolution will take on more clearly recognized forms and limitations.

Violence and the potentiality of violence will at all events remain in the demilitarized world; and its principal reliance against such breakdowns must be the national police forces rather than an international police. All prospectuses for the demilitarized world provide for national police forces—usually described as being so organized and weaponed as to enable them to keep internal law and order, to patrol the national frontiers, to enforce the customs and immigration laws of their national state, and to protect their borders against casual forays. If this ideal description could everywhere be exactly realized, the problem of international violence would be resolved. With domestic law and order everywhere fully maintained and with no nation capable of levying a military threat against any other or having reason to fear such threats, no "cause" for war would remain.

The several national police forces would become so many agents, as it were, for the global order. They would everywhere secure observance of local law, reduce violence everywhere to the minimum (as indeed they now do over much the larger part of the globe), and confine all necessary changes, whether internal or international, to non-violent means of adjustment by adjudication, that is, by negotiation, by agreement, possibly by economic or propaganda pressures. In the absence of the great military threats, this would be quite enough to deal with all conflicts of interest between the nation-states as such, especially since the true conflicts of *national* interest remaining would not be of a nature that could be settled by organized war. The actual situation created would be rather like that which obtains among great American business corporations, which are often in bitter conflict with one another (adjusted only in part by strictly legal or juridical means), which usually maintain large private police and "security" organizations, but which never think of using these forces to wreck one another's factories because the conflicts in which they are involved are not susceptible to resolution by such means.

Unfortunately, the usual picture of the national police forces—all equally efficient in keeping domestic law and order and in patrolling the national frontiers—is quite unreal. In practice, they are bound to vary widely in their competence, in their methods, in their relation to the national political authority, and in their local empowerment. Where local laws differ, the functions of those charged with their enforcement must differ; and the great federal systems, such as those of the United States and the Soviet Union, introduce further complications into a purely police-type organization of legal violence. When the delegates sit down (if they ever do) to put facts and figures into tables of the allowable police forces for the United States and the Soviet Union, one suspects that they will run into considerable trouble.

Yet if the goal—a world policed, rather than regulated by war—is accepted, these will be no more than technical difficulties. The constitutional problem presented by the national police forces seems rather more serious. They are to be the main reliance in the demilitarized world for the maintenance of global order. However nicely balanced and rigorously commanded they may be, they will remain as fuel around which a restored national military power, with all its threats to the demilitarized system, might form. And their varying efficiency as agents of the global system of law and order is bound to raise problems. If one attempts to imagine a demilitarized globe, it is hard to believe that the national police forces that would remain, say, to the Scandinavian states, would be in any way remiss in their duties as agents of the world order, but it is as difficult to believe that the national police in states like Ghana or the Congo would successfully fulfill those duties. Riven by faction, by violent personal ambition, and by conflicts of external interests (like those that the French and British brought to India in the eighteenth century or that the Union Minière left with the Congo in the twentieth), how can one expect them to develop a national police competent to discharge its responsibilities to global law and order?

In areas like the Congo (or even in Palestine), the problem is perhaps manageable through existing international institutions. One is more troubled by the thought of what happens when and if it appears in the great organized states. The Russians and the Chinese believe (or profess to believe) that Western capitalism is doomed to collapse under its own "contradiction"; Westerners in general appear to hope that Soviet and Chinese Communism will collapse under "contradictions" no less evident in those societies. How does the police-type organization of global coercive force operate in such situations? Whether or not we admit it to ourselves, we benefit enormously from the capability of the Soviet police system to keep law and order over the some 200 million Russians and the many additional millions in the satellite states. The breakup of the Russian Communist empire today would doubtless be conducive to freedom, but it would be a good deal more catastrophic for world order than was the breakup of the Austro-Hungarian Empire in 1918. The wits who said that if "Austria did not exist she would have to be created" were rather well justified by the event; similarly, one might say today that if the Soviet empire did not exist, something would have to be created to fulfill its role in the world order. In the interwar and postwar periods, "China" did not exist; now China does exist, and, Communist or not, its existence seems to have an historic inevitability.

A critical question seems to be: does a world organized on a police rather than a military form of coercion try to sustain such great systems of order when they are in difficulties, or does it cooperate with revolution in order to overthrow them? The question runs like a bloody (and interminable) thread through most of modern history since 1776. Let us imagine repetition of something like the Hungarian Revolution of 1956, though on a greater scale. In a completely policed world it would be suppressed, as was the Hungarian Revolution, but with all the global forces of law and order cooperating (as they did not do in 1956) in the suppression. In the imperfectly policed world—which one must posit under any foreseeable system of demilitarization—the national police system might fail in one of the greater powers as in any of the lesser ones. The contiguous states would find their interests involved in violence and disruption; the pressures to intervene with their own police might well be very great. It is difficult to foresee all the complications that might arise out of a situation of this kind, but it is even more difficult to believe that all could be dealt with by an international police force alone.

It is the business of a police—any police—to secure observance of pre-established law. There is no existing, generally accepted, corpus of international law adequate to deal with the case of violent revolution in the Soviet Union—or in the United States, for that matter—and there seems to be no present possibility of developing such a legal structure. An approximation of such law does exist. Military "aggression" by one nation-state upon another is universally considered to be illegal; and it is a legal principle that all disputes *between nations* must be settled by non-violent means. An international police force charged with securing the observance of these two rules would rest upon solid logical and legal foundations. The United Nations police operations in Palestine, which have gone little farther than an insistence upon the observance of these rules, appear to have been reasonably successful. But in the case of major revolutionary dislocation in one of the great organized states, these rules are unlikely to carry an international police authority very far. The "aggressions" that must be suppressed will not be military in character; the disputes will not be between clear-cut national governmental entities, but between groups, factions, ambitious individuals, or impassioned ideologies. The situation will be, on a much larger scale, like that which developed in the Congo. The UN police forces in the Congo began by trying simply to suppress violence, leaving the local political issues to work themselves out. By the end of 1962, they were completing fairly large-scale military operations against Katanga, making a law where available

WALTER MILLIS

law was insufficient. In a greater collapse of a national
police system, any international authority will, in order
to suppress violence and chaos, have to make similarly
political decisions concerning the factions or groups to be
confirmed in domestic power. In the Hungarian case, such
organs of world order as we possessed were unable to make
decisions of this character. Obviously, it is not enough
simply to posit an international police power that will be
capable of making such decisions. To do so is to posit a
global system of law and order so close-textured as to be
beyond any present possibility.

Here one reaches the apparent impasse before the basic
idea of a police-type rather than military type of organization of coercive force in the contemporary world. While
in most affairs of men and nations a world policed basically by the national forces would seem to be quite viable,
situations may arise in one way or another in which only
an international or supranational police can act (without
resort to war) but in which there is insufficient law to
permit a police-type action. For this difficulty there appears to be no *theoretic* solution. The international police
cannot go beyond the enforcement of accepted law without becoming an army; to write a body of law, on the other
hand, would seem to be altogether beyond present possibility. In a way, the very superiority of the modern nation-
state organization in controlling its internal affairs mili-
tates directly against using it as a base upon which to erect
a supranational legal system sufficient in all cases to empower the supranational police in its enforcement. There
is no perfect or theoretically ideal exit from this problem—for much the same reasons that it proved impossible
over many years to devise any form of technically workable disarmament treaty. In such a situation, there seems

300

to be only one recourse. That is to take refuge from the ideal in the possible, from the perfect in the more or less practical.

It is easy to show that a police-type organization of the world is theoretically doomed to failure and that one cannot sit down today and write a treaty establishing an international police force that will infallibly guarantee all the rights of the men, groups, and nations involved. Yet there are large areas of the globe—the Atlantic Union is one of them, but another is the much more turbulent area of Latin-America—where a police rather than a military type of organization does in fact work quite adequately. The general situation in Latin America is certainly far from ideal, and it still knows considerable violence and bloodshed. However, it has not for many years organized international war; broadly, it represents, as no doubt does the Communist empire, a police rather than a military type coercive system.

Many who have considered a demilitarized world have anticipated that its principal dangers will derive from the too great size and efficiency of the national police forces. Too often they are seen as the centers around which new military institutions can form and new military aggressions can proceed—without any real attempt to analyze the question of why they should act in this way. If one does attempt such an analysis, it can be argued that the weakness and inefficiency of the national police will be a greater danger still. For the perils and dislocations likely to flow from their failures, there seem to be two general kinds of answers. One is, simply, that the world will have to accept a certain amount of violence and upset in its affairs. In general, the national police can be expected to keep order, as they now generally do. When they break down, we will not have the law available with which to replace them completely and will have to be able to live with the resultant confusion and possible chaos—up to a point. Beyond that point, we will have to have a supranational police force present to impose such accepted rules as can practically be imposed under the law and the legal institutions as they may stand. How much law will be available for this supranational police to enforce; in other words, what will be its constitutional function in a demilitarized world?

THE INTERNATIONAL POLICE FORCE

The usual concept of an international police force seems to go little beyond the assumption that it will suppress violence and bloodshed—at least organized violence and bloodshed—everywhere in the world by operating against the six-score nation-states in much the same way that the local police operate upon the individuals and corporate groups in a local community. In the demilitarized world, these states will have divested themselves of their military establishments and agreed to resolve all conflicts that arise between them by non-violent means, much as the law-abiding majority in any organized community do not normally carry weapons and at least tacitly agree to settle their disputes without recourse to violence. To facilitate their doing so, there is in the community, a general system of law, or rules, before which all are equal, and some kind of judicial system to apply these rules in specific cases, thus offering an acceptable—or at least generally accepted—alternative to violence in the resolution of conflicts.

In the ordered community, it is essential that there should be at least theoretical equality before the law and at least theoretical impartiality in its enforcement; and most current discussions of international peace and order necessarily begin by assuming that all the six-score national units will be, juridically, on an identical footing, with the international police operating impartially on all hundred-odd entities. Applied to the real world of men and nations, this picture is, surely, quite illusory. It makes no allowance for the enormous actual disparity between the present members of the small "community" of states. It disregards the way in which the world's existing military power potentials are distributed. In present debates over a peaceful world order, few of the participants face the fact that of the world's total present expenditure on weaponry, war potentials, and war establishments about one-third is accounted for by the United States alone, about a third by the Soviet Union, and the remaining third by all the rest put together, from the "powerful" nations like Britain or France or China to the "power-less" ones like Liberia or Costa Rica. To police all conflicts between the United States and the Soviet Union seems a wholly different task from that of policing conflict in all the rest of the world.

The common analogy with a "municipal" police force is seriously misleading in many ways. To lay down general rules governing the conflicts of thousands of millions an individuals and corporate persons is easier than to lay down rules defining the rights and duties in a community of little more than a hundred members, none of whom is an individual or can even be regarded, except by an irrationally extreme extension of legal fiction, as a corporate person. An individual human being is a sufficiently complicated bundle of needs, interests, emotions, and ideas with which general laws, enforceable by the police, can

deal successfully only on basically statistical principles—
that is to say, by the "law of averages." The law of any
community is not an absolute; it is an approximation, so
to speak, developed by tradition and experience, which
"works" only because when applied to sufficiently large
populations its errors tend to cancel out. Applied to a
very small sample, the errors are likely to accumulate.
They are particularly likely to accumulate when the members of the small population are not individual human
persons (and it is from people that all our notions of
law, governance, and conflict are derived) but are themselves complicated summations, as it were, of hundreds of
thousands or hundreds of millions of human individuals.
In trying to establish an inter*national* rule of law, one is
dealing with a population which is drastically reduced in
numbers but of which the constituent members are
inordinately more complicated than are the people of
whom they are composed.

But if the simple analogy between a local and an international police system fails in these and other ways,
it is not without its uses. Complete equality before the
law and impartial police enforcement of law and legal
adjudication are necessary to the theory of the well-organized and non-violent community; but they are obviously theoretical ideals never more than imperfectly realized in practice. Most well-ordered communities include
vast disparities of wealth and power; and while in all of
them the individual members are "equal before the law,"
in most of them some are a great deal "more equal" than
others. Inevitably the law, even the best law, bears upon
the powerful differently from the way it does upon the
weak. When such disparities become very great, there
may be revolutionary violence; but unless and until such

a point is reached, the police fulfill their function very
well. They keep the peace, even though they never succeed in impartially enforcing all law against all involved,
powerful and weak alike. What they do succeed in enforcing with a reasonable degree of impartiality is that
rather minimal body of law that is universally accepted
as indispensable to the survival of the community.

In a demilitarized world society, the role of the international police cannot be to enforce a monolithic law impartially suppressing violent conflict everywhere upon the
globe. As has been said, the general maintenance of "law
and order" is a task that must be left to the national
police systems. The most that the international police
can do—unless, of course, it is to become a conquering
supranational army—is to secure observance of that minimum of basic rules that is accepted as necessary to the
survival of the demilitarized world system.

What these basic rules are, susceptible to impartial international police enforcement, can be estimated only by
considering the peculiar character of the society in which
the international police are to operate. It will be composed, as far as one can foresee, of less than 150 complex
members, varying enormously in size, power, and internal
characteristics. Save in the improbable event that our
investigations of space bring down upon us an attack
from Mars, this society as a whole will be totally free
from the threat of external violence—a condition that no
previous form of social organization has enjoyed. This
absence of external threat to the system as a whole should
simplify the task of those who are to police it as a whole.
On the other hand, the variety and complexity of the
small number of compound "individuals" upon whom the
international police must, at least in the first instance,

operate will tend to aggravate the problem. Or either factor may cut both ways. While a high degree of external threat has created internal police problems, it has also helped to simplify them; and while the simplicity of the domestic organization may have frequently facilitated police work, the high degree of organization to which the modern nation-state has attained can work in the same direction. The most that can be said is that the international society in which the international police are expected to operate is a peculiar one and that it is impossible simply to transfer to it the rules and concepts, the notions of "law and order," appropriate to local society. In order to "fit," the familiar equations must undergo some degree of transformation. For example, the international rule, now well established if not well enforced, against military aggression is closely analogous to the domestic rule against premeditated murder. But it is analogous only. It is not the same rule, in either origin or in effect. The international society will have generally accepted (and therefore have police-enforceable) rules of its own. One must try to see more clearly than most do today what they are likely to be.

It is here argued that these rules will be few. Obviously, the first and most fundamental must be that all nation-states divest themselves of all instrumentalities of military power or military threat and that they do not reassume or rebuild them. A second rule, which is actually no more than a necessary corollary of the first, is that all nation-states are bound to resolve any *national* differences arising among them by non-military and non-violent means. The primary constitutional function of an international police in a demilitarized world would be to secure the observance of these basic world statutes. This is a police function that no national police force or combination of national police forces could hope successfully to perform. It is an inter national—or better a supranational—function that, if it is to remain within the realm of police rather than military action, only a supranational authority could fulfill.

In a constitutionally demilitarized world these tasks of an international police, commonly regarded as presenting difficulties so great as to be insuperable, would, in fact, be relatively simple. In suppressing murder or the carriage of lethal weapons in a local society, the police have the aid of severe penalties ranging up to the death sentence. These are obviously unavailable to those attempting to police nation-states, and the whole concept of a punitive inter*national* police system suggests a profound misconception of the nature of the problem. The true object of demilitarization is to create a non-military system of international relations that will be more or less self-enforcing, without penalties that are in the nature of things impossible to impose. If one considers only the giants—the United States and the Soviet Union—with their well-organized allies and satellites, it should not be difficult to prevent their recourse to military aggression once they had divested themselves of their military establishments. This is especially true since the elimination of weapons and the concomitant military threat system would remove virtually all present incitements to military aggression. It would not, of course, remove conflicts and differences among them; it would eliminate any reason for submitting these to the test of war.

This, in fact, is the situation that obtains today over large areas of the globe, where many nations conduct their mutual relations without war or even recourse to the military threat system. With the great military establishments and threat systems eliminated, the task of policing the resultant situation, so far as the great and stable states are concerned, should not be difficult. The Cuban crisis of October 1962, is at least instructive. Fidel Castro was able to convert Cuba to a Communist satellite, to confiscate large amounts of foreign capital, and to threaten subversive if not guerrilla attack upon his neighbors without raising any significant threat of war in the Western hemisphere. It was only the introduction of the Soviet long-range weapons that brought the crisis even near the danger point. The end of the long-range and other major military weapons will itself supply a policeable international stability.

With demilitarization achieved, however, it must, of course, be maintained; and some supranational police work will have to be devoted to the task. There must be no secret rebuilding of nuclear arsenals and delivery systems; there must be no clandestine conversion of national police ministries into military general staffs; there must be no threatening excess in the production of police weapons. A supranational police system of some kind will be necessary, not only to prevent the occurrence of such things but—much more importantly—to assure all nations that they are not occurring anywhere. So far as the giant states and the lesser stable ones are concerned, this should not be an impossibly difficult police problem. It seems so today because of the mutual (and well-founded) "distrust" of the great armed powers. It is a distrust that cannot be removed by any amount of merely friendly or conciliatory gestures, no doubt; but it can be removed by the establishment of conditions that eliminate the factors that at present incite governments to military threat and attack against one another. It is easy to "trust" a government (as it is to "trust" a man) not to act in ways that are both pointless and highly dangerous to it. And it is not difficult to police relationships resting upon a confidence so engendered.

Surely, it takes no great degree of sophistication to realize that this kind of pointless action could not happen and never will happen. In a demilitarized world, what could possibly impel a government—any government—to embark upon so fruitless and illegal an enterprise? To begin with, while there may be "n" states capable of producing a nuclear weapon, there are not more than half-a-dozen that could produce them, together with effective delivery systems, in numbers sufficient to be of any significant political effect in the world at large. And these, even including the greatest, could do so only by prolonged and massive efforts that would be unconccalable and that would certainly be halted by the rest of the world (using the many means other than military that would be open to it) long before they had reach fruition. The notion that one nation could, by secretly building a few nuclear weapons, hold all the rest of a demilitarized world up to ransom is the sheerest fantasy, born of our gross overvaluation of the effects of explosive destruction in the regulation of human affairs and of our incomprehension of the fluidity and resilience of all human organization.

Even if enough nuclear weaponry could be secretly accumulated to seem to support a ransom demand, it would still provide no way in which the guilty government could collect. Any blackmail threat, of course, defeats its own object if it has to be put into effect. In ordinary life, the power of the blackmailer resides in the fact that he can usually publish without risk to himself. If the demands

WALTER MILLIS

of a blackmailing nation were simply refused, the only action open to it—a mass slaughter of the people of the intended victim—would not only, as usual, defeat the object of the blackmail but would involve the guilty power in social, political, and economic consequences catastrophic to itself. In any actual situation one can imagine, this would be obvious to the intended victim and no ransom would be paid.

The problem of nuclear or other forms of mass-destruction blackmail in a demilitarized world is a wholly unreal one; and it certainly does not call for an international police of a massively military character armed with the colossal weapons that are to be otherwise excluded from international relations. So far as the stable states are concerned—and these alone will possess the material and technical resources necessary for rebuilding a nuclear arsenal at all, to say nothing of rebuilding one in secret— the questions involved are genuinely police and not military questions to be met primarily by the normal police methods of oversight, investigation, and report. Even these methods will be required more in order to give general reassurance to the world at large than in order to provide physical protection against possible dangers. Once the governments have divested themselves of the mass destruction weapons, it will be to the vital interest of all that they nowhere be revived. The international police can count normally on the cooperation, rather than the opposition, of the several national police forces in seeing that such weapons are nowhere revived, rather as Federal police authorities in the United States count on the cooperation of state and local police in controlling such Federal crimes as kidnapping or counterfeiting. These are everywhere recognized as crimes against the United

States as a whole, and the police authorities on all lesser levels combine in assisting the Federal police in their suppression. In a demilitarized world, the revival of mass-destruction weaponry anywhere will be a global crime, and police authority on all levels will be at the disposal of the international police in its suppression.

If the only function of an international police in the demilitarized constitution were to prevent the recreation of nuclear or other mass-destruction weapons, its task would be simple. It is difficult to visualize a situation in which any government sufficiently stable and with enough resources to be capable of rebuilding a nuclear arsenal, would wish to do so. And in even the greatest and richest states, it could not be done except by the government— or at least with governmental consent and connivance. One can say with confidence that if demilitarization breaks down, it will be in some other way than this. Since it is impossible to predict all possible future situations, one cannot say with any precision just what these ways might be. In general, one would expect the danger of breakdown to lie not in any secret or sudden decision by a government to revert to war as an instrument of policy but in a much more gradual and probably much more complex deterioration of the system of national police forces. There can be no direct comparison between the revival of military threat and war in an initially demilitarized system and the revival of war in Europe by Mussolini and Hitler in the thirties (Europe had never been demilitarized to begin with); but even the breakdown of the thirties was a gradual and complex process never fully calculated by anyone, the fatal outcome never clearly discerned (except possibly by hindsight) at any one point. Once the world is demilitarized, it is in these ways, rather

311

than in some one patently criminal outbreak, that one would expect collapse to come, if it ever does come.

One can envisage many possibilities, some of which have already been touched on. The unavoidable imbalance between the large national police forces that must be allotted to the great states and the much smaller ones to which their small neighbors will be restricted is one source of concern. A point that is often overlooked here is that if the national police are confined (as all draft treaties and proposals would require) to genuinely police-type weapons and organization, the imbalance can be of consequence only along contiguous frontiers. The kind of weapons that, whether rocket-borne, air-borne, or sea-borne, today enable the great states to fling their military threats far over the heads of their immediate neighbors will no longer exist. Where contiguous states are of roughly equal size, there will be no imbalance of police forces. Where one neighbor is much greater and more powerful than the other, moreover, there will be slight reason for it to convert its police into the equivalent of an aggressive army, since it will have many cheaper and more effective means—political and economic power, the control of trade, or even more outright non-military subversion—of achieving ends that seem useful to it. No doubt there still remains the possibility of border violence growing into quasi-war between police forces. In the absence of the giant military-threat systems, conflicts of this kind will no longer be capable of fusing a catastrophe; they might, however, promote the deterioration of the police system to a point at which catastrophe could again become possible.

There is the serious possibility of revolutionary violence or civil war breaking out within one of the presently stable great states or great state systems. Conflict would then revolve around control of the national police or various parts of it, with consequent chaos and lapse of the state's constitutional function within the world order. There would be heavy pressures on the police of the contiguous states to intervene, directly or indirectly. If an international police intervened to "restore order," it would be imposing law—in other words, waging war, whatever the weight of weaponry it might employ—rather than policing it; if it did not, contiguous national police might attempt the same thing. In either case, the world might well be on the way to a general revival of war and failure of the police order.

Even if matters in the great states did not reach the point of internal violence, there would be the possibility of politicians or factions arising to demand (for reasons of internal politics) an enlargement of the national police or freedom from the treaty restrictions upon its weapons. One cannot foresee all the complexities of behavior of either men, governments, or nations; and in dismissing the grosser ideas of governments clandestinely preparing criminal assaults upon one another, one cannot deny that there are many other less premeditated ways in which a police-type world order could deteriorate even if it had once been successfully established. It must be a constitutional function of the international police to prevent such deterioration—to the extent that it is able to do so—by means that will not at the same time promote it. The provisos are difficult; and it is, of course, impossible to devise police institutions that will certainly succeed under all conceivable future situations. It should not be impossible, however, to devise institutions that can confidently be expected to tend toward, rather than against, success.

The success of an international police in maintaining a demilitarized order must turn primarily, not on its size, weight of weaponry, or organization, but on its empowerment. An international police empowered, or authorized, to wage war upon the member governments in the event of disarmament violations would be certain to fail, for reasons discussed earlier. It does not follow that empowerment of other kinds might not be both useful and successful. One here meets the question of the possibility or desirability of empowering international authority to reach beyond the national governments in order to operate directly upon persons (natural or corporate) within them. Too little is now known about the decision-making processes in modern government to speak with much confidence here. The way in which decision is actually arrived at within our own "open" government is almost as obscure to us as in the way in which it is achieved in such great "closed" societies as those of the Soviet Union or of China; in neither case is it at all clear what are the effective motivations involved nor, consequently, just what kind of police empowerment and police action might successfully control them. It is rather plain that the motivations usually assumed—nationalistic ambition, military threat, the desire for freedom, economic necessity, population pressure—fail to "fit" the observed facts with any accuracy. Without a theory of governmental decision-making that will more closely fit the results of observation, it is hard to speak dogmatically about the manner in which international police action might best affect governmental decision.

It is both the great weakness and the great strength of

international law today that it can operate directly only upon governments. The weakness resides in the fact that governments, as has already been argued, are not susceptible to police action in the same way as are the individuals within a community. The strength, on the other hand, resides in the fact that this rule devolves upon the national governments nine-tenths (or ninety-nine hundredths) of the colossal task of policing all the affairs of some three billion human beings, making the governments agents of the world order whose authority as such one cannot lightly impair. It is interesting to consider whether, in this situation, international law might not be extended by general consent, and might not usefully be so extended, to make certain defined activities of a war-making or war-inciting nature into international crimes susceptible to suppression by international police action. There have been tentative beginnings in this direction. We already have international conservation treaties, governing migratory birds or the taking of pelagic animals, and their violation is an international crime. Treaties of extradition, in effect, declare that an individual regarded as a criminal in one state will be so regarded in all other states parties to the treaty. It is true that in such cases the enforcement of the relevant international law is left to the national police. Whether or not to apprehend an extraditable criminal is in the discretion of the police of the state in which he has taken refuge; if they do not cooperate, there is no international police to intervene and arrest him. Yet under all usual circumstances, the local police do cooperate, and an international police would be superfluous. And in cases where the local police did not suffice, rudiments of a genuinely international police force have appeared. Long before the general abolition, after 1860, of chattel slavery in the Western world, the international trade in slaves had been recognized as an international crime. The British, American, and other navies joined forces in the suppression of the trade and in so doing became in a real sense an international police force, operating not upon governments that might condone the practice but directly upon the ship captains and owners who engaged in it. And the post-1945 war criminal trials, at Nuremberg and elsewhere, represented a long step forward in the attempt to impose a "policeable" international law upon the individual commanders and leaders within the confines of a nation-state.

Nuremberg was a step forward in the attempt; there is much question as to whether it was not a step backward in realization. It is difficult now to see much "justice" in its verdicts; few can now believe that the condemnations and sentences it meted out upon the Nazi decision-makers will have any significant effect on the decisions of future governments. Since this last was its only rational purpose, it must stand as a warning as to the extent to which genuine international *police* action can be carried out against the activities of individuals or groups within the nation-states.

So far one has been thinking primarily of the role of an international police force in relation to the great stable states and their smaller, but no less well-organized, allies and satellites. Over those great areas of the world that are now well ordered and well policed, the problems of an international police force in a state of demilitarization seem anything but insoluble. But even under the most optimistic assumptions, the demilitarized world will inherit areas of disorder, violence, and revolution—such as those now represented by southeast Asia and sub-Saharan Africa or those potentially quite possible elsewhere. The police problems it will encounter in such areas are quite different from those it will encounter, initially at least, among the great, powerful, and stable states. They are not perhaps so different from those, already discussed, that might be encountered in the event of the breakup of one of the imperial powers; and one might say that if sound police principles can be worked out and applied in situations like that in the Congo, they will be available for dealing with possible greater disruptions in the fabric of the police-type world order.

Some of these principles are beginning to emerge. In situations of this kind, the governments are typically weak in relation to any of the great powers or to the force that international authority could bring to bear upon them; they are internally weak, torn by violent faction and under all the incitements to irresponsible international action that are generated by ambitious men at home; they are rarely armed beyond the levels that would be permitted to a national police in a demilitarized system, but police-type weapons are abundant (as they would be under general demilitarization) and offer ample opportunity for violent outrage, guerrilla war, and bloody destruction. One basic rule for international police action in such a situation seems to be developing: the police power should be applied only when the local anarchy begins to put an unbearable strain upon the fabric of the world community and should then be directed only toward suppressing the violence, leaving the political issues to be settled, so far as possible, non-violently by the parties immediately concerned. The rule is simple to state. The difficulty, of course, is in its application.

In the increasingly integrated modern world, at what point does local anarchy begin to put an intolerable strain upon the global fabric? In the past, unspeakable savageries and destructions were normally perpetrated in most parts of the globe without the more powerful and settled nations paying the slightest attention. The growth of humanitarianism makes this no longer possible. It was, no doubt, the early atrocities in the Congo that gave rise to the first pressures for international police intervention. But atrocities are today hardly a sufficient cause for police intervention, even if they are an increasingly significant one. Quite legitimate global economic interests (as well as somewhat less legitimate private ones) may intensify the strain imposed by the local anarchy. When national armies are as a rule no longer used to protect private property or to collect private debts, it can hardly be the function of an international police to do so. But where global interests importantly depend upon the continued supply of raw materials such as Katanga copper or Iranian oil or upon the maintenance of communication facilities such as the Suez Canal, local anarchy may become intolerable.

There can be little doubt that the most compelling pressure for international intervention in a situation of local violence and chaos is political. This is commonly (though it is believed inaccurately) expressed as the fear of a great war arising out of the little one. There must be an international police authority to prevent the local violence from "spreading" into general conflict. This, however, is a misapprehension that serves chiefly to generate a vast amount of bad argument about which parties stand for "peace" and which are "warmongers." It is more useful to say that in any situation of local anarchy or chaos, political and power interests much wider than those of the immediate area concerned are likely to hang upon the outcome. When police action is demanded in such situations, what is really meant is that there must be intervention by an impartial police to ensure that the outcome is favorable—"impartially," of course—to one's own interest, rather than to others. This, one need hardly say, is beyond the powers of any kind of police action. Even within a well-ordered domestic community, once a conflict has reached the point of violence, the police cannot intervene to suppress the violence without almost inevitably favoring one contending interest over the other. All a police can do is to "restore law and order"—to restore, that is, an existing legal system that has been shown by the very act of violence to be regarded by one party or the other as unfair, partial, and biased against its own just rights and interests. An "impartial" police intervention is almost a contradiction in terms, except under a legal system so just, so subtle, so balanced as to determine unambiguously all the rights and duties involved in the conflicts out of which the violence has arisen. Even the best of domestic legal systems can never achieve more than a rough approximation of this ideal; it will be a long time, if ever, before there develops a structure of international law that can achieve it in face of the intricate conflicts of interest, internal and international, present in situations like that in the Congo or, for that matter, in Viet Nam.

CHAPTER XV

THE IMPARTIALITY OF THE
INTERNATIONAL POLICE

BY HANS J. MORGENTHAU

Four Propositions

THIS paper is divided into two major parts, one analyzing the functions the police have traditionally performed within the state, the other applying this analysis to the international police force in a disarmed world. The first part develops a general theory of police functions; the second part tries to visualize the functions an international police force is likely to perform in a disarmed world in the light of that theory. Thus, the first part is, in a sense, more important than the second one, since it deals with what is known and sheds light upon the functions of any police force, domestic or international.

The inquiry of the first part issues in four propositions:

First, the police perform two different functions for the maintenance of peace and order: (1) a law-enforcing function in the strict sense, concerned with piecemeal violations of the legal order, the survival of which is not in question; (2) a political function, dealing with all-out challenges to the legal order and the political, social, and economic status quo itself.

Second, the issue of the impartiality of the police arises only with regard to the former function, while the latter presupposes partiality of the police in favor of the legal order and the status quo.

Third, there exists a complementary relationship between the political functions and the popular consensus supporting the legal order and the status quo. The more there is of the latter, the less there need be of the former, and vice versa.

Fourth, the quantitative relationship between police and consensus depends upon the quality and the policies of the government. The government can afford to dispense with the use of police to the extent that it has the voluntary support of the people and trusts the people in giving that support.

THE POLICE WITHIN THE STATE
THE POLICE AS LAW-ENFORCING AGENCY

In order to understand the functions an international police force would have to perform in a disarmed world and, more particularly, to assess the conditions for an impartial performance of its functions, it is necessary to guard against too close an analogy with the police as they are known in our national experience. Police as an institution appeared relatively late in the history of the modern state. The creation of a police force coincides with the development of the *Rechtsstaat*, the state whose relations with its citizens are regulated by objective legal rules of general application. Thus, the modern police appeared on the European continent in the eighteenth century and were established in England through Peel's Metropolitan Police Act of 1829.

Under normal circumstances the police perform certain specialized functions for the modern state.[1] Considered in the overall context of the functions that the modern state fulfills, especially for the maintenance of peace and order, these police functions are marginal. The police cooperate in the enforcement of certain regulatory laws

[1] We are using this term here as synonymous with *Rechtsstaat*.

concerned, for instance, with motor traffic, licenses, and closing hours. They try to prevent the violation of criminal laws and concern themselves with the apprehension of criminals. They aid in the administration of justice through the collection of evidence.

Yet it is not upon the performance of these functions that the maintenance of peace and order within the modern state primarily depends. The police can protect peace and order from individual infractions and keep those that occur within tolerable bounds because of the deterrent effect that the likelihood of effective police intervention has upon the prospective criminal. Yet when a national society is rent by deep dissensions over vital issues threatening disintegration, revolution, or civil war, the state does not turn to the police but depends upon the whole range of human and material resources of society. The modern state relies, especially, upon its government and the armed forces.

The state is enabled to assign the police this specialized and marginal place in the overall scheme of things because it can draw for the maintenance of its peace and order upon the psychological resources of unorganized society. The peace and order of the modern state rest primarily upon the psychological predispositions of the great majority of its citizens, supporting that peace and order. Modern society has created networks of interests, of social and economic dependencies, of power relations, and of political loyalties that converge in creating and continuously recreating a consensus in favor of peace and order. The great majority of the citizens of the modern state are committed to the perpetuation of the political, social, and economic status quo, at least in its essentials; insofar as they are not, their interest in the maintenance of peace and order outweighs their desire for change.

In the creation and preservation of this consensus, the quality of government plays a decisive role. This consensus is in good measure a reflection of four qualities of government. The government allows for peaceful change. It is the focus of popular loyalties overriding parochial ones. It creates in the people the expectation that its policies will result in at least an approximation to justice. And it appears to have the power, in the form of the means of organized violence, to make its will prevail. Yet this last quality stands in a subsidiary and complementary relation to the other three. For it remains normally in the background as a general deterrent to be used only in extremis, and it tends to enter the picture as an active force in the measure that the other three qualities are not sufficient to maintain a voluntary consensus.[2]

The impartiality of the police has two different meanings within the context of the modern state. As concerns the legal order and the political, social, and economic status quo, the police cannot be impartial; for it is their purpose to defend that legal order and to maintain that status quo. If they perform their duty, they cannot help but be partial to them; if they violate their duty, as they do when they do not enforce certain laws, such as those against gambling or racial discrimination, they are partial against the legal order. But, in the nature of things, an institution whose purpose is the defense of the legal order cannot be impartial with regard to it. It must be either for or against it.

The appearance of impartiality is here a mere illusion.

[2] Cf. Hans J. Morgenthau, *Politics Among Nations* (3rd ed.; New York: Alfred A. Knopf, 1960), pp. 502ff.

It stems from the almost general acceptance of the legal order, which thus appears as the objective framework within which society functions and in whose objectivity the police partake. The reputation for impartiality that the police enjoy, however unfounded in fact, is important because it fulfills an ideological function. By making it appear as though the police were not an institution of organized violence on behalf of a particular legal order and status quo but somehow the impartial manifestation of the objective order of things, that reputation necessarily strengthens obedience to the law and submission to the police. It becomes an active factor in the maintenance of peace and order. In this respect, the reputation of the police for impartiality performs a social and political function similar to that performed by the reputation of the courts for being the impartial "mouthpiece" of the law, arriving at their decisions by a rational process of logical deduction.

The other meaning of impartiality, as applied to the police, is identical with equality before the law. The police are, in this sense, impartial if they mete out equal treatment to persons and situations that the law requires to be so treated. They lack in impartiality if they discriminate among persons and situations in a manner unsupported by the law or, to use the formulation of American jurisprudence, if they deliberately deny a person the enjoyment of a right that is commonly afforded others in like circumstances.[3]

It then obscures the issue to say with Charles Reith that the democratic police force "gives service wholly to

[3] Cf., for instance, *Barbier v. Connolly*, 113 U.S. 27 (1885), at 31.

law, and not to policy. . . ."[4] It would be more correct to say that the modern police are, of course, the instrument of policy, that is, of that set of policies supported by the consensus of the great majority of citizens, and that the issue of impartiality normally comes to the fore only when policy has to be applied to individual persons and circumstances. Were it not for this consensus codified in objective laws of general applicability, the issue of the impartiality of the police could not arise at all. Without that consensus, the police would simply be an organization of violence through which the state imposes its will upon a recalcitrant or, at best, indifferent population. Then the police would be not the instrument of a national consensus but a substitute for it.[5] Both qualitatively and quantitatively their functions would be utterly different from those they perform in the modern state. This was indeed generally the case before the beginning of the nineteenth century, and it is still the case today in numerous countries.

THE POLICE AS A POLITICAL INSTRUMENT

The functions that the police perform for the maintenance of peace and order in the state that is not a *Rechtsstaat* are entirely different from those discussed thus far, and, in consequence, the problem of their impartiality is posed here in entirely different terms. This observation is true both for the autocratic state, historically preceding

[4] Charles Reith, *The Blind Eye of History* (London: Faber and Faber, 1952), p. 253; cf. Charles Reith, *British Police and the Democratic Ideal* (London, New York, Toronto: Oxford University Press, 1945), p. 6.
[5] There is an inkling of this complementary relationship in Julius von Soden, *Die Staats-Polizei nach den Grundsatzen der National-Oekonomie* (Aarau: Heinrich Remigius Sauerlander, 1817), p. 40, where consensus is equated with religiosity.

the modern state, and for the autocratic and totalitarian states contemporaneous with it. The functions of the police are here neither specialized nor marginal but general and central. They are so central to the state's existence and so persuasive throughout its activities, they are to such an extent the distinctive characteristic of the state, that we call such a state a "police state." For the same reason, in the usage of the sixteenth, seventeenth, and eighteenth centuries, the term "police," as derived from the Greek word for state, covers the sum total of state activities concerned with internal peace, order, and welfare.[6] According to Doctor Johnson, it connotes "The regulation and government of a city or county, so far as regards the inhabitants,"[7] and the *Oxford English Dictionary* defines the term as "A body of men officially instituted, or employed, to keep order, enforce regulations, or maintain a political or ecclesiastical system."[8] One of the most influential nineteenth-century writers on the subject defines police as the sum total of the domestic policies of a state.[9] An eighteenth-century writer defines police as "the ordering of a state with regard to its internal security, beauty, convenience, population, morality, and standard of living."[10] Definitions of this type abound in the literature of the period. Or, as a contemporary writer has put it: *"Police*

[6] Cf. the Imperial Ordinance of 1495, the Ordinance of the Imperial Diet of 1500, and the Imperial Police Ordinance of 1530, in Julius von Soden, *op.cit.*, pp. 6ff.

[7] Samuel Johnson, *A Dictionary of the English Language* (London: W. Strahan, 1755), I.

[8] Sir James A. H. Murray (ed.), *A New English Dictionary on Historical Principles* (Oxford: Clarendon Press, 1909), VII, 1069.

[9] Robert von Mohl, *Die Polizei-Wissenschaft nach den Grundsätzen des Rechtsstaates* (3rd ed.; Tübingen: H. Laupp, 1866), I, 6ff.

[10] Carl Gottlob-Rössig, *Lehrbuch der Polizeiwissenschaft* (Jena: Academische Buchhandlung, 1786), p. 2.

anciently meant policy, social organization, civilization; the art of technic of so organizing a community that a civilized society would be the result."[11] Yet even in contemporary American jurisprudence, police power is defined as the power "to promote the health, safety, morals and general welfare,"[12] or in the words of Chief Justice Taney as "nothing more or less than the powers of government inherent in every sovereignty to the extent of its dominions."[13]

Another aspect of this comprehensive concept of the police force, important for our discussion, is its association with the army and with the exercise of arbitrary, oppressive power. This association exists both in verbal usage and in substance. A modern constable is the diminished successor of the commander of an army and the keeper of a royal castle or fortified town of medieval times. Gendarmes are etymologically "men-in-arms." In Pakistan and in certain parts of Northern India, the officer in charge of a police station is called "Faujdar," that is, military officer, and the central police station of a large city is called "Kotwali," that is, the fort.[14] As concerns the association of arbitrariness and oppression with the police, a bipartisan committee reported in 1818 on the establishment of a professional police force in Great Britain in these terms:

Though your committee could imagine a system of police that might arrive at the object sought for; yet, in

[11] Asher Byrnes, *Government Against the People* (New York: Dodd, Mead and Company, 1946), p. 20.

[12] Edward S. Corwin, *The Constitution and What It Means Today* (Princeton: Princeton University Press, 1954), p. 51.

[13] *The License Cases*, 5 Howard 504 (1847), at 583.

[14] Cf. John Coatman, *Police* (London: Oxford University Press, 1959), pp. 1, 14.

a free country, or even in one where any unrestrained intercourse of society is admitted, such a system would of necessity be odious and repulsive, and one which no country could carry into execution. In despotic countries it has never yet succeeded to the extent aimed at by those theorists; and among free people the very proposal would be rejected with abhorrence; it would be a plan which would make every servant of every house a spy on the actions of his master, and all classes of society spies on each other.

And another committee reported thus in 1822 on Peel's proposal for the establishment of a professional police:

It is difficult to reconcile an effective system of police with that perfect freedom of action and exemption from interference which are the great privileges and blessings of society in this country; and your committee think that the forfeiture or curtailment of such advantages would be too great a sacrifice for improvement in police or facilities in detection of crime.[15]

The facts have borne out this picture that the language and expectations of men have painted of the police. Aside from the primitive decentralized system of what has been called "kin police"[16] in which a chief or other ruler delegates the authority to preserve peace and order on the local level to the community as a whole and aside from self-help, widespread throughout history, this power was exercised until the eighteenth century by organized armed forces that were either identical with the regular armed forces or were, except for organizational or functional peculiarities, indistinguishable from them. This

[15] Quoted after Charles Reith, *op.cit.*, pp. 144, 147-148.
[16] Charles Reith, *op.cit.*, p. 20.

was as true of the *cohortes vigilum* that Augustus established as protection against fires, thieves, and robbers[17] as it was true of similar institutions in later periods of history. These military and paramilitary forces were typically oblivious of those piecemeal disturbances of peace and order that are the routine concerns of the police today, but they were put into action whenever there was a major threat to peace and order. The Peterloo massacre of 1818, for instance, resulted from an attempt by the army to perform what we would regard today as a typical police function, that is, the dispersal of a crowd. The same was true of many of the riots that preceded this massacre for almost a century. The same was true even of the American War of Independence.

It was exactly this disproportionate and indiscriminate use of force, the only one an army is capable of, that revealed to an "enlightened" age the inappropriateness of the army as a routine instrument of police power. Either the army would not act at all, leaving the protection of individual rights to self-help, or its intervention would be so devastating as to make the cure worse than the disease. The search for a modern police force was the result of this dilemma, foreshadowing the dilemma with which the availability of nuclear weapons confronts modern nations in their relations with one another.

Thus, professional police forces were established to replace the army, such as was done in Great Britain by virtue of the Act of 1829. Or a segment of the army was transformed into a professional police force; the Texas Rangers and the Canadian Mounted Police are cases in

[17] Joachim Marquardt, *Römische Staatsverwaltung* (2nd ed.; Leipzig: S. Hirzel, 1884), II, 484ff.; Theodor Mommsen, *Römisches Staatsrecht* (4th ed.; Tübingen: Wissenschaftliche Buchgemeinschaft, 1952), 112, 1055ff.

point. Yet it is worthy of note that even the nations that established professional police forces for the purpose of coping with piecemeal disturbances of peace and order have retained armed forces, one of whose major purposes is to meet a major challenge to the legal order and status quo. We look to our armed forces primarily as a protection against foreign enemies, and it is exactly the all-persuasive consensus, making outright challenges to the domestic legal order and status quo at present unlikely, that allows us to look to them that way. Yet even in our society, the state militias, the National Guard, and the Federal army are the foundation stones upon which public peace and order ultimately rest. This becomes obvious in the rare crisis situations, such as Little Rock and the University of Mississippi, in which the police are not able to maintain peace and order, not only because of the magnitude of the challenge but also and most importantly because they prefer a kind of order other than that to be enforced.

While in the United States the armed forces constitute a kind of reserve power that the Federal and state governments can fall back upon in case of emergency, in other countries the armed forces, backing up the regular police in cases of outright challenge against peace and order, are institutionalized into paramilitary organizations. Thus, in France the *gendarmerie nationale* is under the authority of the Ministry of National Defense. So is the *garde républicaine*, which fought as a unit in the two World Wars and in Indochina. The *garde mobile*, created in 1921 to deal with the revolutionary strikes and disturbances of that period, was transformed in 1948 into the Republican Security Companies. The Italian *carabinieri* and Spanish Civil Guards are paramilitary organizations that symbolize and enforce the authority of the state per se rather than perform regular police duties.

In other words, the functions of such paramilitary organizations are primarily political in the sense that they are a visible and effective demonstration of the power of the state for the benefit of the citizenry and particularly of its actually and potentially recalcitrant members. These organizations are generally, as they are intended to be, reliable instruments in the hands of the government. But they can also become a state within the state, pursuing policies of their own. Thus, the police prefect of Paris has at times been able to pursue his own policies in defiance of the French government, since he commands all the police forces of the Department of the Seine and is, for all practical purposes, the head of the municipal government of Paris.

It is revealing that the political purpose of these paramilitary organizations is perfectly understood by the population at large. Those groups of the population, in particular, who either are opposed to the government or the legal order and the status quo or else are alienated from society altogether hate this type of police as an odious instrument of oppression. It has for long been the favored target of collective violence.[18]

Paramilitary political police, which in the *Rechtsstaat* gives symbolic or emergency support to the government, is in modern totalitarian societies developed into a full-fledged institutional system of oppression, administration of justice, punishment, and terror. In Nazi Germany and in the Soviet Union under Stalin, the police established a second state, duplicating and at times superseding

[18] Cf. Bernhard Weiss, *Polizei und Politik* (Berlin: Gersbach u. Sohn, 1928).

the administrative, judicial, and military institutions of the regular one. It was so powerful that it held in awe not only the population at large but also the officials of the regular government. Both Himmler and Beria commanded large well-equipped elite forces that in quality were at least the equal of the regular army. These potent police organizations owed their existence to the lack of confidence—probably unfounded—of Hitler and Stalin in a voluntary consensus that could have supported their rule. distrustful of the regular officials and the people at large, they created a special organization of violence fanatically loyal to themselves, a special state, as it were, with a reliable consensus of its own. This special state imposed peace and order upon the regular state and the population at large with the methods of the totalitarian police state.[19]

AN INTERNATIONAL POLICE FORCE IN A DISARMED WORLD

Applying this analysis and the propositions deduced from it to an international police force in a disarmed world, one must make two assumptions that are likely to prevail regardless of unforeseeable aspects of a disarmed world.

First, the world could be disarmed only in the sense that no nation will be able to wage a major war after the model of the two World Wars. It is generally admitted that nations will retain police forces for the purpose of law enforcement. But it ought to be obvious as well that nations will also retain the paramilitary and military forces necessary for the protection of the legal order and

[19] Cf. E. K. Bramsted, *Dictatorship and Political Police* (London: Kegan, Paul, French, Trubner and Co., 1945); Ernst Fraenkel, *The Dual State* (New York and London: Oxford University Press, 1941).

the domestic status quo itself. The extent of these armed forces will be proportionate to the precariousness of the legal order and the status quo. The more a nation is lacking in stability spontaneously provided by society, the more will it be in need of armed forces to enforce stability. The two types of police will continue to perform for the individual nations the same functions they are performing now.

Second, the day-by-day enforcement of legal rules in the relations among nations will not be appreciably affected by general and complete disarmament. The multitude of unspectacular technical rules of international law that regulate the relations among nations with regard to matters such as diplomatic immunity, territorial limits of sovereignty, and postal and telecommunications are being enforced primarily by the reciprocal self-interest of the nations concerned and under exceptional circumstances through reprisal, retaliation, and judicial determination. This virtually automatic enforcement of legal rules, which makes the intervention of a special police force unnecessary, is not likely to be affected by general and complete disarmament.

THE ENFORCEMENT OF DISARMAMENT

This being so, there is in a disarmed world only one law-enforcing function in the strict sense left for an international police to perform: the enforcement of disarmament itself. This function can require of the international police the performance of four different tasks: control of production and transport of weapons and of military installations, the ascertainment of facts concerning alleged violations, the restoration of the legal status of disarmament after violations, and the punishment of the culprit either individually or collectively in the form of the nation who has allowed or ordered the violation.

The issue of the impartiality of the international police in the performance of these tasks can arise only on the condition that the binding force of the disarmament provisions as such is not in question but that these provisions are generally accepted as legitimate and valid and that what is at issue are piecemeal violations of individual rules either by negligence or intent. In other words, the situation is assumed to be similar to that facing the national police in the day-by-day performance of its law-enforcing functions. In consequence, the issue of impartiality, too, poses itself in similar terms.

If impartiality is the equal treatment of persons and situations that the law requires to be treated without discrimination, then the impartiality of the police rests on two foundations, one objective, the other subjective: efficiency and fairness. A police force that is slipshod in supervision and control, in the collection of evidence and the apprehension of suspects, cannot be trusted to meet the requirements of equal treatment of equal persons and situations, however impartial it intends to be. Its partiality is a function of its inefficiency. It does not know how to be impartial since it does not have the technical competence to identify the persons and situations deserving equal treatment. The remedy lies obviously in the maximization of technical competence and in the establishment of strict inside and outside controls assuring a continuous high level of performance.

The risk of unfairness is inherent in the multinational composition of the international police. It is likely to manifest itself in two different ways. On the one hand, national loyalties and divergent national interests are likely to survive in a disarmed world, however mitigated and neutralized by more comprehensive loyalties and interests. Thus, an international police force must protect the impartial performance of its tasks against distortions that reflect the national preferences of some of its members.

The other risk of unfairness stems from the very desire of the international police, composed primarily of members of uncommitted nations, to be fair. There has been a tendency among uncommitted nations, such as India, to regard themselves almost by definition to be fair with respect to the disputes of other nations and to take an intermediate position in any conflict that does not concern themselves. It has been said that if nation A takes the position that two and two make four and if nation B takes the position that two and two make six, then the neutralist nation, in order to be fair, will commit itself to the proposition that two and two make five. In other words, such a nation equates impartiality with compromise. Yet when it comes to the enforcement of unambiguous legal rules, as those concerning complete and general disarmament are supposed to be, compromise between the legal and the illegal position, far from complying with the requirement of impartiality, actually meets the illegal position half-way. The temptation to confound impartiality with compromise is likely to be particularly strong when the correct assessment of legal responsibility might conjure up a major conflict among great powers.

The remedy for partiality as the result of national bias lies in a judicious national composition of the international police. Two contradictory patterns have been developed by the United Nations, one through the operations in the Congo, the other through those at the southern frontiers of Israel. The rationale underlying both

HANS J. MORGENTHAU

patterns is the exclusion from the police force of those
nationals that can a priori be presumed to be biased by virtue of their national allegiance. Both patterns exclude nationals of the Great Powers, opposing each other in conflict and competition throughout the world, that can be
presumed to be interested in a particular settlement,
favorable to them, of any local issue.

Yet as concerns the actual composition of the police
force, the application of the same rationale has led to
diametrically opposed standards of selection. The Middle
Eastern operation has excluded members of Middle Eastern nations since the latter are all committed to partisan
views of the local issue. The Congo operation, on the
other hand, has preferred contingents from Africa and
Asia, whose sympathetic disinterest and support for
United Nations policies are assumed, while white contingents, especially from former colonial powers, are regarded as less trustworthy, regardless of whether or not
they actually are.

It follows that an international police force needs to
be impartial not only in fact but also in appearance. If
the nation or nations concerned do not trust its impartiality, its actual impartiality will be of little avail. For its
measures will be received, and it will be treated, as though
it were actually lacking in impartiality. Suspicion, however unfounded, will destroy what the requirement of
impartiality aims to create and preserve: the voluntary
acceptance, on the part of the subjects of the law, of the
measures of the police, of the police as an institution, and
of the legal order on behalf of which the police act.

The application of these considerations might require
a flexible composition of the international police force in
view both of its actual impartiality and its reputation for

it. One can imagine as many patterns for its composition as there are situations requiring special attention to the impartiality of the police. For instance, in order to ensure impartiality, the international police force might on occasion have to be composed of contingents of the great powers concerned, operating on the basis of equality, after the model of the quadripartite police operating in Vienna during the occupation.[20] Aside from the interests at stake, the composition of the international police force will depend upon the nature of the issue as presented by the disarmament provisions to be enforced.

We have thus far tried to answer the question of who shall perform the functions of the international police, in order to guard against one of the two possible types of unfairness. We are now raising the question of what freedom of action the international police should have, in order to dispose of both possible types of unfairness. It is obvious that the opportunities for partiality are proportionate to the freedom of action the actor possesses. The more discretion an actor has, the greater are his chances to substitute his own standards of action for those required by the law. Insofar as the law prescribes the equal treatment of persons and situations under certain circumstances defined by itself, the requirements of legality and impartiality coincide. Exclusively concerned in the context of this paper with maximizing the impartiality of the international police, we must emphasize the paramount importance of strict legal standards reducing the discretion of the police to that minimum compatible with the effective performance of its tasks. Two devices serve that purpose: the rule of law and judicial review.

[20] Concerning different types of impartiality, see Georg Simmel, *Sociologie* (München and Leipzig: Duncker and Humblot, 1922), pp. 76ff.

Strict legal rules that clearly define what the police must do, can do, and cannot do under clearly defined circumstances not only maximize the ability of the police to act with impartiality but also increase its reputation for doing so. The parties affected by the action of the police are capable in large measure to determine for themselves whether or not the police have acted with impartiality. I can tell without the benefit of legal counsel that the police who have singled out my home for a search without warrant have acted not only illegally but also with partiality.

Judicial review of the actions of the police serves the same dual purpose of maximizing impartiality and increasing reputation for it. The availability of judicial review will in itself have a restraining influence upon the police. The actual intervention of judicial review will have a corrective effect upon police actions violating the standards of impartiality. Review procedures could be set up within the police organization in a quasi-judicial fashion, or independent courts could determine the legality of police actions, or the two procedures could be combined. Whatever the procedures chosen, the subjection of the police to clearly defined and enforceable legal standards will assimilate the international police as a law-enforcing agency both in its actual operations and in public esteem for the police in a *Rechtsstaat*. That is to say, the international police would attain the highest degree of impartiality with which we are acquainted in the history of the police.

INTERNATIONAL POLICE AS A POLITICAL INSTRUMENT

Even in a disarmed world, conflicts among nations will continue to occur. This will be so even if the conflicts that at present divide the major powers were to be peacefully settled as a precondition for general and complete disarmament. For even then, the distribution of political, social, and economic power will change within and among nations, and the groups benefiting from the status quo and protected by the legal order will be challenged by groups demanding changes in both. Insofar as these conflicts will take place among nations, the international powers-that-be will require a political international police force strong enough to deter potential challengers and to keep actual ones in check. In other words, the political tasks assigned to an "international" police force require a world government with a supranational police force at its disposal.

As has been pointed out, the issue here is not the impartiality of the police but its effectiveness and reliability and, most importantly, the quality of government and of society. In other words, the issue is here political and military; it concerns the viability and nature of world government. The choice will be between a world-wide police state with unprecedented powers of oppression and an ordering of international society in such a way that it will create and maintain a world-wide consensus in support of the legal order and the status quo. If the latter alternative prevails, the world order will repose, as does the domestic order of the *Rechtsstaat*, upon the twin pillars of a political police, to be used only as the ultima ratio of the world government, and of a political, social, and economic order that allows for peaceful change, commands the loyalties of the great majority of mankind, and holds out to them at least the expectation of an approximation to justice.[21]

[21] See Morgenthau, *op.cit.*, pp. 509ff.

PART THREE

SECURITY IN TOTAL DISARMAMENT

INTRODUCTION TO PART THREE

THE three chapters in Part Three deal with a series of issues relating to the appropriate structure of international society once disarmament has successfully taken place. Prior discussions of disarmament have not given much attention to the distinctive problems of governing a world in which national military force has been eliminated but in which inter nation conflict persists. These chapters are concerned not so much with assuring continuing compliance as with creating a political environment that is suitable for the resolution of conflict and for the promotion of national and human interests in a totally disarmed world.

Buried beneath the speculation about how to maintain order and to secure justice in this drastically altered international society is a sharp and crucial disagreement about whether it is necessary or desirable to preserve the sovereign state as the principal actor once disarmament has taken place. This central disagreement fosters others such as the proper role of and the necessary power and authority for supranational institutions of both regional and global scope. Another center of controversy involves the extent to which the disappearance of national military power necessarily implies an accompanying redistribution of wealth and income among states that is designed to reduce the disparity between rich nations and poor nations. As these essays demonstrate, it is possible to envisage a disarmed world either as one that resembles the present world in all respects except that it lacks military establishments or, in contrast, as a world in which the military transformation is accompanied by a series of comparably radical political, social, and economic transformations. The three writers in this section disagree both about the type of disarmed world that is most feasible and about the type that would produce the most beneficial effects. As might be anticipated, the form of a disarmed world proposed by an author as the most feasible is also, to him, the most desirable.

The projection of models of a totally disarmed world may strike some readers as a somewhat remote exercise. Despite its apparent remoteness, the consideration of total disarmament is relevant to present concerns for several reasons. First, both the Soviet Union and the United States have advanced plans for general and complete disarmament that are being studied around the world. These proposals incorporate contrasting images of a disarmed world. Thus, an awareness of this contrast and its implications may induce critical reflections that will lead subsequent proposals for comprehensive disarmament to express more faithfully the true character of national objectives.

Second, increasingly specific thought about a disarmed world makes the prospect seem somewhat less utopian. It brings general and complete disarmament into the realms of analysis where the respected and respectable social scientist works. This may create a more responsible public attitude toward disarmament and help to build the confidence that is needed to make disarmament a realistic goal.

And, third, differing models of a disarmed world contribute to our understanding of contemporary patterns of international relations. The novelist often studies the normal man by creating abnormal character types that highlight the fundamental attributes of human nature by carrying them to stark extremes. So, too, the political analyst may disclose his more fundamental interpretation of patterns of conflict and order in world affairs if he examines these issues in the imaginary setting of total disarmament. By asking what happens after national military establishments have been abolished, one is more or less compelled to consider the function of national power and its threat in the present world system.

Chapter XVI discusses the problem of providing for peaceful change in a disarmed world. It inquires how change is to be facilitated in international relations once states have lost their capability for coercion. Such an inquiry assumes that force currently plays a legislative role and that, in a disarmed world, a legislative equivalent to force must be developed to assure minimum stability. The author's solution discloses his commitment to the need for and desirability of the growth of supranationalism.

Chapter XVII describes and assesses the contrasting Soviet and American conceptions of a disarmed world as they are expressed in their own disarmament proposals. The author tries to identify the defects that are implicit in each view; he then proposes his own alternative, designed to assure the survival of the sovereign state and yet to provide enough centralized power and authority to enforce the disarmament agreement and, to a lesser extent, deal with threats to the peace arising from boundary disputes and breakdowns of internal order.

Chapter XVIII depicts in considerable detail the contrasting attributes of international and supranational models of a disarmed world. This procedure enables a more informed choice to be made about which kind of disarmed world one should aspire to create. It shows rather convincingly that far-reaching consequences follow from this choice. In view of his appraisal of these differing consequences, the author indicates his own preference for the international model of a disarmed world. Although it is not possible to state his rationale in a single sentence, the author seems heavily influenced by his judgment that disarmament becomes both more feasible and more valuable as a policy objective if it is carried on in such a way as to preserve the autonomy and status of the nation-state as the basic mode of political organization in world politics.

CHAPTER XVI

PROVISION FOR PEACEFUL CHANGE
IN A DISARMING WORLD

BY RICHARD A. FALK

I T is generally conceded that security during disarmament involves more than simply an adequate assurance that present adversaries will not cheat. Some authors have examined the questions whether Communism is more likely to spread in a disarming world and whether the danger of minor aggression is likely to grow as the risk of nuclear war is perceived to decline. There is rather less tendency, however, for authors to examine the wider conditions of political stability during drastic disarmament.

In examining the problem of peaceful change, this chapter deals with the importance of premising security in disarmament upon an improving basis of political stability in international society. This discussion will be divided into three parts. First, attention will be given to the problem of peaceful change as it has been perceived in the history of international relations. Second, peaceful change will be treated in the light of the experience of the League of Nations and of the United Nations. And, third, consideration will be given to the kind of advance disarmament planning that can best cope with the need to improve the procedures for peaceful change in a world of disarming—yet still sovereign and often frustrated—states.

*

A stable social order normally combines an apparatus of social control with adequate mechanisms for social change.

This is primarily achieved in a stable and non-totalitarian domestic social order by means of a legislature empowered to initiate and carry forward changes in the legal and social status quo. The international social order, so far as it can be described as a system of order at all, lacks a regularly functioning legislative organ. Force has often acted as the main substitute for legislation in the history of international affairs; even war has played in the past a legislative role by reallocating wealth, territory, and people to accord more closely with new distributions of power and demand. As C. K. Webster has said, "clearly, then, if war is to be averted something must be devised in the future to do what war has done in the past."[1]

A substitute for war has been generally discussed in the literature of international relations under the title of "peaceful change." The concern with peaceful change is far more encompassing than the perfection of peaceful settlement procedures to assure that disputes between states are settled by diplomacy rather than by force.[2] Mechanisms to settle disputes can only be effective if the social system also provides methods to alter the norms

[1] C. K. Webster, "What is the Problem of Peaceful Change?" in *Peaceful Change—An International Problem*, ed. C. A. W. Manning, 6 (1937) [hereafter referred to as Manning]; Lincoln Bloomfield applies this insight to the contemporary world: "If all-out war has been outlawed by the overmastering facts of life, rather than by fiat or treaty, something is needed in its place—a means of change without war. But this is needed not only because the 'law' suffers from an unfortunate 'gap.' It is needed because there has been no outlawry of human nature, of political interests, of social dynamics, or of the willingness of men in the final analysis to fight against odds for their deepest values." *Evolution or Revolution? The United Nations and the Problem of Peaceful Territorial Change*, 19 (1957) [hereinafter referred to as Bloomfield].
[2] For an historical treatment, see C. R. M. F. Cruttwell, A *History of Peaceful Change in the Modern World*, 1937; cf. also Bloomfield, 4-5, 78-84.

by which such settlement is achieved. The subject of peaceful change implies a willingness to deal with the roots of conflict, not just with its overt manifestations. Arnold Toynbee has correctly observed that "if peaceful change is to become the rule, if, that is, it is to occur not simply as an *ad hoc* expedient for staving off some great war or revolution, you must have some regular method for the perpetual redistribution of power, of wealth, of population, and of the goods of this world as well." Toynbee adds, "I am afraid one sees no precedents for this in the history of the past."[3]

Disarmament, at least if it proceeds to advanced stages, is designed to achieve the elimination of military force from international relations. This emphasizes the importance of providing adequate alternative means to achieve peaceful changes. The US Disarmament Proposals of April 18, 1962, oblige "The Parties to the Treaty" in Stage III to "undertake such additional steps and arrangements as were necessary to provide a basis for peaceful change in a disarmed world." This undertaking is not specified in any greater detail, nor are any suggestions given about how to implement peaceful change in a disarming world. At least, however, the relevance of peaceful change to drastic disarmament has been explicitly recognized by the United States in its current proposals.

It is submitted, however, that Stage III is too late. Unless there is established at least by Stage II a reasonable prospect for institutionalizing control over peaceful change of a scope comparable to that suggested in the statement of the preceding paragraph by Arnold Toynbee, then it would be hazardous for states to proceed to Stage III. Probably the methods of assuring peaceful change should

[3] Arnold J. Toynbee, "The Lessons of History" in Manning, 36.

be intensively studied in Stage I and progressively adopted throughout Stage II, although not necessarily within the structure of the disarmament treaty. Unless such steps are taken, it is hard to imagine that sufficient confidence will exist to proceed with disarmament.

The subject of peaceful change has not been extensively debated thus far at the Geneva Disarmament negotiations. Concern was expressed, however, that the supranational regulation of peaceful change might become a pretext for interference in the domestic affairs of sovereign states in a manner forbidden by Article 2(7) of the Charter. The Soviet delegate made an interesting statement:

> These changes vary from country to country, depending on historical, national and economic conditions, and it would be quite unrealistic to believe that this many-sided historical process can be contained within any predetermined framework. . . . The political purpose of such external regulation of the whole varied process of the historical development of individual nations and countries can only be to delay the progressive development of society and to impede the national liberation movement and the far-reaching social and economic changes which are in progress and which must inevitably come about in the different countries of the world.[4]

This can be construed either as a trust in the spontaneous forces of history or as an insistence that the paths of the "indirect aggressor" be kept clear. Soviet patterns of practice show an unwillingness to tolerate spontaneous political developments, except as a last resort. Certainly, it is

[4] ENDC/P.V. 17 (April 10, 1962), p. 21, quoted by Alan F. Neidle in "Peace-Keeping and Disarmament," 57 *American Journal of International Law*, 46, 52 (1963).

difficult to reconcile the Soviet response in 1956 to the Hungarian uprising with Mr. Zorin's affirmation of the need to protect the dynamics of national self-determination from supranational interference.

From the perspective of the international system, change is "peaceful" so long as international violence does not accompany it. In fact, it is generally the case that coercive tactics are very often employed to make the will of the more powerful state effective with regard to the weaker one. Frederick Dunn has expressed the view that "Since the subject of peaceful change often involves the revision of a treaty or the alteration of a boundary, such agreements are generally very difficult to reach. Hence in the past there has been frequent recourse to various kinds of coercion, including subversion, political agitation leading to local insurrection, and all-out war."[5] As this comment suggests, a nation will often couple its demands for a revision of the international status quo with coercive tactics designed to bring to power an elite willing to accede to the demand. Certainly, the use of the Fifth Columns by Hitler was a means of obtaining peaceful changes of the most sweeping kind. It is obvious that the ascription of the attribute "peaceful" should not necessarily be taken to imply a "voluntary" undertaking by the two states. In the history of international relations, peaceful change has generally meant any change that was not a direct or indirect consequence of an international war, including a major peace settlement. This historical connotation should be kept distinct from the idealistic connotation that conceives of peaceful change as a species of international legislative action. The idealistic usage

[5] Frederick S. Dunn, "Peaceful Change Today," World Politics, XI (1958-1959), 279.

remains a wish, perhaps an expectation, that has been rarely realized to any appreciable extent in the practice of states. States continue to guard jealously whatever legal rights they presently possess, regardless of arguments of social justice or international peace that are advanced to support demands for revision and relinquishment, unless the demands are backed up by a willingness and capability to use or threaten superior force.

The traditional academic treatment of peaceful change has been restricted to revisions of the international status quo involving the rights and duties of more than one state. Typical instances involved the revision of treaties, the redelimitation of boundaries, accommodations of popular pressure, the protection and migration of minorities, access to markets, to raw materials, or to water, restoration of territory lost by conquest, and tariff adjustments. The concept of peaceful change is extended in this essay to include *internal* revisions that concern the rights and duties of only a single state. For example, international efforts to prevent the practice of genocide or systematic suppressions of races are considered here to be part of the subject of peaceful change.

The attainment of the objectives associated with the history of peaceful change has often meant recourse to various forms of minor coercion. This has been even more obviously true since the advent of the nuclear age has made so hazardous the pursuit of national objectives by recourse to war or major instruments of coercion. The use of violence as a political instrument for the conduct of world politics has thus had to conform to the new and more subtle patterns of coercion that we identify as "indirect aggression and subversion." If one considers the changed role of violence, it seems clear that the regulation of indirect aggression and subversion involves far more than meeting "the Communist menace." It demands the fashioning of effective institutions and procedures to make peaceful change increasingly more peaceful. More than this, it requires nations to be willing to allow an unfavorable revision of their legal rights and duties, perhaps to endure a redetermination of the scope of their territorial domain or of their discretion to exclude and admit aliens; it requires deep inroads into the traditional preserve of national sovereignty. Formerly, these inroads were almost always forged by external coercion or its threat. Can states now be persuaded to participate in a system that makes inroads by enforced supranational decision or by voluntary acquiescence? Nothing short of this seems likely to extirpate the roots of international conflict and to create the basis for stability in a disarming world.

Two distinctions have been assumed valid in thinking about peaceful change that warrant added examination now in view of the contemporary international situation: (1) the limited usefulness of the distinction between peace and war in the context of peaceful change; and (2) the diminishing relevance of the distinction between internal and international warfare.

The distinction between peace and war is misleading for the contemporary world since violent change is a pervasive aspect of international relations despite the infrequency of recourse to formal belligerency. In the context of disarmament, peaceful change must come, at least gradually, to mean more than the absence of war in its old-fashioned sense. This extra meaning requires a gradual strengthening of the control exercised over the use of indirect aggression and other forms of minor coercion.

RICHARD A. FALK

Unless, however, we are prepared and, what is even more unlikely, the other more revisionist states are prepared to accept a petrified status quo, with all the dangers of collapse that this implies, we must find new substitutes for the dynamism provided by the threat or use of national force. A significant kind of substitute would be a gradual enlargement of the legislative competencies of regional and global international organizations, together with a commensurate increase in supranational enforcement capability. It is not necessary to banish force altogether from history but merely to increase the community management of its use. The danger to the stability of disarmament comes not from change through force but from changes that are achieved or attempted by unauthorized national applications of force across borders.

The distinction between international and national political violence has lost much of its significance as the pursuit of national power has become a battle for hegemonic influence rather than for territory. The "satellites" of Eastern Europe retain their national identity and international personality although the shift in their political status is a crucial instance of "peaceful change" that has been accomplished and sustained as a consequence of Soviet coercion. Thus, purely "internal" changes may have critical "international" significance and should not be exempted from the subject of peaceful change by reference to the norms or policies that have given rise to the doctrines of non-intervention, self-determination, and jurisdiction. As a concept of international community welfare begins to develop, the adoption or retention of domestic policies and practices that violate fundamental human rights, as defined by a consensus of states, is

354

likely to become increasingly a matter of international concern that generates a demand, supported by coercion, for domestic compliance. That is, the problem of peaceful change includes mechanisms to assure that changes are brought about *within* states by means *other than* the application or threat of *superior national force*, as well as to assure that processes are developed for making changes as a result of disputes *between* states. The acceptance of this interpretation would effectuate a radical transformation of the traditional relationship between national sovereignty and international order.

*

The history of supranational institutions in the twentieth century indicates some awareness that the maintenance of international peace cannot be divorced from the problems of peaceful change. The Covenant of the League of Nations contained Article 19, a heroic bid to confer an inchoate competence upon an international organization to advise on changes in any international status quo:

> Article 19. The Assembly may from time to time advise reconsideration by Members of the League of treaties which have become inapplicable and the consideration of international conditions whose continuance might endanger the peace of the world.

As Lauterpacht remarked, "there ought to be no doubt— although such doubts have been repeatedly raised—that the article is wide enough to embrace all claims for the change of the existing *status quo* arising out of a treaty or otherwise."[6] But despite this apparent breadth of scope, Article 19 conferred on the League Assembly the author-

[6] Hersh Lauterpacht, "The Legal Aspect" in Manning, 153.

ity only to advise upon changes. It is interesting to ponder why states eager to challenge the fundamental status quo failed to invoke Article 19.[7] For instance, as Bloomfield observes, "Article 19 was never once invoked by those who sought to revise the Versailles settlement."[8] Lauterpacht noted that "the potentialities of that article are admittedly small, but recourse to its procedure could not possibly have weakened the case of the State asking for a change in the law—if they had a case." In view of this, why was it not invoked? Lauterpacht gives this explanation: "The fact is that such life as it could legitimately expect to enjoy departed from Article 19 as soon as it became established that force and unilateral change are possible within the League and that their reward is not punishment and repression, but success—which consideration shows the intimate link between peaceful change and collective security."[9] That is, if Hitler and Mussolini can defy the League by the successful use of force to achieve their ends, then there is little incentive for a powerful state to assert its demands through such a dilatory and uncertain medium as Article 19. If the expectations of satisfaction are small under Article 19 and if favorable alternative ways exist to achieve the desired changes, then why bother with an appeal to an international organization?

The United Nations Charter makes a veiled reference to the heritage of peaceful change in Article 14:

Subject to the provisions of Article 12 [Security Council preemption], the General Assembly may recommend

[7] The two instances in which Article 19 was invoked are briefly described by Lauterpacht in Manning, 155-156.

[8] Bloomfield, 40.

[9] Lauterpacht in Manning, 156.

measures for the peaceful adjustment of any situation, regardless of origin, which it deems likely to impair the general welfare or friendly relations among nations, including situations resulting from a violation of the provisions of the present Charter setting for the Purposes and Principles of the United Nations.

Articles 73 and 74 incorporate an anti-colonial bias that should be read as a willingness to accept some changes in the status quo as part of the Charter framework. As Bloomfield phrases it, ". . . the United Nations, instead of being wedded to the *status quo* had a distinct bias in favor of 'change' and of 'progress.' "[10] Certainly, the existence and the activity of the United Nations have hastened the process of decolonialization in the Afro-Asian world by adding its more subtle variety of coercion to the internal and external pressures, often including tactics of violence, that persuaded the colonial powers to relinquish one colony after another.

Nevertheless, the problem of peaceful change is far from solved by the existence and activity of the United Nations. Many nations are dissatisfied with their present situation and display no inclination to refrain from a coercive solution whether or not it is authorized by a consensus of United Nations Members.

The Clark-Sohn proposals for a revised Charter suggest two changes in Article 14.[11] First, the General Assembly's recommending power would no longer be restricted by Article 12. And, second, a provision is added requiring Members "to give prompt and due consideration to any recommendation . . . and to report as soon as

[10] Bloomfield, 14.
[11] Grenville Clark and Louis Sohn, *World Peace Through World Law* (2nd rev. ed), 49-50.

practicable what action it has taken with reference thereto, or, if no action has been taken, its reasons therefor."[12] The Clark-Sohn comment to this provision observes that no sanction is provided for a failure to heed the recommendation, but if the situation is likely "to endanger international peace and security," then the General Assembly could refer it to any of several organs available in their renovated United Nations World Conciliation Board, International Court of Justice, World Equity Tribunal—and thereafter a decision of the Court or recommendation of the Tribunal might then, "under careful safeguards," be enforced.[13]

Presumably, this kind of structure, if effectively implemented, would add greatly to the capacity of the organized community to legislate various changes in the international status quo. Whether these changes would eliminate opportunities to promote change by recourse to indirect aggression is impossible to predict. This would depend, among other things, upon the political control and direction of the organization. Bloomfield's study not surprisingly suggests that "the record of interpretations placed on Article 14 in debates tends to confirm the predominance of political interest over issues of intrinsic legality."[14] It is hard to image reliance upon non-political criteria if the competence involves revising the status quo in light of other considerations. But, if this is true, what criterion is available to distinguish between beneficial and detrimental changes? The answer is left vague in the discussion and practice of international organizations. Practice suggests that beneficial change consists of what the majority of states feel it necessary or desirable to do; peaceful change, in the context of United Nations co-

12 *Idem,* at 49-50.   13 *Idem,* at 50.   14 Bloomfield, 117.

ercion, has been based on the issues that can attract an ardent and overwhelming consensus. When indirect aggression is used by nations to implement this consensus, then the organization has tended to tolerate it, not abet it, for example, on anti-colonial issues.

*

What is generally described as peaceful change includes changes that are brought about primarily by means of indirect aggression, that is, by force that is not so visible as to be perceived as an armed attack by one state upon another. Yet presumably, in the context of disarmament, peaceful change must be increasingly made to mean change that does not depend upon the export of national force across an international boundary either directly or indirectly. But why will a nation be willing to deny itself the benefits of a favorable status quo except by force? It would seem that either a new altruistic disposition must arise among nations or supranational coercion must be made available and effective as a substitute for national coercion. Another alternative would be virtually to do away with change after disarmament commences, although as the world is now constituted the effect would be merely to postpone change until revisionist claims accumulate to a point of explosion. The containment of change does not seem to be a safe way to plan disarmament. This is especially obvious in view of the widespread strife and misery in the Afro-Asian and Latin American worlds. The pressure to change the character of relations between states, within states, and in the overall structure of international society seems likely to induce political violence unless a non-coercive alternative is accepted and developed.

In my view the most constructive alternative involves the gradual endowment of international institutions with legislative functions. This process has started already. It is not without its difficulties, some of them grave,[15] but it is nevertheless the most promising alternative. My argument to authorize international institutions to implement peaceful change can be summarized as follows: significant disarmament requires the development of a legislative substitute for the "peaceful" changes that are now achieved primarily by means of minor coercion, world public opinion, and national interventions. This legislative competence must be located in supranational institutions, most probably in the United Nations. Soviet opposition to the further growth of supranational institutions adds to the difficulty of developing the kind of legislative action that is deemed essential for the stability of the later stages of disarmament. To assert the relevance and necessity for improved methods of peaceful change does not argue for their inclusion in the disarmament treaty itself. The problem should be considered a part of the wider need to establish an international environment suitable for disarmament. This environment can only be created by action and events that are formally independent of a disarmament treaty in every respect. The nature and magnitude of the adaptation of the international environment to a disarming world is such that fundamental shifts in attitudes must take place. It is naïve to suppose that rules and procedures that are agreed upon can lead actors in international affairs to accept a new set of parameters for the perception and pursuit of their interests. A more fundamental reorientation must first take place.

[15] For an elaboration of some of these difficulties see Falk, "Janus Tormented: The International Law of Internal War," in James N. Rosenau, *International Aspects of Civil Strife* (1964).

CHAPTER XVII
CONFLICTING NATIONAL INTERESTS IN
ALTERNATIVE DISARMED WORLDS

BY ARTHUR I. WASKOW

A MONG the major stumbling blocks to the achievement
of disarmament is the uncertainty of national governments as to how the world would look at the end of
the disarmament process. Specifically, two questions seem
most critical: (1) How could national governments without arms protect and advance the national interests?
(2) How could an institution be created that would have
sufficient power to enforce disarmament without illegiti-
mately intruding upon spheres of action reserved by the
national governments as within their own competence?

Close examination of the two most extensive proposals
yet made by national governments on general and complete disarmament (the United States "Outline of Basic
Provisions of a Treaty on General and Complete Disarmament in a Peaceful World" and the Soviet Union "Treaty
on General and Complete Disarmament under Strict International Control") indicates that somewhat different
answers are proposed to these two critical questions.
Neither the American nor the Soviet proposal, however,
is sufficiently detailed to indicate that either government
has fully examined the issue and foreclosed changes in its
position. From a careful analysis of the two plans and
of the various difficulties that might arise if each were
put into effect, it may be possible to construct a third
model that would meet at least some of the possible difficulties.

The United States proposals seem to be based on the belief that, in a world where resort to armed force has been ruled out as a means of pursuing national interests, the only way of coping with national conflicts is to provide for their resolution through international institutions. Further, the American proposals seem to regard punishment by a world institution as the major sanction to be used to prevent rearmament.

The American proposals therefore look toward a transformation of the nation-state system into something approximating a world federal system. The institution intended to enforce disarmament, the "United Nations Peace Force," would be given "sufficient armed forces and armaments so that no state could challenge it." All states would accept the compulsory jurisdiction of the International Court of Justice to decide international legal disputes. "Rules of international conduct related to disarmament" would be codified, as would rules against "indirect aggression and subversion." It is not specified how these rules would be authoritatively interpreted and enforced, but the existence in combination of an unchallengeable peace force and a compulsory international court would indicate that such rules would be interpreted and enforced upon all states by this complex of international institutions. Whatever the legal and constitutional arrangements, the existence of a peace force so strong that "no state could challenge it" would be likely to transfer the power to make many political decisions from the nations to the complex of world institutions.

In addition, the existence of such a powerful peace force would almost certainly require the establishment of a highly effective quasi-governmental institution to control the peace force itself. Such an institution would be necessary for the same reason that there is at present great concern for preserving "civilian command and control" over the military use of nuclear weapons: the fear that unofficial political decisions might be taken within the armed force itself that would transform it into an independent political force, along the lines of the Praetorian Guard or certain elements of the French Army in recent years. To prevent such independent acts, a powerful peace force would need extremely effective controlling political institutions that would, in fact if not in name, comprise a government.

Certain problems can be imagined in the management of a world thus constituted. Most of these problems can be traced to the unlikelihood of achieving among the present conflicting interests in the world a sufficient political consensus on which to construct either a government or a series of peace-keeping institutions with quasi-governmental authority to manage a large army and settle political disputes between nations.

What is meant by such a consensus is either agreement on a future image of the way the world should look and run or agreement on the kinds of political institutions and rules within which a disagreement on the future could be worked out in practice. Either sort of consensus (on political substance or political procedures) would require a partial surrender of the right and power to make independent national definitions of the national interest or of the means to be used in advancing the national interest.

The present outlook does not seem good for such a consensus among many states whose participation would be crucial to a disarmament agreement. Between the Soviet Union and the Federal Republic of Germany, between the

People's Republic of China and the United States, and between Nigeria and the Republic of South Africa, for example, there does not seem to be any likely useful consensus on an image of the future world. Nor does any consensus seem at present to exist on the sorts of political institutions that each major state would think to be worthy of its trust as procedural bases for pursuing its national interest.

It is sometimes argued that the achievement of a worldwide disarmament agreement would itself create a broader consensus on each level—procedural and substantive. It is possible, but not at all certain, that this would occur. It is also conceivable, for example, that states that are now willing to allow to a number of international institutions some limited authority to decide certain limited political questions are willing to do so precisely because they feel that both their own possession of armed power and the international authority's lack of it give them an automatic protection against enforcement of such international decisions, whenever they choose to consider that such decisions threaten their own vital interests. If this situation were to be transformed so that the state had too little armed force to prevent an international institution from enforcing its decisions, the state might be less ready to concede even the present authority to make political decisions to international bodies. In this fashion, the expectation and consideration of a disarmament agreement might bring about in some states a reduction, not an increase, in the willingness to permit certain decisions to be made by international institutions and therefore a reduction, rather than an increase, in the amount of political consensus on which could be built institutions capable of controlling a world army.

It is also sometimes argued that no disarmament agreement will be reached unless and until the political climate in conflicting states has changed so much that not only agreement on disarmament per se but adequate political agreements could be achieved sufficient to establish political institutions capable of controlling a world army. This argument raises the question whether the achievement of disarmament per se is separable from settlement of political conflicts.

In view of the way in which various governments have during the last fifteen years distinguished the problem of arms control and disarmament from the pursuit of their national interests, it is at least conceivable that agreement on disarmament and political agreements are separable. It may well be that many governments now regard disarmament not as a way of establishing a world order acceptable to all nations, but as a way of changing the means of independently pursuing the national interest. This view of disarmament would assume that states had taken into account both the increasing danger involved in using military means of advancing the national interest, because of the scale of modern weaponry, and the increasing difficulty of actually using military means, because of the increasing deterrent effect of the large-scale weaponry. In other words, the interest in disarmament may have arisen from a growing acceptance of "the hypertrophy of war" as a means rather than from a growing acceptance of world order as an end. In the event that this view has directed the attention of some governments to the possibility of achieving disarmament, such governments may not regard it as necessary or desirable to change their political goals as a concomitant of changing from military to other means of pursuing those goals.

If this view of disarmament as a means be taken by several or possibly even one of the major states, it is possible to see that agreement on disarmament could be made an issue separable from agreement on political settlements. And it is thus possible to imagine a situation in which neither as a prerequisite to nor as a result of a disarmament agreement is there any enlargement of the area of political consensus among states. In that case, to recapitulate the previous argument, the absence of sufficient political consensus may prevent the establishment of international political institutions capable of effectively controlling an armed force so large as to be a world army or to be capable of resolving conflicts among nations.

Insistence by the United States on establishing a world army and an approximation of world federation as preconditions to disarmament is likely, therefore, in the first instance to frustrate efforts to achieve disarmament.

If the conditions were accepted, we might expect attempts to be made by each state to protect its national interests by means of penetrating and taking over the decision-making apparatus of the army, with one of two results: (1) Success by one state in establishing control over the world army, so that its decisions favor one major interest in the world against others. (2) Failure of any one of the competing states to succeed, resulting in stalemate and paralysis of the official decision-making apparatus, so that an unofficial political apparatus arises within the army itself and it becomes an independent political force.

The second possibility would clearly be contrary to American interests. The first, however, might either serve or disserve American interests, depending on whether the

United States or some other state were able to establish control over the world army. It may well be that official estimates of probable distributions of world power have suggested to the United States government that it would be more likely than any opponent to establish control over the world army and to dominate world federal institutions. Since the construction of disarmament proposals by all nations is probably heavily influenced by considerations of how to protect the national interests in a disarmed world, it may well be a calculation of American predominance that suggests to the United States the usefulness of a world federal model for enforcing disarmament. If the estimate of American predominance were incorrect, of course, the establishment of a world army would be a disaster to American national interests; and if the achievement of general disarmament were considered among the goals of the United States, the frustration of this goal because of American insistence on a world federal model would be a defeat for American policy.

*

On the Soviet side, rejection of the American model is probably connected with a Soviet estimate of power relations in the disarmed world that is in many ways consonant with the American estimate. The Soviet image of the disarmed world is quite different from that of the United States. The Soviet proposals seem to be based on the belief that, in a world where resort to armed force has once been ruled out as a means of pursuing national interests, intense conflicts can be pursued without either using organized military force or resorting to agreed international institutions for achieving settlements of disputes. Further, the Soviet proposals seem to regard the provision to all states of full information about all military affairs as the major sanction to be used to prevent rearmament. The use of information as a sanction would seem to be based on the belief that nations would realize that a resort to rearmament would precipitate a renewed arms race and on the belief that fear of a renewed arms race would deter any nation from "striking first" to rearm. The Soviet proposals do not mention prohibition of such non-military means of carrying on conflicts as indirect aggression or subversion, nor do they mention the International Court of Justice.

As for the international policing of disarmament, the Soviets suggest that (in addition to the inspection services of the International Disarmament Organization) there would exist only national militia units "placed at the disposal of the Security Council" and under the command of "representatives of the three principal groups of states existing in the world," each group to have equal representation and all questions to be decided by unanimous agreement. Thus, in contradiction to American plans for a peace force that would in effect be a world army, the Soviets do not propose to create any armed forces that would be outside the immediate effective control of the national governments.

This model of the future disarmed world would clearly not create the same problems that would be involved in a federal world government or a world army so large as to require a "government" to control it. Evidently, the Soviets discount the possibility and value of such world institutions, probably, in general terms, on precisely the grounds suggested above—that there is no adequate political consensus in existence capable of supporting such political institutions—and, in specific terms, on the ground of fear that a world army and world federal institution would come under American or Western control. As a substitute for resolution of conflicts between nations by a world quasi-government, the Soviets seem to see the heated pursuit of national ends by all means short of rearmament and the resolution of conflicts by the non-military victory of one or the other party.

The problems that might arise in the management of a world constituted according to the Soviet proposals would be quite different from those that might arise in the American world. Most of these problems can be traced to the unlikelihood of preserving disarmament by the use of information as the sole sanction in a world where the states would be heatedly pursuing a series of intense conflicts.

In the absence of any more powerful sanctions than those of full inspection and revelation by the International Disarmament Organization, the outlook would not seem good for preserving the non-military character of conflicts, say, between the Soviet Union and the Federal Republic of Germany, between the People's Republic of China and the United States, or between Nigeria and the Republic of South Africa. Even if such conflicts were to begin as economic, political, or propaganda struggles, an approaching "victory" by one or the other side might well drive the weaker party into rearmament. The only obstacle to such rearmament would be the knowledge that other states would also rearm. But in the despair bred of an impending defeat, this knowledge would not be likely to deter the weaker state from rearming.

It might be argued that, once accomplished, disarmament would itself so change the internal political structures of many nations that they would find themselves incapable of rearming. Indeed, the belief that this would be the result of disarmament may be the Soviet analogue to the belief held in support of the American approach that disarmament would soften political conflicts between nations and thus contribute to achieving international political consensus. In other words, the assumption behind the Soviet plan may be that disarmament would bring about a transformation in internal politics; the assumption behind the American plan, that disarmament would bring about a transformation in international politics.

Just as the transformation expected by the American proposals is possible but not at all certain, so is the transformation expected by the Soviet proposals. It is quite conceivable that, contrary to this expectation, political groups that now attach themselves to the preservation of arms would find other programs just as useful to their continuation in power. For example, the expectation that control of the populace (in some countries) or expansion of the economy (in others) is dependent upon the preservation of the military system may well be mistaken. Controls over information and expenditures on outer space, to name two possibilities, might well replace the weapons systems as a means of social and economic control.

If powerful political groups were indeed able to make such substitutions for arms a part of their own "armory," then the belief that disarmament would bring such groups tumbling from power is an incorrect assumption. Remaining in power in a disarmed world, these groups might find their ability to reinstitute an arms race little impaired if there were no world institutions challenging a decision to rearm.

It might also be argued that no disarmament agreement can possibly be reached in the first place unless and until there has been a political transformation within present armed states, involving so great a change that present power groups in control of the state machinery of violence would be cast out of power and replaced by groups with deep-rooted commitments to oppose the military system. But during the last fifteen years, powerful political groups in various countries have begun to treat disarmament not as an absurd demand of powerless and irresponsible out-groups, but as an item in their own programs, to be pursued by official agencies and semiofficial pressure groups. In this way, pressures for disarmament have begun to be separated from pressures for radical internal political change. For these reasons, disarmament might be achieved without major political changes in some of the Great Powers. Again there would, in the absence of a world enforcement institution, be little external reason for such politically unchanged states to remain disarmed if they were in desperate fear of losing a political struggle with some other nation in the disarmed world.

The Soviets apparently assume that disarmament would be connected with internal political changes in many nations. This assumption is probably tied to a Soviet expectation that Communist movements would benefit from such changes. Just as the official American (and Soviet) view seems to be that Western interests could predominate in a world federal institution, so the official Soviet view may well be that Soviet interests would prevail in a fluid, no-holds-barred conflict without military restraints. And the United States government may share this view and may be rejecting the Soviet model, in part, for this reason.

Insistence by the Soviet Union upon its model of the disarmed world is likely, therefore, in the first instance to frustrate efforts to achieve disarmament. If the achievement of disarmament be considered among the goals of the Soviet Union, the frustration of this goal because of Soviet insistence on a no-policing model would be a defeat for Soviet policy. In the second instance, if the no-policing conditions were for some reason accepted, the struggle for political power with no holds barred might result in great political gains for the Soviets—or in major political disaster for them. Political disaster could result if the Soviet estimates of success in no-holds-barred conflict happen to be incorrect, if anti-Soviet forces swept over countries presently in Soviet control or alliance, and if in the absence of a police institution such countries decided to rearm. In short, intense competition in an unpoliced disarmed world could conceivably produce a rearmed world in which the Soviets were confronted with a heavy relative disadvantage.

These successive reviews of the American and Soviet proposals for enforcing disarmament and managing political conflict in the disarmed world suggest that there are complementary defects and strengths in the two plans. In terms of the political interests involved, each of the plans seems to include a built-in political advantage for the state proposing it as regards its efforts to advance its political interests in a disarmed world. But each plan, it should be noted, would spell political disaster for the proposing nation if that nation's political estimates happened to be incorrect. Thus, the creation of a world army might be a political disaster for the United States if the United States proved unable to control it; and the absence of any effective institution able to police disarmament might spell political disaster for the Soviet Union if Soviet clients and allies lost an intense political competition whose victors could then rearm without fear of punishment. A workable plan, therefore, would neither offer one side a built-in political advantage nor make total political disaster a likely result if either side's expectations were disappointed.

The specific defect in the American plan is its vision of supranational political institutions capable of resolving political conflicts by making and enforcing its own political decisions; its strength is the assumption that some sort of world institution would be necessary to enforce disarmament. The defect of the Soviet plan is its vision of the enforcement of disarmament solely by means of the provision of full information; its strength is the assumption that political struggle between nations would be carried on without adjudication by international or supranational institutions.

The problem then is whether it is possible to conceive and invent the sort of world institution that could enforce disarmament without becoming the umpire of political disputes. If this is possible, then one may imagine the achievement of world disarmament without either a transformation in the international political system, as envisioned by the United States, or a transformation in the internal political systems of some states, as envisioned by the Soviet Union. If a non-governmental world institution to enforce disarmament cannot be invented, then it seems probable that disarmament will have to await the achievement (or readiness in all states for the achievement) of the one transformation or the other.

The world institution should, therefore, be incapable of adjudging political disputes or of imposing a solution in such disputes, but it should have sufficient power to damp down immediate dangers to the peace that pose an urgent threat of inspiring rearmament and should, further, have enough power to nullify an actual attempt at rearmament. In other words, the amount of power and authority available to the world institution should range from wide authority and considerable power to cope with an actual violation of the disarmament agreement, down to no authority and inadequate power to cope with an international political dispute that does not seem to threaten rearmament.

Neither of the extremes in this range of power and authority is hard to work out. At the one extreme, deterring or putting an end to direct violations of the disarmament agreement would not usually require a large force, if the enforcement effort were directed solely and precisely at ending the violation rather than at punishing the violators or humiliating their government. So long as the violators knew that any resistance to a small initial enforcement effort would be highly likely to encourage other nations to approve the use of a larger force against the violation, escalation by the violator would be unlikely. Thus, the amount of power directly brought to bear in a particular case to enforce disarmament should be closely correlated with the amount of international consensus available to uphold the use of more force. A sizable but carefully limited amount of force would be available to the world institution, and the increasing use of that amount would depend upon increasing levels of agreement by the major powers and interests in the world.[1]

At the other end of the range of power and authority available to the world institution, it would be kept wholly incapable of dealing with most political conflicts between nations. No doubt there would be many occasions on which intense conflict between the still-independent states would lead to confrontations somewhat similar to traditional wars. Having given up traditional war, however, the states would have to settle such disputes by other means.

In such situations, the results might be remarkably similar to those obtained in the 1950's and 1960's when certain kinds of war were "abolished" not by agreement but by deterrence and fear. In other words, the sub-war or quasi-war exercise of national power by means of propaganda, subversion, economic aid, economic embargo or boycott, espionage, bribery, etc., may occur in the disarmed as well as in the hyperarmed world.

Giving the world institution the power to intervene in the use of such non-lethal equivalents of war would almost inevitably be equivalent to giving it world governmental power to interfere in domestic political and economic affairs. In order to avoid giving the world institution power over such activities, many national activities that are now considered illegitimate under international law may have to be made fully legitimate or at least deliberately ignored. In other words, if "violent" and "lethal" activities are spelled out as illegitimate in great detail (as they would be in a disarmament agreement), many "non-

[1] See Arthur I. Waskow, *Quis Custodiet? Controlling the Police in a Disarmed World* (Peace Research Institute, 1963) and see Roger Fisher, Chapter XIII in this volume, for further discussion of this approach to police enforcement of disarmament.

lethal" activities might have to be spelled out as legitimate, perhaps newly so.

Some analogies to the process here suggested may be seen in the way some national governments over the last one hundred years have gone about eliminating violence from labor-management disputes. Just as certain forms of propaganda and economic pressure are of doubtful legitimacy under international law today, so the strike was of doubtful legitimacy under national law a century ago. The result was that when strikes did occur, they frequently involved considerable violence. The process of law-making during the past century tended to make a careful and rigid distinction between the strike as economic pressure and the use of private violence by labor or management. It was made clearer and clearer that sheer economic pressure was legal, and also clearer and clearer that sheer violence was illegal and would be punished. The clear *permission* to engage in economic struggle had a great deal to do with acceptance of the clear *prohibition* on violence. The government was essentially saying that it would allow labor and management to swing their own weight without let or hindrance, so long as they did not use violence. An international agreement along the same pattern would mean the legalization of many forms of pressure now considered only semilegitimate, along with precise outlawry and punishment of violence.[2]

It should be pointed out that in recent years in many Western countries there has been movement in the direction of having governmental or "neutral" settlement of strikes, rather than allowing them to be settled by

[2] For discussion of a similar process in American racial conflict, see Arthur I. Waskow, *From Race Riot to Sit-in, 1919 and the 1960's: A Study in the Connections between Conflict and Violence* (Doubleday, 1965).

sheer exercise of relative power. But this development came *after* that described above. It is not impossible to imagine that in a disarmed world, a succession of economic and political quasi-wars would stir some future generation to turn the "police-only" international institution into a true government, with power to intervene in political and economic struggles between governments. But it should be remembered that such a development could arise only from a far higher level of world consensus than now exists.

In the meantime, between the two poles of lethal behavior (to be strictly forbidden) and politico-economic conflict (to be vigorously encouraged), there seems likely to be a most troublesome gray area. Two sorts of quasi-political disturbances seem most likely to bring on rearmament: border incursions and domestic civil wars.

Let us imagine several possible situations. A small country that is far from its allies and is surrounded by larger hostile states is, simultaneously with its enemies, disarmed. It and its enemies are permitted to keep X men under arms per 1,000 population, in order to keep internal order. But before the disarmament agreement went into effect, the small nation had been armed to the teeth with its own and its allies' men, whereas its enemies had kept a far smaller proportion of its men in the armed forces. Now its enemies can divert their legal internal police to the conquest of the small country, since the small country's internal police are fewer than theirs. Or the larger states can simply have thousands of women and children "walk in" on their neighbor's territory and set up housekeeping. Should the international police force remain quiet, simply because the agreement on arms production has not been violated?

Or again: a major civil war begins in an underdeveloped country with rich but untapped resources. Two separate "governments" claim the right to form from their own adherents the internal police provided under the disarmament agreement and to manufacture the legal quota of arms. Some major states that have been struggling for the allegiance and alliance of the underdeveloped country begin to sell arms to the warring governments, each claiming that it is selling only in amounts legal under the disarmament agreement and only to the true government. Should the international police force remain aloof?

Each of these examples, added to the world history of the last fifteen years, suggests that two missions in addition to arms-elimination are likely to concern an international police force: the restoration of internal order in situations where domestic disorders involve other nations and threaten the peace; and the protection of international boundaries from incursions by lightly armed or unarmed forces.

Neither of these missions is self-evidently essential for an international police force that is primarily concerned with enforcing disarmament. "Walk-ins" by unarmed men into the territory of a weaker neighbor could conceivably be tolerated on the ground that weaker neighbors would have to think up their own unarmed means of defense or suffer the classic fate of weaker neighbors: to lose "wars" to their stronger enemies. Domestic civil wars could conceivably be tolerated on the ground that to intervene would be a worse remedy than the disease, and nations in turmoil could be allowed to suffer their classic fate: bitterness, division, atrocities, misery, and brotherly hatred. Yet both these situations seem more likely to breed re-armament than do propaganda wars, economic embargoes,

378

or even espionage. Somehow threats to the national territory and struggles for control over the symbols of governmental legitimacy seem to release the dammed-up springs of violence more easily than most other forms of conflict. For that reason, it seems likely that there will be a considerable amount of pressure in the disarmed world to cope with a Congo crisis, a Kashmir crisis, and a Sinai crisis before such crises could revive the arms race—just as there has been such pressure in the hyper-armed world to cope with these crises before they could escalate into war.

Political arrangements for an international police force might therefore include arrangements to carry out the missions of coping with internal disorder that becomes a threat to the peace and of coping with boundary incursions. These preparations might be made, even if other sorts of conflict—such as propaganda wars, competitive economic aid and boycotts, and even espionage—are specifically exempted from the jurisdiction of the international police force (as suggested above). But preparing to cope with internal disorder and border incursions that might breed rearmament need not be of as high an order of priority as preparation by the international force to enforce the disarmament agreement itself.

For that reason, it might be made more difficult for international force to be applied to the domestic-order and national-boundary missions than to the arms-eliminating one. In other words, a given level of force could be dispatched to cope with an arms violation upon agreement of fewer nations than would be required if the same level of force were being dispatched to deal with a boundary or domestic-order problem. Such an arrangement would recognize the centrality of the disarmament agreement itself and the secondary nature of the other missions. In a sense, such a graded system of missions would place disarmament per se in the center of a circle, with high-level guarantees of enforcement; boundary maintaining and domestic order (where it concerns the peace of the world) would be in the next outermost circles; and totally outside the enforcement area, economic pressures and propaganda, etc.

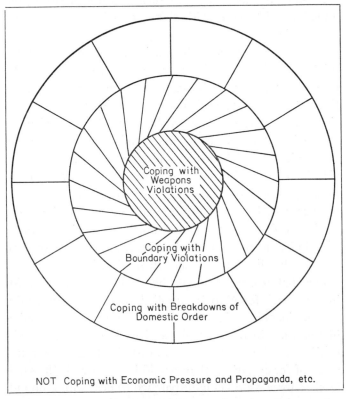

Coping with
Weapons
Violations

Coping with
Boundary Violations

Coping with Breakdowns of
Domestic Order

NOT Coping with Economic Pressure and Propaganda, etc.

In the innermost circle, enforcement is most highly valued, and therefore a given level of force can be ordered into action earlier and with a lower degree of international consensus than in the proximate and mediate circles. In the outermost area, enforcement is not desired and thus no force can be ordered into action.

To constitutionalize such an arrangement would probably require a separation of the forces required to deal with each of the three major missions. For one thing, the three missions themselves require considerably different sorts of training and equipment. Making a tank factory inoperative is an operation quite different from that of defending a border against lightly armed or unarmed invaders or infiltrators, and both of these operations are quite different from that of managing a city in turmoil. In some instances, the types of work involved might overlap, but the basic training required for forces intended to carry out each mission would be distinct. Second, the very existence of the total force levels in international hands that would be required to be prepared for all three missions might well arouse some fear in national governments of a coup by the international force itself, if it were able to take concerted action. Separation of the police force into three quite distinct services with three separate chains of command would minimize the likelihood of concerted action and make such a coup less likely. Finally, the gradation of the three forces as to consensus levels necessary to order action undertaken might make it wise to have three separate councils or courts, voting under different procedures, for the control of each.

Some precedent for this sort of arrangement exists in the proposals of the United States and the USSR (in their draft treaties on general and complete disarmament) for separate organization and control of the proposed International Disarmament Organization (an inspection and verification system) and the proposed peace or police forces. A separation of the police force itself into three separate institutions to cope with three separate problems would simply build upon this already recognized approach.

*

We may now review the model of a disarmed world that has been proposed above. It would contemplate: (1) the enforcement of disarmament itself by a small police institution designed for that end alone; (2) the creation of two other small police forces intended to cope with such border incursions and such internal disorders as threatened to cause rearmament; and (3) the independent pursuit by every nation of its national interests by various means, however "tough," "underhanded," or "cunning," so long as they did not threaten to bring on rearmament.

The major objection to this model is that possession by a world police institution of a monopoly over the legitimate use of violence could not long be separated from possession of the power to make political decisions and that such a police institution would soon either collapse into inanition or turn itself into a world government. That objection, at first glance, seems historically well founded, since the transfer of military or quasi-military power from such units as French baronies, California vigilante committees, and Italian city-states seems to have been inextricably connected with the transfer of political decision-making authority.

But the objection should be examined more closely, especially through intensive historical research on periods of transition in the carrying out of such transfers of military and political authority. Research also needs to be done on the transitional periods in which strikes grew at the same time less violent and more legal and into periods like that from 1805 to 1812 when British-American conflicts were pursued by the use of economic pressures as "non lethal equivalents of war."

The emphasis on transitional periods in this proposed research is based on the belief that an agreement on disarmament per se, with no surrender of political independence, may represent a transitional period—possibly a long one—between national and world sovereignty. Or it may, if the police institutions are carefully constructed, represent the establishment on a permanent basis (so far as any political institutions are permanent) of what might have been merely a transitional state, national sovereignty without military forces. Since such a model of a disarmed world may promise a release from the mutually exclusive and jointly problematical models now officially proposed by the United States and the Soviet Union, further research on the possibility seems highly desirable.

CHAPTER XVIII

SUPRANATIONAL VERSUS INTERNATIONAL MODELS FOR GENERAL AND COMPLETE DISARMAMENT

BY KLAUS KNORR*

Writers on disarmament differ considerably on the nature of the disarmed world they envision, even when they all start with the same assumption of "general and complete disarmament" (GCD). This is to say that their positions are less sensitive to the degree and extent of disarmament than to their conceptions of the prerequisites and consequences of GCD. My reading of the literature suggests that most of these positions can be grouped in two clusters, one describing a supranational and the other an international model of the disarmed world. For brevity's sake, I will call these two groups of authors the "supranationalists" and the "internationalists," without, of course, implying that they are necessarily supranationalists or internationalists in any respect other than serves my classificatory convenience.

*

The *supranational* model of the disarmed world calls for a powerful world police force that, in terms of authority and capability, would effectively centralize the use of military force on behalf of a disarmed and warless world. In order to facilitate peaceful change, the supranational-

* For helpful criticisms of a first draft of this chapter I am indebted to Richard J. Barnet, Richard A. Falk, Mohammed Guessous, and George Modelski.

ists further specify strong supranational organs authorized to undertake supranational legislation extending to such matters of fundamental national interest as human rights and economic welfare. Accordingly, the extreme supranational model implies broad as well as deep inroads on national sovereignty, or, to put it another way, a sweeping as well as radical transformation of the present world order. If the nation-state survived for long at all, it would become a definitely subordinate form of organization. This position is perfectly consistent. The powers to make and to enforce political decisions are usually organized in a consonant manner. In the present world, both powers are diffused. The supranationalists propose that both be concentrated in central institutions. Richard A. Falk and Arnold Toynbee are among the writers representing the "supranationalist" position.[1]

The *international* model of the disarmed world specifies weak or no supranational institutions, including a weak or no international police force, and leaves change to be wrought by national pressures, though pressures other than international war. Accordingly, this model implies a deep but narrow reduction of national sovereignty, one confined to the abolition of national armaments; and, except for their elimination, it requires no formal alterations in the present international order. The nation-state would continue to function as the major organization for administering a large range of values. Lincoln P. Bloomfield and Arthur I. Waskow are authors representing the "internationalist" position.[2]

[1] Cf. Falk, present volume, Chapters II, XI, XII, and XVI, and Arnold Toynbee, "Change in a Disarmed World" in Arthur Larson (ed.), A *Warless World* (New York: McGraw-Hill, 1963), Chap. III.
[2] Both in present volume, Chapters VI and VII (Bloomfield), and Chap. XVII (Waskow).

It has been observed that, according to their current official positions on GCD, the Soviet Union favors the international model, whereas the United States adheres to the supranational model.[3] According to the United States proposals, all nations would settle disputes peacefully and refrain from using force and from indirect aggression. An authority would decide on acceptable changes in the status quo; and a supranational police force would deal with recalcitrant states. On the other hand, Soviet proposals reject any encroachment on national sovereignty, leave peaceful changes in the status quo to national bargaining, and want international police forces—equipped only with small firearms and commanded by a troika committee acting in unanimity—organized on an ad hoc basis from national units. The utility of such international forces would be limited by their weak military capabilities and the possibility of the refusal by member states to supply contingents, a veto in the command structure, and presumably also a veto in the council that must authorize the organization of such a force.

However, this sharp contrast between the positions of the United States and the Soviet Union may be deceptive. The Soviet position seems to accord well enough with its extreme sensitivity to national sovereignty in a world largely composed of non-Communist states. In the case of the United States, on the other hand, there seems to be a deep and broad gulf between official position on GCD and actual behavior on matters affecting its own national sovereignty. It is hard to detect evidence of a strong United States disposition to accept any supra-

[3] Cf. Bloomfield, present volume, Chapter VII; Waskow, Chapter XVII; also J. I. Coffey, "The Soviet View of a Disarmed World," *Journal of Conflict Resolution*, VIII, No. 1 (March 1964), 1-6.

national control over its policies and welfare. For example, the Connally Reservation to the acceptance of the compulsory jurisdiction of the International Court of Justice expresses a strong reluctance to do so. Perhaps the disarmament position of the United States is a direct linear descendant of the Wilsonian vision of squaring the circle and safely combining the advantages of both supranationality and national sovereignty. Indeed, Messrs. Clark and Sohn[4] do propose a hybrid model that is internationalist as well as supranationalist, and they have designed a constitutional blueprint intended to serve both these ends. In the light of prevailing political attitudes and forces, however, the necessary world-wide consensus would be very hard to establish and preserve. It would require, as Richard A. Falk puts it, ". . . a new altruistic disposition . . . among nations."[5] Perhaps the United States position has not been thought through sufficiently well and would quickly crumble once its implications were fully understood.

Why particular authors favor one of these models or the other is not always clear from the literature. Obviously, mixed motivations may be at work, and to speculate about them extensively would scarcely be profitable. Instead, I wish to point to one rationale for favoring one model or the other that is built into the logic of each position. It can be inferred from the conclusions, if not from the premises, of the various authors.

The supranationalist position is appealing if the overriding objective is to minimize international war—ideally, to achieve a dependably warless world. The international-

---

[4] Grenville Clark and L. B. Sohn, *World Peace Through World Law* (2nd ed.; Cambridge, Mass.: Harvard University Press, 1958).
[5] Chapter XVI.

KLAUS KNORR

ist position is attractive if the prime objective is to maximize the chances of establishing disarmament in a world in which the present prospects of establishing a supranational structure are assumed to be very small. Both posit the same degree of internationalist disarmament: general and complete. Yet disarmament is, after all, an instrument of policy, not an end in itself. To the supranationalists the obvious end of disarmament is a world without war, and in order to achieve this objective they require sweeping and drastic changes in the existing international order. In order to abolish war they are prepared to go far toward abolishing the nation-state. This is logical, for if, at the extreme, the nation-state ceased to exist, internation war would be sure to be impossible.

The "internationalists" may share the desire for a completely warless world as an ultimate goal. But, excepting for specifying GCD, their model is protective of the nation-state as an institution. Whether or not they themselves favor the eventual abolition of the nation-state, their writings express the view that the present world is not ready for so radical a move. Accordingly, the "internationalists" posit a more modest reform of the existing order and, logically, are prepared to tolerate residual violence and an appreciable risk of rearmament. This shows that the achievement of disarmament and the achievement of a completely warless world are not necessarily the same thing.

*

Having set out, in a simplified form, the essential differences between the supranationalist and internationalist approaches to a disarmed world, I will now proceed to explore some of their implications. In doing so, we must frankly accept the fact that we are dealing with imaginary constructs. We lack all experience of the world described in either model and are free—too free, perhaps—to form hypotheses without any possibility of putting them to a test. Under these circumstances, any proposals and argumentation depend crucially on personal power of imagination and judgment, and on personal values. This does not mean that the exercises involved are worthless, for it is only by means of such probing forays that we can begin to understand what a disarmed world might be like. This understanding—uncertain and fragmentary as it must be—is essential to any decisions on whether, and how much, we want a disarmed world, and which, if any, of several possible disarmed worlds we should attempt to bring about. Because of the highly personal nature of the reconnaissance, however, I feel it advisable to clarify briefly my own relevant position.

First, since I believe that a large-scale nuclear war would be almost inconceivably destructive of human life and other values, and since I also believe that the chances of such a war are appreciable in a world of highly armed nation-states, I favor, in principle, an international order in which nations could not settle their disputes by resort to war. Second, I favor the development of such an order by voluntary agreement of states. Third, for reasons stated at the end of the paper, I do not believe that such agreement is likely to come about in the foreseeable future.

✧

In order to throw some light on the implications of the two alternative models for a disarmed world, I will at first disregard the question of which looks more attractive from the viewpoint of achieving disarmament or a warless world, in order to focus on their other properties. To the extent that these *other* properties indicate substantial changes in the present world order, they can be viewed as indicating the price we may be asked to pay to make disarmament or a warless world possible. They will represent a cost as long as they are valued only as instrumental to achieving a world without war, and not for their own sake.

The supranational model, as stated, foresees a more far-reaching abridgment of national sovereignty than is required for abolishing the ability of nations to prepare for and engage in international war. A strong international force may have the military *capability* to enforce on nation-states various decisions that a supranational legislature would have the constitutional *authority* to pass. The supranationalists suggest that this legislative competence be extended to many matters now left to national communities to decide. Arnold Toynbee points out that a disarmed world cannot hope to remain warless if the status quo is "frozen," because ineluctable pressures for change would generate violence unless they could be channeled by suitable procedures for "peaceful change." Thus, Toynbee observed that there must be "some regular method for the perpetual redistribution of power, of wealth, of population, and of the goods of this world as well."[6] Falk adds that peaceful change may include *internal* revisions that concern the rights and duties of a single state; for instance, nation-states may have to be prevented from practicing genocide and racial suppression.[7] In order to curb the incentive to commit indirect aggression and subversion in the disarmed world, nations must be "willing to accept unfavorable revisions of their

[6] Quoted in Falk, Chapter XVI.   [7] *Ibid.*, p. 352.

legal rights and duties, extending even to enduring re-determination of the scope of their territorial domain or of their discretion to exclude and admit aliens. . . ."[8]

The supranationalists regard these deep and broad in roads on traditional sovereignty as indispensable to the achievement of a world without war. War, they point out, has in the past substituted for alternative but absent procedures as the agent of change. Since change is irrepressible and war too destructive to be tolerated, supranational legislation and, presumably, enforcement of change are instrumental to achieving the warless world.

The proposed changes in the international order will not be registered as a cost by persons and groups who are now deeply disillusioned with the traditional nation-state on other grounds than its ability to conduct war, and who prefer to have some sort of world-state administer world community welfare regardless of traditionally organized nationality. Moreover, these persons may assume that they are a vanguard more sensitive than others to a strong secular trend that, as it is consummated, will result in a spreading of their own preferences. Though the requirements of effective disarmament may represent a bonus rather than a cost to these people—or not merely a bonus, but a value as important as, or more important than, disarmament—they must admit to themselves and others that there are, even from their point of view, risks to be entered on the debit side of the scheme. The risks are, first, that the supranational authority will legislate in response to other values than are deemed just or acceptable by the supranationalists, and, second, that the strong supranational police force will defy or capture ultimate authority, again in order to enforce change in

[8] *Ibid.*, p. 353.

contradiction to the values cherished by the supranational-ists. Even if aware of these risks, they may, of course, be prepared to pay this price for the extirpation of traditional international conflict—a source of appalling risk at the present time. Furthermore, they may argue, war as a traditional agent of change has often been more subservient to military prowess and destructive ruthlessness than to what might be termed "justice" by supranationalist standards. The supranationalists may regard the incidence of injustice to be substantial in either world order, yet expect a degree of improvement from supranationality.

The supranationalists may be accused of naïveté if they assume that supranational legislation will necessarily render change smooth and peaceful. They seem to believe sometimes that the pressures for change will fail to generate dangerous tensions and breed violence if only the proponents of change are allowed to have their way. Yet may not the opponents of any particular change resist, and perhaps resist violently? The supranationalists will doubtless retort that the opponents as well as the proponents of change would be duly represented in the supranational legislature and bow to legitimate authority. Except in fairly homogeneous communities, however, majority rule can be unenlightened, unjust, and brutal. It is not clear how the supranationalists propose to cope with this cost of making the world warless. But they might argue, once again, that pressures for change produce plenty of violence under the traditional world order, and that we can hardly lose, and stand an excellent chance to gain, by proceeding to the supranational regime.

The problem of costs is altogether different for the vast number of people who are less moved by the vision of a supranational welfare system, or do not subscribe to it at all. Confining my remarks chiefly to the population in the Western world, I will divide this large group into two categories. Most of them by far are not knowledgeable about nuclear war or, if vaguely acquainted with this contingency, prefer to ignore it or, in any case, to ban it from the range of their active preoccupations. These people tend to be traditionalist, whether active or passive, prefer to make the best of existing institutions, and are not easily persuaded to exchange the world with which they are familiar—far from satisfactory though they may think it to be—for a new model, no matter how glittering its promises. A rare combination of inspired leadership and the hard knocks of major adversity may be capable of jarring such persons from customary attachments, but they are not especially susceptible to subtle calculations and reasoning. It is my guess that, by and large, they would be inclined to reject the supranationalist model if it were put to them.

The other category is a smaller but perhaps strategic group. It is composed of those who—by dint of office, avocation, or expertise—know as much about war and nuclear weapons as the supranationalists do, but who are less sanguine than they about the consequences of supranationality regarded as an instrument for achieving a world without war. This group includes the "internationalists," except for those who favor the internationalist model only for tactical reasons and, by ideological preference, subscribe to the values of the "supranationalists."

The people in this second category are not only aware of the danger that, if implemented, the supranationalist model may be subject to perversion and not as likely to render change peaceful as the supranationalists tend to assume. They are also sensitive to the question of whether

KLAUS KNORR

the implementation of the supranationalist model, even
if it resists perversion and does not breed violence, would
not seriously threaten the welfare of their own nations.

This group may agree that, in the nuclear age, international warfare has become extremely and, perhaps, in-
tolerably destructive. Some of its members may, therefore,
be interested in the idea of arms control and disarmament.
But otherwise they may think well of the nation-state as
an institution for ordering human affairs—not perhaps a
very good institution, let alone a perfect one, but not bad
when compared with conceivable alternatives, and having
the great advantage of familiarity as against the larger
uncertainties of alternative arrangements. Especially in
many countries of the West, the nation-state, since it
came of age, has not done too badly by historical standards in terms of providing domestic peace and order, freedom and opportunity for its citizens. Though there may
be plenty of room for improvement, the prospects may
not seem bleak, since, after all, a great deal of betterment
has been accomplished within the framework of this organization. If the members of this group are interested
in international welfare, they may doubt that the supranational order would achieve what, by their lights, could
and should be done, and prefer that international welfare
measures be promoted through interstate channels and
multilateral institutions.

In fact, they may be fairly pragmatic, rather than rigid,
in their attachment to the nationalist principle of managing political affairs, and favor experimentation with at
least supplementary institutions. This inclination is evi-
denced by support for the UN and its specialized agencies;
the members of the movement for European integration
are of this general persuasion; and the United States,

though chary of bold experimentation on its own part, has lent considerable support to regional integration moves elsewhere. Yet most members of the group under discussion prefer safe experiment to a headlong plunge into the unknown; and it is scarcely discreditable to be careful before undertaking irreversible commitments.

What about the threat to their own welfare, including that of the persons and groups with whom they strongly identify? Neil W. Chamberlain has spelled out some of these consequences of supranationality.[9] As he perceives them, Western dominance would be superseded by the dominance of the underdeveloped Asiatic and African nations over the economically developed West, including the Soviet Union. This would, he thinks, lead to a compulsory redistribution of the world's wealth. The Western, highly industrialized societies would have part of their income channeled to the less developed countries by means of a system of progressive taxation. According to Chamberlain, this draft on the West would not be too uncomfortable, since it would be limited by the capacity of the underdeveloped areas to absorb outside resources for the purpose of effective economic development. He estimates the draft at from 8 to 10 per cent of the Gross National Product, or about the proportion now being allocated to national armaments in the United States.

As foreseen by Chamberlain, these consequences are fairly reassuring.[10] To put up with them would seem to be paying a small price for escaping from the deadly incubus of the nuclear bomb. The question is whether or not Chamberlain's expectations are realistic. If disarmament, according to the supranational model, would en-

[9] Neil W. Chamberlain, *The West in a World Without War* (New York: McGraw-Hill, 1963), pp. 25ff.
[10] *Ibid.*, pp. 51ff., 79f.

gender the redistribution of international power that he foresees, it is not clear why the majority of poor countries should be so moderate in exploiting that power by taxing the rich. Why must their take be limited by their absorptive capacity for economic development? Why could redistributive finance not be applied toward raising consumption levels; and why would they stop at redistributive finance? What if they wanted to redistribute population? Free migration could quickly destroy the way of life of recipient communities. I am not, of course, predicting that such inroads on the lives of nations would take place. But if decisions are made by a majority of the countries represented in the supranational authority, I can easily think of particular majorities that would have little regard for any injury inflicted on the small minority of highly developed nations. Most of the countries in the majority have little experience in government and, for reasons perhaps historically justified, harbor strong resentment against the Western nations.

There is the further problem that the present international "community" is far more intensely political in its interrelations than are many national societies.[11] Especially in the economically developed non-totalitarian societies, the scope of political authority is carefully delimited, thus affording precious freedom for private decision-making. Relations between national governments are, in contrast, highly politicalized. It is to be feared that under a supranational order this tendency would persist, at least for a time, and give the abuse of power an appalling range.

It may be contended that the highly developed nations

[11] Cf. Werner Levi, "On the Causes of Peace," *Journal of Conflict Resolution*, VIII, No. 1 (March 1964), 27f.

would not lack bases of power for putting up effective resistance if a majority of less developed nations joined forces against them and pressed their advantage with little regard for their nations' welfare.[12] But in a supranational world provided with a powerful police force, military power would be likely to be dominant, particularly if it was acting within its constitutional role; and rearmament—for which the rich nations are well endowed with material and intellectual resources—would probably face prohibitive odds. This is, after all, precisely why the supranationalists favor their model of a warless world.

Nobody can demonstrate convincingly that the aforementioned fears will be realized if mankind marches down the unfamiliar path indicated by the supranationalist signpost. Nor can anyone convincingly demonstrate the opposite. There simply is no adequate basis for predicting the consequences. The uncertainties loom too large to permit any attribution of probabilities. Yet, under these circumstances, anxiety is bound to be profound in the nations that have a great deal to lose—namely, those now enjoying prosperity, order, and personal freedom. In fact, the awareness of the risk they would face surprisingly leads one full circle to rediscovering a strong rationale for national military forces. After all, such forces do have a protective function.

The supranationalists may contend that the wealthy democratic nations need not be too frightened of the redistributive consequences of supranationality, since these countries have, after all, during the last two hundred years

[12] Those developed nations that governed overseas colonies until recently did not, after all, display much regard for their colonies' welfare—at least not in terms of the welfare function of the colonial populations.

undergone an *internal* series of redistributive changes, and have not only survived but grown more stable and much wealthier. Yet this analogy will strike the skeptic as not very reassuring and, besides, misleading in two important respects.

The analogy fails to be reassuring because, in the course of Western history, domestic changes in the direction of lesser inequality of influence and status, wealth and income, was frequently accompanied by a great deal of domestic violence, revolutionary and counterrevolutionary; one has only to think of the history of France, Germany, and Russia to realize this fact. Domestic change also inflicted on the previous beneficiaries of inequality losses of life, wealth, power, and status that, subjectively, were no doubt extremely painful for each generation concerned. However much we may approve of the end result, the costs of transition were far from negligible.

Furthermore, when the process of change was going on, these national communities may be assumed to have been more homogeneous politically and culturally than mankind is at this juncture. Redistribution occurred within a well-established polity. During, say, the first part of the nineteenth century, the English gentry may have felt little in common with the English farmer, or the Manchester mill owner with his worker, but it is plausible that there was more mutual identification than is felt today between the Russians and the Chinese or between Americans and Saudi Arabians. And mutual identification facilitates concession and compromise.

The analogy is also misleading because redistributive change took place gradually over a long period of time, whereas the supranationalists propose to rush headlong into supranationality, if only because the threat of devastating international war is immediate and hence requires immediate action. This difference in time scale is extremely important. As individual Western countries progressed slowly and haltingly toward lesser inequality, there was time for the beneficiaries of each redistributive installment to acquire education and political experience—that is, to become moderate and realistic in their demands. Thus, destabilizing effects were often kept within tolerable bounds, although, as we have observed, the history of several West European nations is marked by sharp bouts of revolutionary and counterrevolutionary violence.

The analogy could perhaps be made more reassuring if supranational institutions would be modified to protect the more developed countries from excessive taxation and interference. For instance, the supranational legislature might be constitutionally required to pass on certain sensitive specified matters by a qualified majority; and control, as well as the finance, of the world police force might be entrusted to a minority of nations which, at any one time, led in terms of per capita income. But would such an arrangement be acceptable?

If serious threats to the welfare of the most developed countries are admitted, it might still be said that the cost of nuclear war is infinite and that no price is therefore too much to pay for rendering war impossible.[18] Yet this advice is perhaps gratuitous because of the observable tendency of people to refuse to choose in a coolly calculating, rational manner when confronting a choice of major calamities. It is, furthermore, misleading since the future occurrence of a catastrophic nuclear war is far

[18] Thus The New Republic referred to the "Last Big Bang" which would end all human life (March 14, 1964), p. 3.

399

from certain. The real question is whether the *risk* of such a war presents us with infinite costs. I doubt that this is the case. Statesmen are well aware of the horrid destructive potentialities of unlimited nuclear war. *If* nuclear war is precipitated, it may be of short duration and limited destructiveness—that is, it may inflict casualties that, although appalling, are within, or not much beyond, the range of historical experience. There could even be some compensation in that, acting as a sufficiently traumatic event, the experience might induce more people to come to realistic terms with the world we live in, face unpleasant choices, and facilitate speedy progress toward disarmament. In other words, though we have no way of measuring this particular risk of continuing with the present international order, the costs involved need not be felt by informed people to be so enormous as to propel them forthwith toward choosing supranationality sight unseen.

There is little evidence that "world" peace and welfare rank high among the goals and preferences of people anywhere. On the contrary, most of the underdeveloped and ex-colonial societies seem to be entering or going through a phase of political identication focusing on the nation-state or quasi-nation-state; and even the Communist states do not seem immune to its integrative appeal. Does this not suggest a near-universal tendency to appreciate "world" peace and welfare less for their own sake than for what they are expected to contribute to the peace and welfare of the individual nation? Being derived values, they may be appreciated only as long as they promote national welfare.

Nevertheless, if the supranationalists are right in describing the conditions and consequences of supranationality, the fears of the richer nations may be paralleled by redistributive hopes of the less developed ones. What may be registered as the "costs" of supranationality by the highly developed nations may look like "gains" to their poorer neighbors; and it may be on these narrowly self-regarding grounds that the supranationalist model finds more admirers in the less developed areas. But even if this were true, the question would remain of whether the construction of the supranationalist world is possible without the cooperation of the developed societies.

To conclude, the supranational approach to disarmament is not now acceptable, in my judgment, even if, as assumed, mankind is, in principle, ready to adopt GCD—a condition that implies substantial shifts in attitude from the current pattern. This opinion is based on three beliefs about relevant patterns of motivation among the majority of people, especially in the Western world. First, these populations are not powerfully attracted by the non-disarmament values of the supranational model—that is, by the expected utility of world-wide supranational institutions and by the redistribution of means to welfare through such institutions. Second, to the extent that they ponder the implications of such institutions and redistributive actions, they are repelled by uncertainty about, or fear for, their own welfare. Third, these motivations are reinforced by the availability of other approaches to disarmament. Some of these approaches can be subsumed under the internationalist model.

*

The internationalist model under discussion also posits general and complete disarmament. As pointed out in the introduction, it does not, like the supranationalist model, promise to make the world warless or render GCD permanent. Nevertheless, it offers three valuable advantages over the present world without disarmament.

In the first place, it is very likely, though not certain, that international wars would diminish in number under conditions of general and complete disarmament. Given the adoption of GCD, such diminution is probable as the result of several associated changes. First, nations would hardly proceed to GCD unless they were politically and morally prepared to resolve conflicts by other means than war; the class of international conflicts arising directly from requirements to bolster national military postures (e.g., the Soviet installation of missiles in Cuba, the flights of the U-2) would suffer appreciable shrinkage; and national attitudes, institutions, and organizations supportive of national military establishments would likewise decline. Secondly—and this is very important—wars that occurred under conditions of GCD would be far less destructive than is likely under present conditions. They would be waged with small military and paramilitary capabilities and a relatively primitive or quickly improvised technology. Thirdly, even though disarmament might not be final, and substantial national rearmament might well occur involving military capabilities based on weapons that are conventional, or nuclear, or neither conventional nor nuclear, this is only a risk and, as such, less immediately dangerous than the risk of major warfare that we are running at present.

The extent to which these benefits would accrue in a world patterned on the internationalist model for disarmament is impossible to predict. International wars between disarmed states waged by means of police or other paramilitary forces *could* be frequent and, though they would tend to be localized for lack of the military means to exert remaining, or quickly improvised, military capabilities over long distances, they might spread if nations formed alliances. However, if this were to happen, rearmament would be sure to ensue; and the experiment with a disarmed world would be doomed to failure. At the other extreme, the disarmed states might learn how to shun violence and perhaps eventually reinforce stability by strengthening world-wide institutions.

A stable outcome would obviously be very sensitive to the restraint that interested parties observed in pushing for such changes in the status quo as would redistribute values across national boundaries. Restraint would mean that, whether for aggressive or defensive purposes, nation-states would stick to non-violent means of settling conflict, making do with adjudication and arbitration, diplomacy and propaganda, and economic blandishments and reprisal. Restraint would also mean that the proponents of change refrained from pressing too hard, lest the prospect of serious defeat by non-military pressures provided the status-quo country with a powerful incentive to consider resort to military or quasi-military force. Restraint would be especially important in foregoing such forms of indirect aggression as the organized support from outside of contending factions in nations divided by, or on the brink of, violent internal strife.

The internationalist model for disarmament cannot, of course, provide as much security from international violence as is built into its supranationalist counterpart. The greater freedom of self-direction that nations retain under the internationalist dispensation they pay for by a lesser security from war and rearmament; and, since instability and rearmament cannot be ruled out as possible outcomes, nations with a low potential for rapid rearmament would assume a special risk. Yet, even though these residual dangers and risks are indisputable, they seem small when compared with the risks and dangers of the highly armed world.

The supranationalist model implied side-effects that, depending on subjective modes of perception and subjective values, constituted a bonus to some but, in our estimate, to most people in the West a serious cost to be borne for the elimination of war. Does the internationalist model foreshadow similar costs? As in the preceding discussion of supranationality, we focus on side-effects that are consequences, not of the transient process of implementing GCD, but of completed national disarmament.

The internationalist model seems to me to imply two major side-effects that, among some nations at least, might be registered as fairly serious drawbacks. One relates to shifts in the international influence wielded by individual nation-states. The bases of non-military power or influence are not distributed among nations in proportion to military capabilities. Military power, to be sure, is associated with stages of scientific, technological, and economic development, with powers of organization, with numbers of population, and with many other factors that may also affect international influence. As the contrasts among the United States, Western Europe, and Soviet Russia reveal, however, the association is not one of strict proportionality for any one basis of military power. There are, furthermore, bases of international influence that are more obscurely associated with military strength and potential, or are wholly dissociated from them. Ideological attraction, moral reputation, diplomatic finesse, and cultural achievements are examples. GCD, therefore, would be likely to cause some nations to rise above and others to fall from the relative position of influence which they currently occupy. This might be a matter of serious concern to nations anticipating a decline. GCD would not render nations indifferent to their position of influence. On the contrary, with national armaments abolished, other means of international influence would tend to appreciate in value.

The other drawback is suggested by the question of whether—under the absence of strong supranational institutions and a strong supranational police force—the near-elimination of military force might not plunge international relations into unpredictable disorder, if not chaos. What if some nations exploited a monopolist position (e.g., national control over a canal or straits) in order to obtain extortionate dues, or to put pressure on a nation with which they were in conflict? What if some nations mistreated the nationals, and confiscated the property, of other nations? What if piracy reappeared on the seas? What if bloody and prolonged border fighting took place in remote areas? As Richard Falk reminds us, a degree of force often serves as a basis indispensable to order between as well as within national communities. The supranational model for disarmament recognizes this condition. The internationalist model, intent on protecting disarmed nation-states from the misuse of supranational authority and force, does not. Hence, this drawback is the logical concomitant of the model. The burden of such disorder would not, of course, be borne equally by all nations. It would hurt most those nations that are least self-sufficient, particularly in terms of economic or moral well-being.

On the other hand, we are again dealing with imaginings, not prediction. The degree and incidence of international disorder might turn out to be slight. Even in a largely demilitarized world, the victims of disorder would not be lacking in means to press for the abandonment of delinquent behavior; and the vast majority of nations might well perceive that cooperation on behalf of orderly conditions is in the long-run interest of all states. Indeed, the internationalist model is compatible with, if not conducive to, a growing practice of international cooperation. Cooperating toward "peaceful change," especially in matters promoting the welfare of the less developed areas, should appeal as a means of minimizing international conflict and, thereby, also minimizing the chances of serious relapses into war and rearmament; and an expanding network of international cooperation should create a climate favorable to the maintenance of international order.

Whether the drawbacks just discussed would inspire enough doubt and resistance to make the internationalist model desirable is a highly speculative question. It is reasonable to guess, however, that—in terms of acceptability—the internationalist model is superior to the supranational.

But at this point, it becomes interesting to withdraw our initial assumption that mankind is ready to adopt GCD. The application of either model is obviously resisted by the inertia of existing institutions or, more precisely, of human attachments to them. These attachments seem to have three primary roots. First, societies indoctrinate their members with a firm loyalty to their vital institutions. Second, many members receive direct benefits—in terms of political influence, social prestige, income, etc.—from these institutions and thus have an incentive to support them. Finally, existing institutions tend to be protected by fear of the unknown and the uncertain results of institutional experimentation.

Action on the internationalist model seems less infeasible than pursuit of the supranationalist scheme because it runs less counter to these attachments. It does not degrade the nation-state nearly as much as the alternative course and does not imply side-effects as threatening to many people as those implied in the supranational model. In my opinion, indeed, the less any specific scheme appears to tamper with existing institutions, the more the political acceptability of GCD rises. This opinion is shared by some of the internationalists.[14]

*

The choice between the two models is, of course, largely academic as long as nations are unable to bring about GCD. That they can manage to do so was the starting point of this essay as well as of several others in this volume. In making this assumption, the authors relied heavily on a deus ex machina. If national governments ever seriously contemplate proceeding to a significant degree of disarmament, they must grapple with the issues explored in this paper. But their decisions will hinge not only on how they evaluate the relative merits and demerits of the two models—the internationalist and the supranationalist. They must settle in addition whether and how GCD can be safely brought about. This further question raises problems of phasing, verification, inspection, and enforcement—a range of issues analyzed elsewhere in this volume but beyond the scope of the present paper.

[14] Cf. Arthur Waskow, "Alternative Models of a Disarmed World," *Disarmament and Arms Control*, ii, No. 1 (Winter 1963-1964), 59-73.

There are numerous proposals or models for solving these problems of immediate implementation, each—in its direct consequences and in its various side-effects, domestic and international—exhibiting different merits and demerits that, in turn, raise grave uncertainties and inevitably involve subjective perception and evaluation.

It was these problems raised by the processes of negotiating and implementing GCD that caused my pessimistic confession at the outset of this paper. Unless a deus ex machina does intervene—perhaps by letting us blunder into a deeply traumatic crisis, close enough to disaster to shock us out of our preoccupation with problems of a less fateful order, or out of our sheer complacency— I cannot regard general and complete disarmament, formulated in one compact "package," as a practicable proposition. Of course, this estimate may be wrong. But even if it is not, we are not necessarily condemned to inaction. There is, in my opinion, a chance for reaching agreement on lesser measures of arms control. Although they would not abolish national armaments, they might, with cumulative impact, appreciably reduce the risk and destructiveness of war and, thus having gained time for a protracted learning process, we might—in some distant and as yet obscure future—suddenly discover that GCD has moved into the realm of the feasible.

This leads one to refocus on a more intermediate model, politically more feasible than the supranationalist and the internationalist, for mitigating without GCD the grave risks with which the armed nation-state confronts mankind in the age of nuclear affluence. This model invites us to learn how to lessen their risks by means of many small but perhaps increasing and cumulative moves —unilateral, bilateral, and multilateral—in order to gain time for gradually reforming the present international system and for gradually developing the desire for experimentation that is the prerequisite of such reform.

*

The three models I have discussed—the internationalist, the supranationalist and, more sketchily, an intermediate model—amount to a useful ordering device at this stage in the quest for understanding the problem of how mankind is to be relieved of the dreadful risk of nuclear destruction. As this intellectual effort is pursued, however, one must design and study more complex models of possible, as well as desirable, future worlds. This is indispensable if we want to understand more clearly the contingent character of institutional innovation.

If one were to accord to the elimination of highly destructive war an absolute priority over all other goals, the problem would approach one of simple maximization—i.e., of minimizing the probability of such war regardless of price. Despite the misgivings expressed in this chapter, one would then see the supranationalist model as representing the logical, and most desirable, objective—and perhaps think of the successive progression from the present world to worlds patterned on the intermediate, internationalist, and supranationalist models as the least improbable course of innovation. I doubt, however, that the problem approaches one of maximization. Individuals and nations have many other goals and preferences and, as we have shown, disarmament greatly affects their achievement. The problem is to find an optimum solution, and this is precisely why we will need models that are more sophisticated than the ones thus far explored in the literature.

The foregoing analysis also revealed that—in terms of important side-effects—the costs of GCD may fall more heavily on the economically advanced than on the less developed countries, especially if the supranationalist solution is at issue. Practical progress, therefore, would demand that the less developed nations participate more than they have done in seriously exploring the entire range of relevant problems and proposed solutions. It is not enough for them just to favor GCD. That is too easy and self-serving. Mankind requires order and justice as well as the absence of destructive war; and the concepts of order and justice prevalent in the developed societies must be taken into account if these nations are to agree to bold and risky innovation. There can be no GCD without their co-operation.

APPENDIX I

VERIFICATION AND RESPONSE IN

DISARMAMENT AGREEMENTS*

INTRODUCTION

THE Woods Hole Summer Study focused on verification[1] and response,[2] but necessarily considered a number of related topics as well. The emphasis on verification reflected the view that while the problem of verification is by no means the only obstacle to disarmament, divergence on how verification shall be obtained has been sufficient to block progress. Response to suspected or proven violations was considered to be integrally related to the determination of what kind of verification is needed.

The examination of verification and response proceeded on the basis of two assumptions. The first is that the pursuit of arms control and disarmament measures in the interest of United States security is a primary objective of US policy. The second assumption is that, for the foreseeable future, verification and response procedures which require either drastic reductions of national sovereignty

---

* Summary report on the Woods Hole Summer Study of 1962.

[1] As used in this report, "verification" refers to the totality of means, of which inspection is just one, by which one nation can determine whether another nation is complying with obligations under an arms control or disarmament agreement. "Inspection" will refer specifically to agreed procedures by which individuals either as representatives of national states or of international organizations conduct activities for the primary purpose of verifying compliance with arms control and disarmament agreements.

[2] "Response" refers to any course of action taken by a nation or an international body on the basis of information indicating that another party to an arms control or disarmament agreement is not acting in conformance with obligations contained in, or implied by, the agreement.

or major transformations in Soviet society will not be acceptable or attainable.

Purposes of Verification

The Study examined the purposes of verification in disarmament and attempted to determine how they could be served without requiring unrealistic institutional and political changes. For the present context and the foreseeable future the purposes which verification is intended to fulfill are as follows: (1) to induce compliance with disarmament obligations by creating a credible threat that violations will be detected and will result in undesirable consequences for the violator; (2) to enable the United States to take timely and appropriate action in response to violations; (3) to build confidence among parties to the agreement by establishing a history of demonstrated compliance.

Verification procedures should be a source of reassurance when the agreement is being maintained and a source of accurate, usable information giving the United States adequate opportunity to protect its interests should another party evade or end the agreement. However, in assessing the extent to which any verification technique fulfills these purposes, it is important to bear in mind the following propositions:

1. *Verification acts as a deterrent to evasion only to the extent that a potential violator is concerned with the risks of exposure.* Where the would-be violator is prepared to accept these risks, verification has little deterrent effect. The violations of the Versailles Treaty, the Washington Naval Arms Limitation Agreement, and the Korean Armistice were widely known. However, the evading nations were convinced that, even when the fact of non-compliance

became known, no serious consequences would result. Verification as such cannot guarantee compliance, and its deterrent effect is directly determined by the effectiveness of the likely response.

2. *National self-interest, rather than fear of detection, will remain the principal inducement to compliance.* A nation will not enter into an arms control agreement unless it perceives that agreement to be in its interest. Similarly, national self-interest will be the principal inducement for maintaining the agreement. No attainable system of verification or enforcement can induce a sovereign nation to observe disarmament obligations which, in its view, jeopardize its national interests or contradict its long-term objectives. Confidence must ultimately rest on the judgment that each party will perceive compliance with the agreement to be in its own self-interest.

3. *The successful operation of verification procedures builds confidence in the disarmament process.* The flow of accurate and timely information concerning the compliance of other nations and evidence of their willingness to permit verification will tend to provide reassurance that continued compliance with the agreement is in the national interest. Further, a conviction that violations will be detected with sufficient speed and accuracy to allow effective responses enhances confidence in the disarmament process. Successful verification of compliance will also reduce overall suspicion and distrust and improve the prospects for further agreements.

4. *Verification to support responses is less essential for informal arrangements than for long-term, formal commitments.* Verification should provide information on which to base responsive action and to justify this action to others. This function of verification varies with the

nature of the agreement. A tacit arrangement, or one rev-ocable at will, does not require verification to justify its termination or any other response. A treaty, on the other hand, constitutes a public, international commitment which can be abandoned only at a high political price unless other nations are persuaded that a violation has occurred. If attainable verification arrangements cannot provide a basis for response within the context of a formal agreement, substantive arms control measures may never-theless be desirable and feasible with less commitment and formality.

Verification Requirements

Since absolute verification can never be achieved, the level of verification to be sought becomes a matter for military and political decision. The need for verification varies from measure to measure, agreement to agreement, and context to context.

ASSESSING THE REQUIREMENTS

For all arms control measures three sets of con-siderations will principally determine the verification re-quirements. These are the military factors affected by compliance or non-compliance with the measure, the responses which would be desirable and available in the event of violation, and the political atmosphere surround-ing the arrangement.

Military Verification Requirements. The risk to US security of undetected violations establishes the basic military verification requirement. For many measures sub-stantial undetected violations would not seriously affect the military balance, while for more far-reaching measures small violations could be significant. Ordinarily the significance of violations depends upon the vulnerability of the victims of evasion. Clandestine production of a small number of delivery systems could not give the violator a decisive advantage if the United States retained a large retaliatory force, but such production could become important if the United States had divested itself of all but a few delivery vehicles. The incentive to comply should also be taken into account in determining verification requirements. Violations may be more or less predictable according to the degree of self-interest served by the measure, and the verification that is needed will be affected correspondingly.

Response Verification Requirements. The United States would generally find it desirable to be able to choose from a wide range of responses to violations including military and diplomatic actions and economic and political pressures, depending on the character of the violation. An important response might be to institute procedures for gaining more information concerning a suspicious event. Occasionally no response may be intended or available.

In various circumstances the appropriate response may be unilateral, multilateral, or international, requiring different kinds of evidence to support it. The response which is contemplated for violations of any particular measure, therefore, partially determines the kind of verification which is needed for that measure. For example, international responses would ordinarily call for more stringent verification of a violation than would unilateral responses; responses to development or production violations set lower verification requirements than responses to stockpiling violations, since the former violations usually involve lead times before they become significant. The availability of responses to non-compliance in large part determines whether a given arms control measure is consistent with the demands of national security. The time required to make the response affects the sensitivity and timeliness which must characterize the verification procedures.

Political Verification Requirements. The assurance of compliance demanded for any particular measure depends in part upon the mutual distrust of the parties involved. That is, at the present time verification requirements for an agreement between the United States and the Soviet Union are obviously higher than those relating to an identical agreement concluded with, say, Canada. Verification will be demanded by the United States and its allies to the extent that there is reason to be fearful of the intentions as well as the capabilities of the Soviet Union.

Verification requirements will not necessarily increase as disarmament progresses. While it is true that in later stages of disarmament the parties become more vulnerable and the need for confidence is greater, increased verification alone cannot supply that confidence. Indeed, unless increased confidence is generated in other ways, it is doubtful that advanced stages of disarmament will be reached. In view of these considerations, verification requirements may well be greater at earlier stages than at later ones which, if they occur at all, will be preceded by an increase in the level of trust. The inability to predict levels of trust or distrust in advance suggests that the verification requirements for each stage should be determined only in the light of the political conditions existing at that time.

REQUIREMENTS FOR SPECIFIC MEASURES

The Study examined the verification requirements associated with a range of illustrative arms control measures.[3] The findings in these specific areas may be summarized as follows:

Strategic Delivery Vehicles. The verification requirements of an agreement with the Soviet Union involving strategic delivery vehicles will depend upon the strategy that is adopted in conjunction with the limitation. If agreements or adjustments in other areas should permit the United States to adopt a second strike or purely retaliatory posture, then a series of measures involving a minimum of access to Soviet territory would become possible. These include a ban on the testing of long-range missiles, an agreement not to develop specific new weapons, and a reduction of the strategic forces of each side to a level of about one thousand vehicles. The last measure could be adequately verified by inspecting destruction of arms and declared facilities. For reductions in strategic delivery vehicles to a level of about two hundred vehicles, greater inspection would be needed, but it appears that several hundred inspectors with limited access rights could provide adequate assurance of compliance. They would inspect declared facilities producing delivery systems or subsystems, would conduct sampled inspection for clandestine production and stockpiles, and would verify the level of defensive measures. The maintenance by each side of a diversified force including missiles, aircraft, and submarines impels a violator to evade in a number of different ways if it is clandestinely to develop a capability which

[3] See *Verification and Response in Disarmament Agreements,* Woods Hole Summer Study, Washington, D.C.: The Institute for Defense Analyses, 1962, Annex Vol. I, Pt. I.

can nullify such a deterrent force. Restrictions on defensive armaments could also help to limit the possibilities of nullifying the deterrent. Restrictions on flight testing further increase the difficulties of evasion and lessen the verification requirements.

Chemical and Biological Weapons. Chemical and biological weapons have marginal strategic significance so long as nuclear weapons are maintained as a deterrent. Their current significance lies chiefly in tactical uses. While development and production of such weapons seem virtually uninspectable, most uses of them can be readily detected. At the present time an agreement restricting or outlawing their use would be desirable and need not require inspection to verify control on development and production.

Conventional Armaments and Armed Forces. Clandestine changes in the level of manpower or conventional armaments that are large enough to be significant during the early stages of disarmament can be easily detected. Measures restricting military deployment in specific regions often have greater significance than gross numerical restrictions and, correspondingly, have more severe verification requirements. In some cases an agreement would entail no greater requirements to detect the massing of troops or other unusual preparations than are necessary in the present environment.

Military Research, Development, and Testing. Restrictions on the testing of weapons systems seem the best means of controlling military research and development. Such restrictions can usually be verified by procedures requiring a degree of access comparable with that required for the verification of production. Because of the possible consequences of research and development on

418

stability, agreements for monitoring research and development by means of scientific exchanges, joint space programs, and so on should be sought as early as Stage I.

Nuclear Weapons and Fissionable Materials Production. An agreement to reduce the nuclear weapons stockpiles of the United States and the Soviet Union would be difficult to verify, but even substantial stockpile cuts need not impose stringent verification requirements if the prime military consideration is the maintenance of strategic deterrence. Since large stockpiles are now in existence, violations of a bilateral agreement on a cutoff of production of fissionable materials would not be militarily significant, and verification requirements would be nominal. A production cutoff involving other countries may have relatively stricter verification requirements because diversion of small amounts of material is more significant. Measures such as nuclear-free zones require little verification since compliance primarily benefits the side adopting the restriction by reducing the likelihood of unauthorized use, while violations can be easily countered.

Inspection As a Method of Verification

Just as verification is not the only source of confidence in compliance, so inspection is only one means of verification. Other means include intelligence, open sources, voluntary self-disclosure, and "common knowledge." Inspection, which has often been used synonymously with verification, has appeared to be a key principle of US disarmament policy and the focus of Soviet resistance to the Western position. However, inspection is not a principle but a particular method of obtaining information necessary for verification. Depending on the nature of the specific measure and the level of confidence demanded from verification, sources other than inspection may provide a part or all of the required information.

In addition to the verification requirements, the following general propositions are relevant to the determination of the degree and kind of inspection which should be called for in any US arms control proposal:

1. *A policy of insistence on inspection only when needed to satisfy verification requirements enhances the possibilities for achieving arms control and disarmament.* In meeting verification requirements for any particular measure it is essential to use inspection only insofar as other sources of information are unable to supply information needed for acceptable verification. The need for inspection is thus determined by the reliability, vulnerability, and usability of such other sources, that is, whether they require the active or passive cooperation of the adversary or of other governments, whether they are subject to "jamming" or other interference, and whether they can be used to support intended responses. The demand for greater inspection than this may impair the achievement of otherwise acceptable arms control arrangements.

2. *The pursuit of other gains from inspection must be weighed against specific arms control objectives.* Past proposals for inspection have sometimes emphasized objectives beyond the essentials of verification. Examples of such objectives are the following: (a) promotion of the concept of the open world and the open society; (b) development of international institutions; (c) establishment of a precedent and experience for the subsequent acceptance of inspection where it may appear necessary for verification.

To the extent that these objectives might be considered in US proposals, they must be recognized as competing with the substantive arms control measures to which they are attached, for they can be served only by increasing the extent and complexity of inspection and thereby decreasing the chances for Soviet acceptance. In each case these gains, if they are regarded as valuable, must be weighed against interest in obtaining the specific arms control measure as priorities in US policy.

3. *There are significant arms control measures which can be verified with little or no inspection.* The Study examined a wide range of arms control measures with a view to ordering them on a scale of increasing requirements for inspection.[4] The categories having relatively low inspection requirements include many measures which have been or might be proposed by the United States or the Soviet Union. This suggests two implications for policy: that such measures might be individually negotiable ahead of others that are blocked by Soviet rejection of American demands for inspection; or that, in a disarmament plan composed of many measures requiring varying degrees of inspection, the United States might be willing to place less emphasis on high-inspection measures if this would win agreement on low-inspection measures that are judged to be in the mutual interest and that lead toward more comprehensive disarmament.

THE RELATION OF VERIFICATION TO RESPONSES

The problem of responses is not peculiar to arms control agreements; it exists today. In the ordinary course of events, without any arms control agreement, governments constantly make policy choices in response to changes in their strategic situations. The existence of an arms control agreement, however, restricts the choices

[4] See *Verification and Response* . . . , Annex Vol. I, Pt. II.

open to governments. Most obviously, an agreement identifies as "violations" some forms of conduct which would otherwise be wholly within the national discretion. The agreement may also bind nations not to take steps which they would otherwise take in response to a suspected violation. Termination of an agreement is the most obvious response a nation may wish to make, but it is sometimes difficult to carry out. Express reservation of this option could make termination easier, but it makes it easier for all parties to abrogate. In many cases, abrogation would be an inappropriate response. For example, non-compliance by a smaller ally of the Soviet Union or of the United States or minor violations by a major power would not appear to justify termination of an agreement. Similarly, abandonment or violation of only a part of a disarmament agreement need not make a case for complete abrogation. The Korean Armistice was not terminated even though certain provisions were violated; rather, the response was reciprocal non-compliance with respect to those provisions only.

Whatever responses to various violations are contemplated,[5] it is important to recognize the ways in which verification and response are mutually interdependent. These include the following:

1. *Verification conditions response.* Governments, and particularly Western governments, must explain their policies. If a government wants to terminate or to take other responsive action in respect to an arms control agreement, it must be able to persuade both its own public and that of its closest allies of the basis for this

[5] See *Verification and Response* . . . , Annex Vol. II, Pt. I, for a discussion of responses and their relation to substantive arms control measures.

decision. The verification process can contribute to persuasion, or interfere with it, depending upon the authenticity of the information it develops.

2. *Verification must facilitate the decision on response.* Verification procedures must provide information in the form in which it will be must useful to those who will decide on responses. When decisions must be made by national governments, relevant information must reach the governments concerned in a way which allows prompt and accurate evaluation. When the information is to serve as a basis for an international response, or international support for a national response (for example, debate of alleged violations in the United Nations, international support for US termination of an agreement not being observed by the Soviet Union), the information must come from sources and flow through channels which will be acceptable to the international community.

3. *Obstruction of verification may itself require response.* If verification procedures are specified in an arms control agreement, it is probable that there will be frequent disputes over the operation of the verification system while the substantive measures to be verified are actually being observed. Inspection involving territorial access within an adversary nation may lead to particularly serious friction. An agreement should be so formulated as to provide for responses to obstruction that deal directly with the verification process. It may serve the agreement to establish in advance the procedures for adjudicating disagreements over the operation of inspection systems.

4. *Verification should inhibit overresponse as well as a lack of response.* If militarily significant violations are discovered or are suspected to exist, responses which

redress the military balance may be required. However, if the response is not to upset the balance or unnecessarily endanger other aspects of the arms control agreement, it is in the interest of all parties that the verification system give a clear picture of the military environment and of the apparent violation.

THE DESIGN OF INSPECTION SYSTEMS

If inspection systems are to facilitate the achievement and maintenance of some measure of arms control in the near future, then such systems must require little change in the present form of international relations and must involve minimum penetration into the social systems of participating countries. The inspection arrangements should also permit all parties to continue in compliance with the agreement even if further progress in disarmament should be temporarily halted, as when the accession of other militarily significant states cannot be obtained. Finally, inspection systems should ensure that essential information is accurately and promptly communicated to each party to the agreement since the inspection system, aided by collateral sources of information, must provide the data on which intelligent national decisions can be based. The following judgments concerning inspection systems are particularly to be stressed:

1. *To be acceptable, an inspection system should embody a gradual increase in access privileges.* If the arms control agreement is to be acceptable in the present political environment, or to evolve from it, the rights of access for inspection personnel must develop out of those which are accorded foreign nationals today. At the same time, access rights must be such as to permit adequate verification of compliance with agreements at each step of

the disarmament process. Access should be accorded on the basis of activities or facilities which require inspection and should increase in gradual steps as the disarmament process develops, beginning with rights little greater than those presently given to foreign nationals and expanding into broad access with peremptory inspection rights throughout the territory of the parties to the agreement. Such a procedure would facilitate a more rational relationship between inspection and disarmament than a procedure calling for total access, even if only in a single zone, at the very beginning of the disarmament process. The need for expanding access would be affected by changes in the political environment, especially in the later stages of disarmament. The flexibility available through distinguishing various forms of access on a functional basis permits the monitoring of a variety of arms control measures in different settings of hostility or mutual confidence.[6]

2. *For many measures "adversary" inspection systems may be superior to international inspection systems.* It is true that international inspection systems making use of either impartial civil servants or neutral-nation inspectors may be more acceptable to some nations than adversary systems. International inspectors are less likely to encounter interference, their findings may be more widely regarded as authentic, and their numbers can be easily expanded to include nationals of additional countries. However, experience has shown the difficulties of negotiating an international organization, finding competent impartial personnel, and developing and meeting a budget. International or neutral personnel may frequently err on the side of finding no violation in order to forestall crisis or

[6] See *Verification and Response* . . . , Annex Vol. I, Pt. II.

recrimination, or they may regard their role as mediators rather than as judges. By comparison, adversary systems, involving mutual inspection of each party by other parties to the agreement, require a minimum of negotiation, have few personnel and budgetary problems, give a greater sense of security to the inspecting country, and require only that the population of the host country accept the inspectors as partisan observers, not as legitimate authorities.

3. *"Mixed" systems have advantages over both international and adversary systems.* Each kind of inspection system can be made more useful by adding an element of the other. The addition of international personnel to an adversary system may make the findings of the inspectors more useful as a basis for international action. Participation by adversary personnel in an international system would give each party increased confidence in the system and give a basis for unilateral responses to discrepancies or clear violations. Appropriate mixtures of these differing organizations can enhance both the effectiveness and the acceptability of the system.[7]

[7] See *Verification and Response* . . . , Annex Vol. II, Pt. II.

CONTRIBUTORS

Richard J. Barnet, born in Boston in 1929, is the Co-Director of the Institute for Policy Studies in Washington, D.C. He is the author of *Who Wants Disarmament?*. Until 1963 he served as Deputy Director of Political Research in the United States Arms Control and Disarmament Agency.

Lincoln P. Bloomfield, born in Boston in 1920, is Professor of Political Science and Director of the Arms Control Project in the Center for International Studies at the Massachusetts Institute of Technology. He is the author of *Evolution or Revolution?*, *The United Nations and U.S. Foreign Policy*, and *International Military Forces*.

Richard A. Falk, born in New York City in 1930, is Associate Professor of International Law and Faculty Associate of the Center of International Studies, Princeton University. He is the author of *Law, Morality and War in the Contemporary World* and *The Role of Domestic Courts in the International Legal Order*.

Roger Fisher, born in 1922, is Professor of Law, Harvard University. He is the editor of *International Conflict and Behavioral Science* and is completing a volume on the subject of compliance with law.

Louis Henkin, born in the Soviet Union in 1917, is Hamilton Fish Professor of International Law at Columbia University and was an officer in the Department of State from 1948 to 1957. He is the author of *Arms Control and Inspection in American Law, Disarmament: The Lawyer's Interests* (The Hammarskjöld Forum), and the editor of *Arms Control: Issues for the Public*.

427

Klaus Knorr, born in Germany in 1911, is William Stewart Tod Professor of Public Affairs, and Director of the Center of International Studies, Princeton University. Among his publications are *British Colonial Theories* and *The War Potential of Nations, 1570-1850*.

Hans A. Linde, born in 1924, is Professor of Law, University of Oregon. He has held various posts with the United States government and has been a frequent consultant to the Arms Control and Disarmament Agency.

Walter Millis, born in Atlanta in 1899, is Staff Director of the Center for the Study of Democratic Institutions, Santa Barbara, California. Among his books are *Road to War* and, with James Real, *The Abolition of War*.

Hans J. Morgenthau, born in Germany in 1904, is Albert A. Michelson Distinguished Service Professor of Political Science and Modern History and Director of the Center for the Study of American Foreign and Military Policy, University of Chicago. Among his books are *Politics Among Nations, The Purpose of American Politics,* and *Politics in the 20th Century* (3 volumes).

Louis B. Sohn, born in Poland in 1914, is Bemis Professor of International Law, Harvard University. He has worked closely with the Arms Control and Disarmament Agency since its inception. He is the co-author (with Grenville Clark) of *World Peace Through World Law*.

Arthur I. Waskow, born in Baltimore in 1933, is a Resident Fellow of the Institute for Policy Studies, Washington, D.C. He is the author of *The Limits of Defense* and *The Worried Man's Guide to World Peace*.

SELECTED BIBLIOGRAPHY

Brennan, Donald G. (ed.), *Arms Control, Disarmament, and National Security*, New York: George Brazillier, Inc., 1961.

Buchan, Alastair and Philip Windsor, *Arms and Stability in Europe*, New York: Frederick A. Praeger, Inc. (for the Institute for Strategic Studies), 1963.

Bull, Hedley, *The Control of the Arms Race*, New York: Frederick A. Praeger, 1961.

Clark, Grenville and Louis B. Sohn, *World Peace Through World Law*, 2nd rev. ed., Cambridge: Harvard University Press, 1960.

Etzioni, Amitai, *Winning Without War*, Garden City: Doubleday & Co., Inc., 1964.

Finklestein, Lawrence S., "Arms Inspection," *International Conciliation* No. 540, November 1962.

Henkin, Louis (ed.), *Arms Control: Issues for the Public*, New York: Prentice-Hall (for the American Assembly, Columbia University), 1961.

Larson, Arthur (ed.), *A Warless World*, New York: McGraw-Hill Book Co., Inc., 1963.

Melman, Seymour (ed.), *Inspection for Disarmament*, New York: Columbia University Press, 1958.

————, *Disarmament—Its Politics and Economics*, Boston: The American Academy of Arts and Sciences, 1962.

Mendlovitz, Saul H. (ed.), *Legal and Political Problems of World Order*, New York: The Fund for Education Concerning World Peace Through World Law, 1962.

Millis, Walter and James Real, *The Abolition of War*, New York: The Macmillan Co., 1963.

Noel-Baker, Philip, *The Arms Race*, New York: Oceana Publications, Inc., 1958.

SELECTED BIBLIOGRAPHY

Schelling, Thomas C. and Morton H. Halperin, *Strategy and Arms Control*, New York: The Twentieth Century Fund, 1961.

Singer, J. David, *Deterrence, Arms Control, and Disarmament*, Columbus: The Ohio State University Press, 1962.

Verification and Response in Disarmament Agreements, Woods Hole Summer Study, Washington, D.C.: The Institute for Defense Analyses, 1962.

INDEX

233, 236, 240, 241, 242, 296,
297, 299, 307, 314, 331, 344,
345, 350, 360, 361, 363, 367,
368, 369, 370, 371, 372, 373,
381, 383, 386, 395, 398, 404;
attitudes toward inspection,
127; attitudes toward international organization, 124; and
Cuban missile crisis, 139, 140,
146, 148, 149
United States (US), 12, 15, 16,
22, 26, 27, 45, 47, 50, 51, 53,
70, 73, 75-79, 81, 86, 89, 91,
92, 93, 94, 107, 108, 109, 123,
124, 126, 130, 131, 137, 157,
163, 166, 170, 175, 214, 217,
218, 219, 220, 221, 222, 223,
233, 240, 241, 242, 245, 251,
252, 265, 296, 299, 307, 310,
344, 345, 361, 362, 364, 366,
367, 369, 370, 372, 373, 381,
383, 386, 387, 395, 404; Bill
of Rights, 251; Constitution,
251, 254; and Cuban missile
crisis, 140, 142, 143, 144, 146,
147, 148, 149; Treaty Outline
of April 18, 1962, 54
Uniting for Peace Resolution of
1950, 196, 201

verification, 18, 83, 147; cooperative external, 112; existing internal, 112; increased internal,
113; of military expenditures,
112; procedures, 79; techniques
of unilateral external, 111
Versailles Treaty, 20, 158
veto, 131, 132, 196; role in inspection process of, 133, 136
Vienna, 337
Viet Nam, 165, 167, 319
violations, 8, 17, 20, 21, 25, 27,
31, 33, 35, 39, 40, 42, 46,
56, 57, 58, 59, 60, 61, 63, 64,
77, 84, 86, 89, 90, 93, 109,
110, 111, 115, 116, 119, 121,
123, 125, 131, 132, 135, 136,

147, 149, 150, 156, 157-177,
213, 214, 229, 232, 236, 248,
249, 250, 251, 254, 259, 262,
374; ambiguous, 171, 174;
"creeping," 173; as frustration
of expectations, 167; impact of
on disarmament agreement,
48; incentives for, 40, 43, 228;
justification of, 159; militarily
insignificant, 71; militarily significant, 116; non-inspectable,
41; as probe, 169, 179; as revision of agreement, 174, 175;
as signal of intentions, 167;
temptations of, 227; unintentional, 169, 171, 172, 174, 191
violence, 295, 296, 301, 302,
313, 316, 317, 318, 320, 323,
376, 379, 392, 398, 403, 405,
406; impact of on disarmament agreement, 166
Virginia, 285
Von Soden, Julius, 325

war, effect of on disarmament
agreements, 162-165
war criminals, 188
warning, 6, 57, 65, 91
Wars of National Liberation,
293
Washington Treaty on Naval
Arms Limitation, 16, 20, 170
Waskow, Arthur I., 375, 385
weapons, development of chemical, 233; limitation on transfer
of, 112
Webster, C. K., 348
Weimar Republic, 158
Weisner, Jerome, 37, 38, 45, 46,
47
Weisner Curve, 38, 39, 40, 41,
42, 43, 230
Weiss, Bernhard, 331
Western Europe, 404
Western European Union
(WEU), 87
withdrawal, 26; punishment of,

441